best hikes

COLORADO

best hikes with KIDS

COLORADO

Maureen Keilty

Photographs by Dan Peha

THE MOUNTAINEERS BOOKS

THE MOUNTAINEERS BOOKS
*is the nonprofit publishing arm of The Mountaineers, an organization
founded in 1906 and dedicated to the exploration, preservation, and
enjoyment of outdoor and wilderness areas.*

1001 SW Klickitat Way, Suite 201, Seattle, WA 98134

© 2012 by Maureen Keilty
All rights reserved

Previous editions published as *Best Hikes with Children in Colorado* by Maureen
Keilty. Current edition: first printing 2012, second printing 2019

No part of this book may be reproduced in any form, or by any electronic, me-
chanical, or other means, without permission in writing from the publisher.

Manufactured in the United States of America

Copy Editor: Jane Crosen
Cover and Book Design: The Mountaineers Books
Layout: Ani Rucki
Cartographers: Ani Rucki & Jennifer Shontz
Photographs © Dan Peha, unless otherwise noted

Cover photograph: *Balance games create a fun log crossing for kids hiking Junction Creek (Hike 90) in Durango. Junction Creek is the southern end of the nearly
500-mile Colorado Trail threading the Rocky Mountains to Denver.*
Frontispiece: *Stunning views captivate a young mountaineer in the San Juan
Mountains.*

Library of Congress Cataloging-in-Publication Data
Keilty, Maureen, 1952-
Best hikes with kids Colorado / Maureen Keilty ; photographs by Dan Peha.—
1st ed.
    p. cm.
"Previous editions published as Best Hikes with Children Colorado by Maureen
Keilty."
Includes index.
ISBN 978-1-59485-687-7 (ppb)
1. Hiking—Colorado—Guidebooks. 2. Hiking for children—Colorado—Guidebooks.
3. Family recreation—Colorado—Guidebooks. 4. Children—Travel—Colorado—
Guidebooks. I. Title.
GV199.42.C6K46 2012
796.5109788—dc23

                             2012007546

ISBN (paperback): 978-1-59485-687-7
ISBN (e-book): 978-1-59485-688-4

CONTENTS

NORTH

WEST/SOUTHWEST

I care to live,
only to entice people to look
at Nature's loveliness.

—John Muir

DEDICATION

To Niko, who continues leading us along new trails

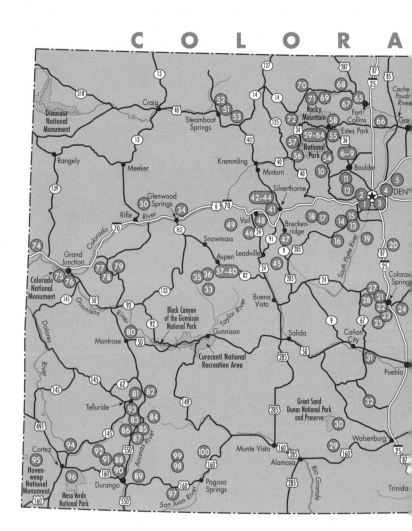

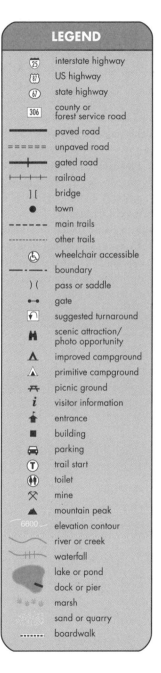

LEGEND

⑤ 25	interstate highway
⑧ 87	US highway
⑥ 67	state highway
306	county or forest service road
▬▬▬	paved road
======	unpaved road
▬┼▬	gated road
┝┼┼┼┥	railroad
] [	bridge
●	town
– – – – –	main trails
- - - - - -	other trails
♿	wheelchair accessible
–··–··–	boundary
) (	pass or saddle
•–•	gate
⏎	suggested turnaround
👓	scenic attraction/ photo opportunity
▲	improved campground
⩑	primitive campground
⊼	picnic ground
i	visitor information
⚑	entrance
■	building
🚗	parking
Ⓣ	trail start
⊕	toilet
⚒	mine
▲	mountain peak
6600	elevation contour
∿	river or creek
┼┼┼	waterfall
🝙	lake or pond
	dock or pier
🌾	marsh
	sand or quarry
········	boardwalk

A QUICK GUIDE TO THE HIKES

To quickly select a hike your family will like:

- Pick the region where you intend to hike.
- Narrow down your choices by difficulty level. (E= easy; M= moderate; C = challenging). Note that some hikes include options of varying difficulty.
- Make sure the trail is accessible at this time of year.
- Browse the highlights to get a sense of the hike.
- See the full hike description for distance, elevation gain, seasonal specifics, and other details. Happy trails!

HIKE NUMBER AND NAME	DIFFICULTY	SEASON	HIGHLIGHTS
METRO: Denver, Boulder, and Colorado Springs			
1. Highline Canal Trail	E	Year-round	Family-friendliest section of Denver's 66-mile pedestrian pathway
2. Lake Loop and Nature Trails	E	Year-round	City wildlife oasis for kids big and small
3. Bluff Lake	E	Year-round	Wildlife pocket with cottonwood-rimmed pond
4. Rocky Mountain Arsenal National Wildlife Refuge	E	Year-round	Revitalized prairie, fishing pond, interactive museum, and guided tours
5. Niedrach Nature Trail and Gazebo Boardwalk	E	Year-round	Prairie-edge pond lures water birds and bird-watchers of all sizes
6. Lichen Loop Trail	E	Apr thru Oct	A gentle creek begins and ends this forest-prairie-canyon path
7. Anne U. White Trail	E	Year-round	Follow a creek that falls, pools, and meanders—delighting all
8. Pines-to-Peak Loop Trail	E	Year-round	Easy "I made it to the top!" hike with views of Denver and Boulder valley
9. Canyon Loop Trail	M	May to Oct	Canyon hike through flowered meadows, lush streambed, and dense forest
10. Mud Lake Open Space	E	Year-round	Spot moose and ermine or discover new wildflowers while circling a lake
11. Rattlesnake Gulch Trail	M	May to Oct; in winter	Views of Continental Divide, historic railroad, and rock climbers
12. Horseshoe Trail to Frazer Meadow	M	June to mid-Oct	Brookside hike through aspen and pine to homesteader's forest cabin

HIKE NUMBER AND NAME	DIFFICULTY	SEASON	HIGHLIGHTS
METRO: Denver, Boulder, and Colorado Springs			
13. Red Rocks Trail	M	Year-round	Flowered meadow leads to red rock panoramas and yellow hogback formations
14. Lair o' the Bear Park	E to M	Apr thru Nov	Three trails thread habitats of creek, pine, meadow, and fishing pond
15. Meadow-Castle Loop	E	Mar to Nov	Mountaintop castle, summer White House, and Red Rocks park
16. Pine Valley Ranch Park	E to M	Apr to Nov	River and mountainside trails lead to fishing and bird-watching satisfaction
17. Alpine Garden Loop and M. Walter Pesman Trails	E	Late May to early Oct	Above treeline pageantry descends to ancient tree artistry
18. Chicago Lakes Trail to Idaho Springs Reservoir	M	Mid-June to Oct	Gentle descent to Echo Lake promising fishing and picnic pleasure
19. South Rim Loop Trail	M	Year-round	Walk a geologic showcase of yellow cliffs and red rock wedges
20. Inner Canyon–Lake Gulch Loop	M	Year-round	Boulder-scrambling, pond-probing, quiet canyon getaway
21. Central Garden Trail	E	Year-round	Garden of the Gods Park's most stunning red rock spires
22. Red Rock Canyon Loop	M	Year-round	Stone slabs jut sky-high with geologic and historical insights
23. Bear Creek Trails	E to M	Year-round	Interactive nature center with hikes through four foothill ecosystems
24. Cattail Marsh and Fountain Creek Trails	E	Year-round	Spy on turtles, cormorants, and herons; multi-sensory center, guided hikes
25. Columbine Trail	M	Mar to Nov	Downhill to two waterfalls and views of prairie and red rock formations

26. Paint Mines Interpretive Park	E	Year-round	Sherbet-colored rocks melting into a canyon
27. Waldo Canyon Loop Trail	M to C	Apr to Nov	Pikes Peak views while following a stream through forests
28. The Crags Trail	M to C	Late May to mid-Oct	Awesome pinnacles to reach, streams to cross, and rocks to climb
CENTRAL: Great Sand Dunes National Park, Central Colorado, Aspen, Vail, and Summit County			
29. Zapata Falls	E to M	Year-round	Tumbling waterfall nestled in rock near the Great Sand Dunes National Park and Preserve
30. Dunes Exploration and Montville Nature Trail	E	Year-round	Fun sand dune climbing and leaping in a national park
31. Newlin Creek Trail	E to M	Mid-May to Nov	Mini-waterfalls and fern-laced cliffs along historic logging road
32. Bishop's Castle	E	Year-round	Castle-in-the-woods exploration
33. Judd Falls Trail	E to M	June to Oct	Wildflower lover's delight at the "best of" Copper Creek
34. Hanging Lake Trail	C	Year-round	Waterfall/lake destination as beautiful as the hike is geologically interesting
35. Maroon Lake Trail	E	Mid-June thru Sept	Easy lakeside stroll with dramatic mountain views
36. Maroon Creek Trail	M	Mid-June thru Sept	Downvalley hike through woods, rocks, and wild flowers
37. Hallam Lake Loop Trail	E	Year-round	Heart of Aspen wildlife sanctuary
38. The Grottos Loop Trail	E	June to Oct	River's playful route beside boulders, ice caves, and a sandy beach
39. Weller Lake Trail	M	Mid-June to mid-Oct	Creek-probing, boulder-climbing, and lakeshore-exploring fun along Roaring Fork River
40. Linkins Lake Trail	M to C	Late June to mid-Oct	Physically and visually breathtaking hike to an alpine lake

HIKE NUMBER AND NAME	DIFFICULTY	SEASON	HIGHLIGHTS
CENTRAL: Great Sand Dunes National Park, Central Colorado, Aspen, Vail, and Summit County			
41. Lily Pad Lake Trail	M	June to Oct	Forests of aspen and lodgepole lead to beaver ponds and lily-blanketed lakes
42. Rock Creek Trail	M	June to Sept	Hike through bird nesting area to historic site with mountain vistas
43. Surprise Trail	M to C	Mid-June to Oct	Staircase of forests leads to pleasant lake near Gore Range Trail
44. Lower Cataract Loop Trail	E	June to Oct	Waterfall view lures hikers around lake, through meadows, and into deep forest.
45. Mount Sherman	C	July to Sept	A "fourteener" for healthy, well-rested, prepared kids and parents
46. Missouri Lakes Trail	M to C	Late June to Sept	Wildflower-rimmed cascades lead to pristine lakes in Holy Cross Wilderness
47. Spruce Creek Trail	M to C	June to Oct	Waterfalls and historic mining cabins in an alpine cirque
48. Eagles Loop Trail	E	Mid-May to Sept	Gondola ride leads to views of Vail's mountains and wildlife
49. Browns Loop	E	June to Oct	Catch a fish or spot a moose on a trail through forests, brooks, marshes, and meadow
50. Coyote Trail	M	Year-round	Rifle Falls State Park's showcase of waterfalls, caves, and suspended viewpoints
NORTH: Steamboat Springs, Rocky Mountain National Park, and Fort Collins Area			
51. Fish Creek Falls	E	Year-round	Two trails to Steamboat Springs' spectacular cascade
52. Mad Creek Trail	M	Mid-May to Oct	Spring's first hike above a stampeding creek to a pleasant meadow

Hike	Rating	Season	Description
53. Rabbit Ears Peak	M to C	Mid-June to Sept	Spectacular flower fields and grand views lead to two rock pillars
54. Blue Lake Trail	E to M	Late June to Sept	Tranquil trek then brisk hike; both lead to alpine lakes
55. Lily Mountain Trail	M	Mid-Apr to Oct	Ideal "first ascent" with great views, fun climbs, and interactive visitor center
56. Adams Falls and East Inlet Trail	E to M	Mid-June to Sept	Valley hike to Lone Pine Lake with waterfall, beaver ponds, mountain views
57. Holzwarth Historic Site	E	Mid-June to Oct	Original homestead of early Colorado dude ranch
58. North Fork Trail to Deserted Village	M	June to Oct	Scenic trail, excellent fishing, and camping along North Fork of the Big Thompson
. Old Ute Trail Tundra Walk	M	Late June to Sept	Tundra trek beginning in alpine garden descending into deep stands of conifer
60. Alluvial Fan Trail	E	Mid-May thru mid-Sept	Waterfall, boulders, and sandy pools to explore in path of 1982 flood.
61. Wild Basin Trail to Copeland and Calypso Cascades	E to M	Mid-May thru Sept	Two waterfall destinations; short and serene, or Falls steep and lush
62. Fern Lake Trail	E to C	May thru Oct (Pool); June thru Oct (Fern Lake)	Multi-destination hike with misty waterfall, fishing lake, boulder maze fun
63. Sprague Lake Nature Trail	E	June to Oct	Fully accessible nature trail with views of the Continental Divide
64. Bear Lake and Glacier Gorge Loop Trails	E to M	Late June to Oct	Trail network featuring the "best of" Rocky Mountain National Park
65. Poudre River Trail	E	Year-round	Fort Collins's "in-town" trail designed for the stroller-bound to those bound-to-explore
66. Chapungu Sculpture Park	E	Year-round	Stone sculptures gracing grassland, meadow, and forest, in urban setting

HIKE NUMBER AND NAME	DIFFICULTY	SEASON	HIGHLIGHTS
NORTH: Steamboat Springs, Rocky Mountain National Park, and Fort Collins Area			
67. Well Gulch Loop	E to M	Year-round	Cool grotto, sparkly rocks, grand views, and eservoir wading
68. Hewlett Gulch Trail	E	May thru Oct	Stream-crossing fun to homestead in lush canyon
69. Kreutzer Nature Trail and Mount McConnel Summit	M to C	May to Nov	Looped nature trail to summit views of Mummy Range
70. Montgomery Pass Trail	M	Mid-June to Sept	High-country hiking from stately spruce to alpine gardens
71. Lake Agnes Trail	M to C	July thru Sept	Alpine odyssey for anglers, rock scramblers, and silence seekers
72. State Forest State Park, Nature Trails	E	June to Oct	Spot a moose, hook a fish, go geocaching in Colorado's largest state park
73. Pawnee National Grasslands	E to M	Year-round	Prairie gem home to hawks, eagles, falcons, and more
WEST/SOUTHWEST: Grand Junction, Black Canyon of the Gunnison National Park, Durango and the San Juan Mountains, and Mesa Verde National Park			
74. Trail Through Time	M	March to Nov	Discover dinosaur remains along an interpretive trail
75. Alcove Nature, Canyon Rim, and Window Rock Loop Trails	E	Year-round	High desert rambles to canyon rims, cliff views, and rock spires
76. Mica Mine	E to M	Year-round	Glittering trail to treasure cave in desert canyon
77. West Bench Trail	E to M	Year-round	Powderhorn's forest-threading trail for hikers and skiers
78. Mesa Lake Shoreline Trail	E	Mid-June thru Sept	Grand Mesa destination for hikers, anglers, and little explorers
79. Crag Crest National Recreation Trail	M to C	Late June to mid-Sept	High forested ridge with options for gentle or vigorous hikes

80. Warner Point Nature Trail	E to M	May to Oct	View Black Canyon's depths from a rolling path through a desert garden
81. Box Canyon Falls and High Bridge Trails	E	May to Oct	Stand in the mist of a thundering waterfall in a canyon alcove
82. Baby Bathtubs Trail	E	Mid-May thru Sept	Water-scoured pockets in colorful rock streambed
83. Ice Lake Trail	C	Mid-June to mid-Sept	High-country climb via switchbacks to waterfall, mine remains, and alpine lakes
84. Highland Mary Lakes Trail	M to C	Late June thru Sept	Broad tundra basin jeweled with lakes, streams, and wildflowers
85. Crater Lake Trail	M to C	Late May to mid-Oct	Top-of-the-world views to forest-edged lake at mountain base
86. Pass Creek Trail to Engineer Meadows	M	Mid-June to Oct	Forested climb to wildflower-studded meadow
87. Potato Lake Trail	E	May to Oct	Aspen-forest hike to lake for fishing, camping, and picnic fun
88. Animas Overlook Trail	E	May to Oct	Accessible trail featuring southwest Colorado's unique geology and history
89. First Fork Trail	M to C	May to Oct	Forested climb to ridge with many streamside destinations
90. Junction Creek Trail	E to M	Apr to Nov	Streamside stroll with pools to wade and forest nooks to explore
91. Highline Trail to Taylor Lake	E	Mid-June thru Sept	Wildflower-rimmed lake destination near Kennebec Pass
92. Sharkstooth Trail to Centennial Peak	M to C	Mid-June to Oct	Encounter mini-waterfalls, a rock glacier, and a mining camp on the way to an easy summit

NUMBER AND NAME	DIFFICULTY	SEASON	HIGHLIGHTS
WEST/SOUTHWEST: Grand Junction, Black Canyon of the Gunnison National Park, Durango and the San Juan Mountains, and Mesa Verde National Park			
93. Bear Creek Preserve	E to M	Late Apr through Oct	Abandoned jeep trail leads to grand views of Telluride's waterfalls and peaks
94. Dominguez-Escalante Trail	E	Year-round	Accessible trail to ancient dwelling site overlooking mountain ranges
95. Sand Canyon and East Rock Creek Loop	M	Year-round	Sandstone trail loops around cliff dwellings and ancient towers
96. Petroglyph Point Loop Trail	M	Mid-Apr to Oct	Canyon to mesa-top loop around Ancestral Puebloan homeland
97. Great Kiva and Chimney Rock Trails	E to M	May 15 thru Sept	Imagination-provoking guided hikes to ancient dwellings
98. Piedra River Trail	E	Mid-May to mid-Oct	Streamside descent passing cliffs, meadows, and excellent fishing/camping destinations
99. Piedra Ice Fissures Trail	E	Late May to mid-Oct	Old wagon road leads to source of underground ice
100. Lobo Overlook and Continental Divide Trail	M	Mid- to late June to mid-Sept	Wolf Creek Pass's easy access to spine of Rocky Mountains

ACKNOWLEDGMENTS

Thanks to the employees of the United States Forest Service, National Park Service, and the divisions of parks and recreation in numerous cities throughout Colorado for providing both verbal and written trail information. Tips on trails from many friends are likewise appreciated. Special thanks go to my husband, Dan Peha, and our son, Niko, my favorite hiking partners.

INTRODUCTION

It's been more than twenty years since I wrote the introduction to the first edition of this book, marking a significant passage for the book and my family. The day after completing the hikes for the first edition, I gave birth to our son, Niko. On his twenty-first birthday I submitted the manuscript for this edition.

Hundreds of "Best Hikes" later, including the trails for two editions of *Best Hikes with Children in Utah*, my family and I are still hiking. My husband, Dan, and I recently celebrated his sixtieth atop 19,341-foot Kilimanjaro, and we're planning a similar ascent in South America later next year. Niko, on the other hand, hikes in whitewater safety gear with a kayak strapped to his back, bushwhacking to remote, boulder-studded descents that he paddles, so far, successfully. (And I keep repeating, "This too shall pass.")

Despite my terrors about Niko's whitewater "creeking," his kayaking introduced me to another type of kid-friendly trail: a community's multi-use riverside trail. In the early kayaking days, Niko trained and competed in a river's whitewater park while I walked alongside on a broad, paved path enjoying a river reprieve. I noted how each walk provided parking (usually free), restrooms, easy access to shops, and fun diversions like a fishing dock, elegant stone sculptures, or a ropes course. Nearly every Colorado community edging a river or creek has recently developed its own riverside trail, and while they all rate as

ideal family destinations, I've described four to six "Best Riverside Walks" at the end of each regional section of the book.

For this edition's twenty-four new hikes, Dan and I circled the state like hunters on an expedition, stopping to hike, photograph, take notes, and ask about other trails. Our research trips totaled 2100 tire miles and about 200 on our feet, but we returned with an assortment of trophy trails for kids. From the ghost-like hoodoos of Paint Mines Interpretive Park (Hike 26) in the east to the triple sixty-foot waterfalls of the Coyote Trail (Hike 50) in the west, from spotting moose on the Ranger Lakes Nature Trail (Hike 72) in the north to "discovering" the ancient dwellings of Sand Canyon (Hike 95) in the south, we found a hike for the Colorado kid in everyone.

Our new collection reflects a welcome trend of trails developed by a community's parks and recreation department, often in conjunction with a private or public entity, such as the United States Forest Service (USFS) or a park. Most of these trails are multi-use, requiring cooperation between walkers, joggers, bikers, skaters, equestrians, and roller-bladers.

Equally pleasing is the increase in respect among different trail users. Trails I had previously dismissed due to heavy bike use are now user-friendly for all. Dog walkers are increasingly leashing their pets. Moms pushing strollers are staying to the right. Joggers pant, "On your left" when passing. We're all learning to share the trails. Learn more about trail etiquette below.

Also satisfying are this edition's new, user-friendly features, like the "Quick Guide to the Hikes" chart, and the "Great Getaways" sidebars—features designed to encourage more families to experience the joys of hiking with kids.

Overall, I'm delighted with the new edition, knowing it's the start of countless little feet exploring Colorado.

KEEPING IT FUN
Keeping the hikes fun for everyone in the family requires some forethought.

Set the Scene
Enthusiastically introducing a hike sparks eagerness in your kids. They'll sense your co nfidence and desire to discover nature and will want to join the outdoor venture.

Opposite: Hiking pals play creek-crossing games on logs and rocks.

Describe the hike with words such as "explore," "walk," or "along the way, we'll see. . . ." Try not to use words such as "hard," "easy," or "difficult." **Tell kids about the destination** and, more importantly, that they'll stop to look at animal tracks, smell flowers, or maybe listen for the bugle call of an elk. **Exploring the sights, sounds, textures, aromas, and even flavors along the trail can be as rewarding as the destination itself.**

Encourage Spontaneity

Spontaneity can redirect your trip or simply season it with a variety of interests. A child's natural curiosity leads to examining insects under a rock or discovering a flower that smells like peanut butter. Once, while walking through a spruce forest with a small group of young girls, I heard the *hoo-ooo* of an owl. Looking into the dark canopy overhead, my eyes caught the movement of a large bird fluttering its wings. I gathered the girls near a tree where, for nearly an hour, we watched a downy young barn owl take its first flights while its mother observed from a distant branch. We never made it to the hot spring as planned, but we were warmed by the gift we shared.

No doubt **your child will discover something** you simply know nothing about. When your son asks the name of a snail captured in his palm and you respond with, "I don't know," enhance his discovery by asking *him* questions, such as, "How does it see? Can you find its mouth? Think it hears us talk?"

Assign Hike Leaders

Somehow **the revered status of hike leader gives kids an energy boost** and encourages them to pay closer attention to the map and watch for landmarks. Switching the title to a child whose energy is waning keeps the group moving at a steady pace. It's a good idea to let your young leaders know in advance where this "change of command" is to take place.

Bring Along a Friend

Complaints, aches, and pains are lessened considerably when your child **brings a friend.** Neither will want to appear slow in front of the other, and the two will concoct unheard-of games.

Make Frequent but Brief Rest Stops

Frequent fuel stops—"We'll have a drink of water and some gorp when we reach the top of this hill"—also keep the hike moving. But **keep the rest stops brief.** Breath-catching stops during high-altitude climbs should be thirty seconds to a minute and a half. Breaks in hiking that last longer than five minutes can defeat the purpose of stopping. Not only do they increase the hiking time considerably, but they cause kids, and adults, to lose their motivation. This is because the drive to get going again diminishes as the cardiovascular system slows down. You have to start all over to attain the efficiency your climbing muscles had prior to stopping. Have your crew **stand during rest stops** so everyone will want to keep moving.

Use Patience, Praise, and Playfulness

As most parents know, **kids thrive on praise and patience.** On a hike, be liberal with both. Plan the trip so there's time to play a balancing game while crossing the creek or to watch a beaver reappear from its den. It's more effective to **give compliments early in the trip** rather than later to encourage tired hikers. Your interest in your kids'

discoveries fuels their energy. Let them know you are proud of their hiking strength and their trash collecting along the trail. Praise given in the presence of other kids and adults has a lasting influence.

When children lose interest during a hike, **turn the trip into a fun stroll.** Try skipping or walking backward. Walk in bare feet. (Be sure the trail surface is free of sharp objects.) Sing a song the kids know and can join in on. Encourage the hike leader

Southwest Colorado's sandstone cliffs are a perennial lure for hikers young and old.

to make up his or her way of walking that the others should copy. Or try any of the following techniques, which are sure to eliminate tedium from most any trek.

Silent fox walk. Instruct kids to place each step with their weight coming down on the outside of the foot and rolling to the inside. With practice they'll move with fluidity and silence.

Color match. Have kids look for colors in nature to match the colors of the clothing they are wearing.

Open house. Insect and animal homes abound in the forest. Have kids watch for examples of woodland creatures' homes, such as bird nests, spiderwebs, insect galls (growth-like swellings holding insect eggs, which are attached to twigs in a bush or leaf stems), a ground squirrel's entrance hole, a creek, rotten logs, and others.

Sniff a tree. Hug a tree and discover its aroma; the ponderosa pine has a delightful vanilla-like scent.

Aspen whitewash. Kids like to paint a theatric white mask on their face by rubbing their cheek on an aspen tree's smooth bark. Try finger-painting with the aspen bark's powder.

Bird music. Listen for birdcalls and try to mimic their melodies and rhythms.

Fantasy fun. Mark Twain once said, "You can't depend on your eyes when your imagination is out of focus." During a long hike, you can lift tired spirits by skipping along the trail, pretending it's the yellow brick road. Salute the rocks guarding the mountain. Compliment the creek for its song. Introduce yourself to the Engelmann spruce and gently shake hands with its branches. Sing to the mushroom. Keep your imagination in focus—it can be contagious.

What in the woods . . . ? In your mind, select a natural item your group sees frequently while hiking. Ask kids to guess what the item is by asking questions that require a yes or no response. The winner picks the next "what in the woods . . . ?"

Nature's Food Web. Living creatures depend on each other for their food. A squirrel scampering through the woods with a pinecone in its mouth, a red-winged blackbird alighting on a cattail, and a mushroom erupting from a rotting log are examples of one species feeding another. Point out a few examples, and then ask your kids to watch for others as they walk.

Finding feelers. "Touch something smooth." "Feel a fuzzy thing."

"Find something slippery." Hands-on touching energizes tired minds and feet.

Wait Out the Rain

Sudden weather changes are the norm for Colorado's mountains. The storm's severity and your kids' ages will determine whether you gather your group under cover of shrubs to wait it out or turn everyone around to walk quickly back to the trailhead. Whatever your choice, **your positive attitude will keep fears at bay.**

It can be **fun for youngsters to wait out a rainstorm,** whether you are huddled beneath spruce branches or under the "porch" of a tent tarp. A magnifying glass, tucked away in your backpack for just such occasions, will occupy fidgety young hikers. A string laid across the forest floor gives little fingers a pretend nature trail for ants to walk along. That apple left over from lunch can be put to good use while waiting for the storm to subside; before showing it to your listeners, tell them a colorful version of the following story:

One day a little boy had nothing to do, so he asked his mother for a game. The mother told him to go outside and find a "little red round house without windows or doors and a star inside." (Describe the places in the forest where the boy searched, using the plants and animals you saw on the day's hike.) The little boy wandered through the forest, asking questions about where the little red house might be. As the boy headed for home, still puzzled, he stopped in an orchard and asked the wind to help him find the little red round house. Just then, the wind shook an apple from a tree. The boy realized it was little, red, and round, and it had no windows or doors. (Present your apple.) To find the star inside, he cut the apple in half (cut yours horizontally) and, sure enough, there was a star (formed by the seed and core arrangement)!

Kids enjoy eating segments of the "little red round house" as much as they like listening to the story.

OF MOUNTAINS, MESAS, AND FORESTS

It's your choice: a gentle saunter along a babbling creek deep in a forest, a rigorous trek across the flower-dappled tundra, a sandy walk past prehistoric sites and thorny cacti. Hikes in Colorado cross the biological,

An adventurous hiker "bum-skis" down a snowy slope above Silverton.

geological, and even historical spectrums. Having even a tad of understanding about these worlds makes each hike all the more memorable. A staircase is perhaps the simplest way to describe the arrangement of Colorado's plant and animal life zones.

Beginning at Colorado's eastern border, the bottom step, at 3500 feet to 5500 feet, is the **Upper Sonoran life zone.** Characterized by grass-blanketed prairies, sandy bluffs, and a few marsh areas, this relatively dry life zone is canyon sculpted in many places. In its forests grow drought-resistant pinyon and juniper trees with a wide variety of grasses, cacti, and yucca adding soft greens and yellows to the landscape. Birds of prey feed and nest in the canyons of this region, and bands of pronghorn race across its plains. For a sampling of this life zone, see Hike 73, Pawnee National Grasslands.

The next stairstep to the west, at 5500 to 6500 feet, is called the **Foothills.** Ponderosa pine and scrub oak trees dominate its south-facing slopes, while Douglas firs take hold on the hilltops. Blue spruce, cottonwood, and willows can be found along its streams. Many of the hikes taking place in and around the Denver, Boulder, and Colorado Springs areas can be considered Foothills hikes.

The **Transition zone** extends up to 8000 feet, covering a large portion of western Colorado. Although much of it is considered sagebrush country, which is generally dry and sun-exposed, fingers of lush streambeds and dense forests weave this region. A classic example of this diverse terrain can be found on Hike 27, Waldo Canyon Loop Trail.

One stairstep up and to the west of the Front Range (the first chain of the Rocky Mountains seen from the eastern plains) is the **Boreal region**, which includes the state's mountains. With a range of 8000 to

14,000 feet, this zone is divided into three sections: the Canadian, at 8000 to 11,000 feet; the Hudsonian, or timberline, at 11,000 to 11,500 feet; and the Alpine, which includes the frosty, windswept terrain above timberline.

Wildflowers and aspens proliferate in the **Canadian zone,** which is also home to several varieties of spruce and pine trees. A large percentage of the hikes in this book take place here, considered by many the prettiest of Colorado's many ecosystems.

The narrowest of the life zones, the **Hudsonian zone,** displays stands of beautifully wind-sculpted bristlecone pine trees. Engelmann spruce and subalpine fir are also shaped by the strong winds and heavy snow of the region. A good example of this timberline world is found on Hike 17, Alpine Garden Loop and M. Walter Pesman Trails.

The **Alpine zone,** which begins where the trees end, consists of pockets of tiny wildflowers tucked into a rocky, treeless tundra. Most hikers come this far to feast their eyes on the mountaintops' magnificent vistas, only to discover that equally precious sights are at their feet. Several ecosystems exist in this land above the trees, which can be discovered on Hike 59, Old Ute Trail Tundra Walk.

BEST RIVERSIDE WALKS

Everyone enjoys walking along a river. Strolling to the water's soothing, sometimes playful sounds while the kids explore wooded nooks and quiet pools, helps us all relax—especially if the trail is paved, easily accessed, and provides restrooms and parking. Such is the case in many Colorado communities.

Historically, towns often established themselves with their backs to the river, regarding it as an irrigation source, transportation hub, and unfortunately, a place to dump all manner of waste. That trend has reversed. Today's communities proudly preserve their waterways as a year-round source of relaxation and recreation.

Typically, a riverside trail reflects years of community teamwork with recreation specialists and engineers to create a multi-use route that highlights the river's natural features while incorporating educational and fun elements. Funding from federal and state agencies like Great Outdoors Colorado (GOCO), along with private donors, allows these universal-access paths to continue growing.

Families walking a Colorado riverside trail may spot a beaver lodge, climb a ropes course, take kayak lessons at a whitewater park, admire trailside sculptures, or learn something new at an educational kiosk. With kids in tow, it's best to stay to the right on crowded trails, allowing bikers and joggers to pass on your left. (As in driving, slower walkers stay to the right.)

When visiting any Colorado city, consider its riverside trail the go-to place for the family. You'll find a brief description of Colorado's best riverside walks at the end of each regional section of this book.

GREAT GETAWAYS

The trails in this book thread together the best of Colorado's outdoor destinations for families. However, countless more kid-friendly trails and attractions surround them, so the "Great Getaways" sidebars found throughout the book highlight hiking, camping, and outdoor fun destinations that are close to the featured hikes. Note that reservations are a must at many of the recommended campgrounds. Where reservations are not required, plan to arrive early in the day to claim a site. The getaways' variety of outdoor attractions—be they a historic gold mine tour, a four-wheel-drive ride to a friendly ghost town in the mountains, or a soak in a natural hot-spring pool—will appeal to all ages and will add a unique flavor your family's adventures.

WHAT TO TAKE

Starting from the feet up, outfit young hikers well to ensure enjoyable outings.

Hiking Shoes

Properly fitted and broken-in hiking shoes are a prerequisite. Sneakers or running shoes work well for the short, paved trails in this book, and they may also be adequate for longer treks on trails relatively free of rocks and tree roots. However, hiking shoes or boots are a necessity for full-day hikes and backpack trips. For kids, wearing them gives the hike a special importance.

Unfortunately, hiking boots for youngsters are expensive—especially since some children outgrow footwear in one season. The least costly hiking shoes, other than boots found at used clothing stores or at yard sales, are simply high-top sneakers. Those made of leather or a similar, stiff material provide the needed ankle support but may be too heavy. Look for lugged soles to grip slippery rock surfaces and provide traction on muddy terrain.

Little and big feet appreciate properly fitted hiking boots.

Timing is the first consideration when buying hiking boots for kids. Plan to shop well in advance of a hiking trip. Have your child **wear the new hiking boots for several days before the hike.** Try the boots on wearing heavy socks. Make sure the boot is snug enough to prevent rubbing but not so tight that it pinches the toes. Boots improperly fitted or not broken in can ruin the most spectacular summit climb. I still remember, at the top of the first 14,000-foot peak I climbed, the miserable, teary-eyed face of a young hiker in our group who said her new boots were "torture chambers." Kids forced to hike under such conditions won't relish doing it again, regardless of your enthusiasm.

Socks

It's amazing how **well-fitted, tightly knit socks support feet** in even the most minimal hiking shoes. A thin liner sock worn underneath a cushioning sock provides the best long-hiking support. Replacing sweaty socks with an extra pair midway on the trip magically revives tired feet.

Trekking Poles

Once a requirement mostly for long-distance hikers, trekking poles have become increasingly popular with day hikers too. Poles or walking sticks make stream crossings, steep descents, and traverses across loose rock less taxing on muscles and joints. Youngsters may not be interested in "one more thing to carry," but their big companions appreciate how the **poles increase the body's efficiency** by transferring some of the load (up to 20 percent) to their arms. Telescoping trekking poles are ideal, and a pair is less awkward to use than a single stick. A low-cost option is a pair of used ski poles; suitable walking sticks can sometimes be found near the trailhead or at creek crossings.

Packs

Another hiking requirement, even for day hikes, is a pack. Most beginning walkers like shouldering at least some of the group's gear as well as their very own raincoat or water bottle. Even a waist pack gives the smallest hiker a way to share the load. For longer treks, especially those that involve an overnight camp, use a larger day pack or a backpack.

Make the packing process a group project, giving each hiker an opportunity to select what he or she carries. Take time to **show kids how to load their pack evenly** and how to securely attach bulky items such as a sleeping bag or the tent fly. Once the pack is loaded, fit it properly to the child by adjusting straps and buckles. Remind your hikers that once the pack is loaded, they should not sit on it—unless, of course, they like eating squashed sandwiches for lunch.

Let each child carry something the entire group needs, whether it's the energy bars or the map and first-aid kit. If young hikers believe the items in their pack are important, they will feel like a valuable member of the group. Tell your crew that they need to remember what's in their packs. This prevents repeatedly asking questions such as "Who's got the gorp?" or "Where's the map?" which whittles away rest stops.

Raingear

During the summer months in the high country, thunderstorms can be expected, so regardless of how clear the sky looks, raingear—including a waterproof hood or hat—is a must for every hiker.

The Ten Essentials

The Mountaineers, over years of teaching classes, have developed a systems approach to items that should be carried on every hike. The Ten Essentials provide comfort and the necessities for coping with emergencies caused by foul weather, an injury, or other unexpected incidents.

To make the preparation process quicker, keep as many of these essentials as possible gathered together in one location.

1. **Insulation** (rain protection and extra clothing): Raingear is an essential layer when hiking Colorado's trails. Bring another layer of warm clothing as a hedge against wet or torn clothing or sudden weather changes. Include a knit hat.

2. **Hydration** (extra water): Bring plenty of drinking water for each hiker, and if necessary, bring along a means of treating water from natural sources (see "Drink Treated Water" under Backcountry Safety, below).

3. **Sun protection** (sunglasses and sunscreen): It takes less time to sunburn in Colorado!

A sunhat and long sleeves protect a beginning hiker from sun exposure.

Sun intensity increases about 4 percent for every 1000 feet in elevation. For instance, at Rocky Mountain National Park (9400 feet) ultraviolet radiation (UV) is 38 percent higher than at sea level. Sunscreen, sunglasses, and a brimmed hat are essential in Colorado. Bright, high-altitude sunshine can tire and potentially damage eyes. Even overcast days may result in serious sunburns for unprotected skin. Select a sunscreen lotion formulated for children, and test it for allergic reactions before leaving home. A lip balm with sun protection should be carried in most every hiker's pocket.

4. **Fire** (firestarter candle or chemical fuel and matches/lighter): During an unforeseen overnight camp, a campfire can be a lifesaver. A fire is not possible without reliable matches in a waterproof container, available at sporting-goods stores.

5. **Nutrition** (extra food): An extra high-energy bar per person (preferably hidden in your pack) is a reliable measure against

hungry, irritable hikers should the trip take longer than planned.

6. **Repair kit and tools** (including a pocketknife): One of the most useful items is a pair of pliers; for overnight trips, you might also include duct tape and other simple repair items.

7. **First-aid supplies:** Check to make sure your first-aid kit is complete, and hope it's not needed. Pack your first-aid kit with additional medicine or supplies your child needs.

8. **Illumination** (headlamp or flashlight): Carry fresh batteries, and plan not to guide children down a trail at night.

9. **Navigation** (map and compass): Always carry a map of the overall area you are hiking in. Orient yourself with the compass and the map before setting foot on the trail.

10. **Emergency shelter:** An extra rain tarp is useful, even on a day hike, if you get caught in a rainstorm.

Good to Have

Besides the Ten Essentials, additional items will come in handy.

The three-dollar Colorado Outdoor Recreation **Search and Rescue Card,** available online and at most sporting goods stores, covers the cost of a rescue in the event of an emergency.

Insect repellent, such as the tiny one-ounce squeeze-bottle type, is worth several times its weight. No-see-ums, common in sagebrush country, prowl invisibly around the ears. Protect ears from these insects' irritating welts by dabbing a few drops of the repellent around the neck area.

A **whistle** can be carried by each child; make sure they understand that it should be used only in an emergency. This can aid in locating a lost little one.

Toilet paper and extra **plastic bags** for carrying out used toilet paper are a good idea. A shovel or trowel for digging cat holes is also recommended. For young kids, a change of underwear and socks can help erase the memory of an embarrassing accident and allow the trip to continue.

If you feel it is necessary to carry and use soap, bring only **biodegradable soap.** Be aware, however, that all soap pollutes lakes and streams, and instruct children to carry water at least 200 feet away from natural sources and wash there.

A **bandanna,** a **magnifying lens, paper and pencil,** a **small paper bag, a piece of string or shoelace,** even a **tiny book of stories** are useful tools for examining the environment or passing time during a summer storm (see "Wait Out the Rain," earlier in this chapter).

Trail Treats

For some hikers, special **trail food** is the biggest attraction to the sport. Extreme hikers—those who hike fast, far, and for a long time—rely on lightweight, easy-to-digest energy bars. However, kids enjoy combining nuts, M&Ms, and other more healthy nibbles into a trail mix. They can bag the carrot sticks, fill water bottles, or make a treat collection for each hiker. Encourage kids to pack a stash of their favorite finger food.

For overnight trips, plan a one-pot meal such as macaroni and cheese, tuna and noodles, or chili. For the most part, kids don't like freeze-dried dinners. Stay with their favorite packable, prepared foods like canned soup or a package of tortillas and can of refried beans. Or, check out the quick-cooking grains and dehydrated vegetables in the bulk isle at a health food store. Try the new concoctions at home before introducing them to hungry hikers on the trail.

After packing and dividing the trip's food, show kids how and where to pack their allotment. Make sure it's accessible, in a somewhat crush-proof location in their pack. Also coach them on making their portion last for the duration of the hike.

BACKCOUNTRY SAFETY

Just as walking to school entails some risk, so does hiking any "Best Hike." Safety is not a measure of how easy or challenging the trail is rated to be. It's a product of common sense coupled with preparation and a positive attitude.

Every effort has been made to describe these trails as accurately as possible. Weather and trail use, however, alter the trail condition from day to day. Trail maintenance, or lack thereof, can also influence the trip considerably. Your physical condition has as much bearing on the hike as does the weather or the route. If a youngster is showing signs that hiking is doing more harm than good, be prepared to turn around. Before doing so, help your child feel that a destination has been reached and that the trip was a success.

Drink Treated Water

Start each hike with a day's supply of drinking water for each person. One quart per person is sufficient for most hikes less than four hours long; strenuous, high-altitude treks require up to four quarts per person. Adults should plan to drink at least two quarts of water during a day's hike.

Encourage hikers to drink at each rest stop, even if they don't feel thirsty. Keep in mind that at 6000 feet elevation your hikers exhale and perspire twice as much as they do at sea level. Watch for loss of stamina, headache, and dark yellow urine, all signals for dehydration. In order to keep tabs on each hiker's water intake, discourage your companions from sharing their water. Perhaps the best system for staying well hydrated is a water bladder that fits in a daypack with a sip hose hanging near a hiker's chin. Hydration packs encourage drinking frequently and generously, in an almost-hands-free, no-stopping style.

No matter how pure a mountain stream or lake appears, the water in it should be considered unsafe for drinking until it has been properly treated. Do not drink or brush teeth with any water that is untreated.

The most common threat to backcountry water sources is the presence of microscopic *Giardia lamblia* cysts, transmitted primarily by animals, including humans. Flu-like symptoms of giardiasis—from stomach cramps to severe diarrhea—appear in five to fourteen days and can last as long as six weeks if untreated. Taking prescription medication is the only cure for this potentially serious disease.

Day hikers should be able to carry all the liquids they require. If you are backpacking, use a water filter or a chemical treatment system or bring water to a boil before drinking. According to Buck Tilton, a wilderness emergency medical technician and coauthor of *Don't Get Sick: The Hidden Dangers of Camping and Hiking* (The Mountaineers Books, 2002): "Once the water is hot enough to produce one rolling bubble, it is free of organisms that will cause illness."

Prevent Hypothermia

Hypothermia is the lowering of internal body temperature, a serious threat to hikers exposed to cool temperatures. Wind, dehydration, exhaustion, and wetness aggravate this number-one killer of outdoor recreationists. Few novice hikers realize that most hypothermia cases develop in air temperatures of 30° to 50°F.

Due to their relatively small body size, children show signs of hypothermia sooner than adults exposed to the same conditions. Whiny,

Opposite: Father and son stop mid-hike for some blister prevention.

uncooperative, or listless children could be exhibiting the **first signs of hypothermia.** More advanced symptoms include uncontrollable fits of shivering, slurred speech, frequent stumbling, memory lapses, and apparent exhaustion even after a rest. Many hypothermia victims, particularly young people, deny feeling cold, so watch for these other signs.

Probably the best way to prevent hypothermia is to **stay dry and well-hydrated.** Wet clothing loses about 90 percent of its insulating value. Wool loses less heat than cotton and some synthetic fabrics. Thunderstorms can be expected during the summer months in the high country, especially in the afternoons, so it's best to start your hike early in the day. Prevent getting wet before rain starts—it's next to impossible to get dry during a rainstorm.

Treatment for hypothermia begins with getting the victim out of the rain and wind. Remove all wet clothes and replace them with warm, dry ones. Provide water, preferably warmed, to sip. A warm sleeping bag may be needed, and skin-to-skin contact is necessary for serious hypothermia cases.

Avoid Lightning

Lightning is a serious threat to all hikers. If, while following a trail above timberline, you notice clouds building, head down below tree level pronto.

During storms, a thick stand of trees is one of the safest places to hunker down. A lone tree on a rocky slope is like a lightning rod—avoid it.

Prevent Altitude Sickness

Lowlanders, children in particular, should spend at least two to three days acclimatizing to Colorado's high altitudes. For treks beginning at 9000 feet or higher, plan to ascend **no more than 1000 feet per day.**

Severe headaches, nausea, a cough, lack of appetite, or a staggering gait indicate a person not acclimatized to high altitudes.

Encourage your companions with these signs of altitude sickness to breathe deeply, rest, and eat high-energy foods. Over-the-counter pain relievers can alleviate headaches. If symptoms persist, head for lower elevations.

Stay Found

Ardent butterfly chasers are apt to lose their way. All kids, be they adventuresome or stay-on-the-trail types, should know what to do in case they discover they have been separated from the group.

Tell them to **stay in one place** rather than going in search of the trail or other people. Encourage kids to use their whistle; three blasts is an international distress call. Remind them that if they feel lost, they should wait and sit in an open area, knowing someone will find them soon. Kids wearing brightly colored caps will be more easily spotted, even in dense brush.

Prevent lost hikers: Assign partners to keep track of the other. Remind kids to stay on the trail at all times. If they hike ahead of the group and the trail meets another trail, tell them to wait rather than try to decide which trail to take. Advise the hike leader to stop at prescribed intervals, such as at the top of every other switchback, to make sure everyone is keeping up.

Show kids the boundaries in camp, where they can explore on their own. Walk to the water pump and toilet with them so they know the way back to your campsite.

ENVIRONMENTAL ETIQUETTE

Hiking in Colorado's forests and mountains brings a great sense of freedom, but with that comes the responsibility to leave the land in its wild state. The following reminders are in no way all-inclusive. Above all, enjoy the grand vistas of the mountains as well as the intimate panoramas at your feet.

Stay on the Trail

Walking alongside the trail widens it and tramples vegetation; stay on the trail itself. Do not allow youngsters to cut across switchbacks to go downhill faster—water will follow their new path, and erosion will soon damage the trail.

Pack It Out

Trash of any kind, including toilet paper, **must be packed out.** After a fuel stop, check for discarded nutshells, orange peels, or cellophane wrappings. A potato chip, though it may decompose, can also cause a serious digestive upset for an unlucky chipmunk.

Teach How and Where to "Go"

Take a potty stop before starting any hike. While on the trail, teach your crew to pee at least 200 feet from a water source or campsite. It is no longer acceptable to bury toilet paper; animals dig it up. Carry it out in a plastic bag. Human waste should be deposited at least 200 feet from a water source, in a hole six inches deep, capped by the sod or soil taken from the same spot.

Don't Pick the Flowers

Little hands are prone to pick bouquets of wildflowers. To prevent this innocent elimination of trailside beauty, explain to young hikers that wildflowers are like us; they cannot live

A spotted moth alights on the lush magenta flowers of Parry's Primrose, an alpine marsh plant with a surprisingly unpleasant odor.

if their bottom half, the stems, are broken off or put in a glass of water. Tell children that it is sad to see flowers taken from their home. (It's illegal to pick Colorado's state flower, the columbine, on public lands.) When your child finds other alluring **items along the trail,** such as sparkly rocks or deer antlers, say, "I wonder, will the next hiker have eyes as sharp as yours and see this pretty rock (or whatever) that you leave here?"

Walk and Speak Softly

These trails take you into the homes of deer and elk, marmots and pikas, eagles, hawks, and hummingbirds, even bears, mountain lions, and foxes. Noise destroys the tranquility needed to see forest creatures. **Speak in a quiet tone** to remind kids that they are visiting wildlife homes. Perhaps spotting a coyote or family of ermine will reward their hushed behavior.

Watch for Wildlife

Edge-of-light hikers, those patient, quiet wildlife watchers during the first and last hours of the day, see and hear the most forest dwellers. Remind your companions that wildlife needs food, water, and space. The closer we get to them, the farther they go away. Stay on the trail or at designated overlooks. Bring binoculars to see elk grazing on a distant slope. (Before hiking, give kids a chance to practice using the binoculars by finding familiar landmarks in your neighborhood.) Wear dark greens and browns, clothing that blends in with the environment. Never chase or try to feed wildlife.

Leash Your Dog

Increasingly, land management policy requires keeping dogs on leash at all times, to avoid disturbing wildlife. In many wilderness areas, dogs are prohibited, as well as in most areas of national parks. Regardless of regulations, courtesy to other hikers and environmental sensitivity suggest that pets be on a leash and that you bag your pet's poop. Few hikers appreciate meeting someone else's dog on the trail, even if it is a "good dog." Consider leaving your

dog at home, especially if you wish to increase your chances of sighting wildlife.

Camp Wisely

Camping in Colorado's (and any) forests requires minimum-impact practices. To avoid harming plant life, **choose a campsite in an established site** well away from the trail or on a nonvegetated patch.

Use a camping stove for cooking; if your hikers want a campfire, follow area regulations, checking the current fire danger to make sure the conditions allow a campfire. Keep it small and in an established campfire site. Use only fallen dead wood; don't break limbs off trees. Let the fire burn down to ashes before drowning it with water. Stir the ashes with a stick and leave the remains in the firepit. Scatter leftover wood.

Dishwashing should take place at least 200 feet from the water source. A smidgen of wet sand applied with a bit of elbow grease makes a great pot scrubber. If soap is used, be sure it's biodegradable. Pack out any leftover food.

Careless campers leave a "hurtful sight," as one young hiker told me. Your group will feel better if they **contribute to cleaning up the natural environment.** Many kids at the end of a hike proudly empty their pockets of gum wrappers and cigarette butts found along the trail. Alert the rangers at the nearest Forest Service office if you see any serious or dangerous violations along the trail.

HOW TO USE THIS BOOK

The hikes described in this guidebook represent the best of Colorado's diverse ecosystems. All the trails selected are near or en route to popular destinations in the state. The Great Getaways sidebars sprinkled throughout the book serve as a resource for extending your day's hiking pleasure with visits to nearby attractions.

The book is arranged into four geographic regions, with twenty-two to twenty-eight hikes in each. The Metro region includes trails in and around Denver and the Front Range. The Central region lists trails in areas around Summit County, Vail, and Gunnison, plus two hikes featuring the Great Sand Dunes, southwest of Pueblo. The North region's access points are Fort Collins, Rocky Mountain National Park, and Steamboat Springs. The West/ Southwest region's starting destinations include Grand Junction, Durango, Silverton, Telluride, and Mesa Verde National Park.

Meadows of columbine reward this high-country hiker.

About the Hikes

Each hike description begins with information blocks summarizing the trail's location, type (day hike or backpack), difficulty, distance (one way or loop), hiking season, elevation gain (starting elevation and high point), maps, information sources and fees, and accessibility for wheelchair users. Driving directions to the trailhead are given under the heading "Getting There." Under "Logistics" you will find trail restrictions, recommended times to visit, and the availability of water and toilet facilities. "On the Trail" summarizes what you can expect on the hike, including human and geological history, optional turnaround points to shorten the hike, trail and environmental cautions, and natural history highlights. The last four items are noted by symbols alongside the trail description. See below for a key to these margin symbols.

Difficulty. Hikes are rated easy, moderate, and challenging. **Easy** hikes are relatively short, smooth, gentle trails suitable for small children or first-time hikers. **Moderate** hikes are 2 to 4 miles total distance and feature more than 500 feet of elevation gain. The trail may be rough and uneven. Hikers should wear lug-soled boots and carry the Ten Essentials. **Challenging** trails are often rough, with considerable elevation gain or distance to travel. They are suitable for older or experienced children. Lug-soled boots and the Ten Essentials are standard equipment.

Distance. All of these hikes range in length from 0.5 mile to 10.5 miles round-trip and can be completed in one day. Whenever possible, loop trips were selected. Turnaround spots indicated can be ideal destinations for a shorter hike or a picnic lunch stop. Many of the hikes can be extended into overnight or backpack trips.

Hikable. This listing in the information block refers to the approximate months the trail is snow-free or open to the public. Winter snowfall and spring temperatures can alter the optimal season considerably. It's a good idea to call the nearest ranger station or other information contact for an update on the trail's condition before attempting the hike early or late in the season.

Maps. Each hike description is accompanied by a map showing the featured route, using symbols to locate key landmarks mentioned in the text (see the hike map legend, just after the table of contents). In addition to these simple route maps, hikers interested in using more detailed topographical maps should refer to United States Geological Survey (USGS) maps, available at www.store.usgs.gov. Not every trail in Colorado is marked on these maps; however, the trails in this book with a USGS listing can be found on the map named in the information block. Other sources for detailed recreational maps can be found at websites hosted by national and state forests and parks, as well as at county open space and parks sites. It's a good idea to become acquainted with USGS and other topographical maps by orienting yourself with a compass while on a well-marked, perhaps familiar, trail and land area.

Accessibility. The accessiblity listing at the end of the information block indicates whether all or portions of a trail are level enough for limited wheelchair use. A wheelchair symbol placed at the start of the trail indicates the entire trail is accessible. Otherwise, an arrow between wheelchair symbols marks the accessible portion. Having spent six months in a wheelchair recuperating from a severe injury, I know the need for wheelchair-accessible trails, also called "ADA-accessible" (American Disabilities Act). Accessible trails are ideal for families with hikers of differing ability, including toddlers and their grandparents. Many of these trails reflect state-of-the-art interpretation and design techniques, creating enjoyable paths for the entire family. At the time of this writing, Forest Service districts throughout the state were proposing numerous barrier-free or wheelchair-accessible trails.

Key to Margin Symbols

 Turnarounds. These are places, mostly along moderate trails, where families can cut their hike short yet still have a satisfying outing. These optional turnaround points usually offer picnic opportunities, views, or special natural attractions.

Trail cautions. These mark potential hazards, such as cliffs, stream or highway crossings, unfenced overlooks, poison ivy, and the like, where close supervision of children is strongly recommended.

Environmental cautions. These are warnings of fragile natural or historical features; be extra careful not to disturb these special spots.

Environmental close-ups. Each of these natural history notes provides a fun, often sensory-based approach to involving kids in nature, alerting them to the trail's unique environmental features. This helps all hikers have fun while learning about and respecting nature.

Trail Tales

Some of the funniest, most amazing, challenging, and heart-warming events happen while hiking, especially with kids. Preserve those moments by jotting them down in the "Trails Tales" pages at the end of the book. In doing so, you'll create a companion volume to this book, which will become your family's cherished record of their outdoor adventures.

A NOTE ABOUT SAFETY

Safety is an important concern in all outdoor activities. No guidebook can alert you to every hazard or anticipate the limitations of every reader. Therefore, the descriptions of roads, trails, routes, and natural features in this book are not representations that a particular place or excursion will be safe for your party. When you follow any of the routes described in this book, you assume responsibility for your own safety. Under normal conditions, such excursions require the usual attention to traffic, road and trail conditions, weather, terrain, the capabilities of your party, and other factors. Keeping informed on current conditions and exercising common sense are the keys to a safe, enjoyable outing.

—*The Mountaineers Books*

Opposite: A wading toddler watches for "fishies" in Fourmile Creek.

METRO

DENVER, BOULDER, AND COLORADO SPRINGS

1 HIGHLINE CANAL TRAIL

BEFORE YOU GO
Map Guide to the Highline Canal Trail
Information For current conditions and more information, contact Denver Water Board, www.denverwater.org or (303) 893-2444

ABOUT THE HIKE
Location Denver metro area
Day hike; Easy
0.2–1 mile one way
Hikable Year-round
Starting elevation/High point 5380 feet/5400 feet
Accessibility Wheelchair-accessible

GETTING THERE

The Highline Canal can be reached from many streets, as shown on the "Guide to the Highline Canal Trail" (see map listing above). An especially kid-friendly 1-mile section of the 66-mile trail begins at mile 24, where the canal loops around DeKoevend Park, located between Franklin Avenue and University Boulevard north of the Southglenn Mall. Accessible parking and a bridge to the canal are at the South Suburban Ice Arena, 6509 South Vine Street.

LOGISTICS

The entire trail is wheelchair-accessible; however, curb cuts are not provided at every street crossing. During inclement weather, the 19-mile section of the trail south of Hampden Avenue is not suitable for wheelchair use. Wading, swimming, boating, and fishing are not permitted along the Highline Canal. Walkers, joggers, bikers, in-line skaters, and parents with strollers use the trail. Horseback riders enjoy all but the Denver portion of the trail.

ON THE TRAIL

For a refreshing pause amid Denver's bustle, enjoy a quiet walk along the Highline Canal. Conceived in 1870 by James Duff, a Scotsman determined to bring water to the farms east of Denver, the 76-mile waterway is still an irrigation canal, but for Denverites it is better known as a swath of nature that runs through the heart of the city. Beginning in Waterton Canyon (south Denver), the canal, which carries water 4 to 7 feet deep, follows the natural contours of the land, dropping

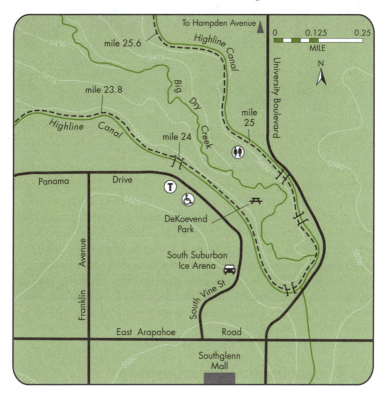

only 300 feet in elevation for its entire length. The 58-mile-long, 8- to 12-foot-wide pathway (paved in urban areas, hard-packed south of Hampden Avenue) parallels the canal. The trail's southwest–northeast course traverses open plains and urban sections and passes near beautiful residential areas, parks, and golf courses. Tall cottonwoods line most sections, affording shade in the summer and a splash of bright color in the fall.

Each section offers a calm reprieve from the city and a chance to savor a slice of the natural environment. DeKoevend Park's playground and three bridges spanning the canal appeal to kids; parents appreciate the area's restrooms, covered picnic tables, and ease of parking. Designated open-space areas border either side of the park, providing destinations for hikers and bird-watchers. Spot foxes and great blue herons at the open space to the west at mile 23.8, a short walk that is fine for very young hikers. For a longer walk, head east, then west, to circle the park

Ducks drift on the waters of Highline Canal.

 (crossing over Big Dry Creek) to mile 25, an area where eagles and great horned owls are known to soar above.

Edge-of-light hikers, those late-evening or early-morning watchers, are the most likely to spot the area's wildest inhabitants, be they squirrels, sparrows, or foxes. Along the trail children run freely, hiding behind trees, chasing squirrels and birds darting across the path. Magpies and meadowlarks are among the birds that alight on branches that canopy the trail. Squirrels sprinting up a tree trunk are common along the residential sections. Prairie dogs and pheasants have been sighted in the open areas. Geese and a variety of ducks flock to the reservoirs and lakes that the canal feeds.

After your walk, return the way you came.

 ## 2 LAKE LOOP AND NATURE TRAILS

BEFORE YOU GO
Map Crown Hill Park
Information For current conditions and more information, contact Jefferson County Open Space, www.jeffco.us/openspace or (303) 271-5925

ABOUT THE HIKE
Location Crown Hill Park
Day hike; Easy
1.9-mile loop
Hikable Year-round (wildlife sanctuary closed March 1– June 30)
Starting elevation/High point 5280 feet/5280 feet
Accessibility 3.5 miles of paved loops, including 1-mile fitness course; 0.7-mile ADA-accessible loop

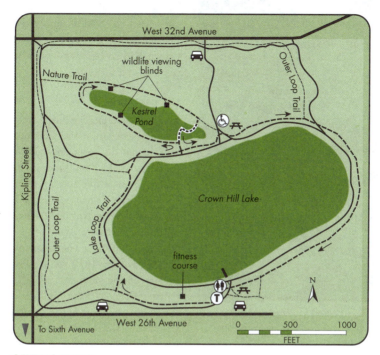

GETTING THERE

From Sixth Avenue, take a right onto Kipling Street and follow it north to West 26th Avenue; turn right to reach the main parking lot, located on West 26th Avenue between Garrison and Garland streets. A secondary lot is at West 32nd Avenue and approximately Garrison Street; an equestrian lot is located on 26th Avenue just west of Garrison Street.

LOGISTICS

Toilet facilities, drinking water, and a picnic shelter are available near the main lot on West 26th Avenue. A Crown Hill Park map is available at the trailhead. The 1.2-mile Lake Loop Trail around Crown Hill Lake features an accessible fishing pier near the main parking area. A second picnic shelter is situated between Crown Hill Lake and Kestrel Pond. Joggers, walkers, and people on horseback and in wheelchairs frequent the 6.5 miles of trails that circle the park and the lake. During the peak nesting period, March 1 to June 30, the wildlife sanctuary surrounding Kestrel Pond is protected from human visitation; even during the open visitation months, horseback riders and pets are not

Wildlife and kids are drawn to the shores and marshes of Crown Hill Park.

allowed in the wildlife sanctuary. These regulations have allowed Crown Hill to become a wildlife watcher's paradise.

ON THE TRAIL

Nestled between two large suburban tracts, this wildlife refuge is as much an oasis for wildlife watchers as it is for the animals that migrate or live there. Crown Hill Park was dedicated on Earth Day 1990 as a Natural Urban Wildlife Sanctuary, and it more than lives up to its commitment. Established in 1979 as a joint project of the Jefferson County Open Space Program and the cities of Wheat Ridge and Lakewood, the park consists of shallow Kestrel Pond and Crown Hill Lake situated on 177 acres.

From the main parking lot on West 26th Avenue, the recommended hike follows a clockwise loop that begins on the soft-surface trail leading north, then west. Continue on this equestrian trail, or take the adjacent paved Lake Loop Trail; both follow Crown Hill Lake's west shore. At about 0.4 mile both trails meet the 0.7-mile accessible trail around Kestrel Pond; turn left to follow this clockwise as well.

The marsh habitat here draws a variety of nesting birds and wildlife. Encourage your companions to walk quietly as they approach the three viewing blinds around the pond; turtles like silence when sunning on a rock. You might see the pond's namesake, the American kestrel, a small (9-inch length, 22-inch wingspan) falcon with cinnamon and blue-gray coloring and a black stripe down the sides of the cheek. When perched, a kestrel frequently "pumps" its tail. Keen-eyed observers are more likely to spot a red-winged or yellow-headed blackbird perched on a reed above the water. Have young hikers look for their nests: woven cups fastened to tall grasses. Geese and red-headed and canvasback ducks stop over here. Watch for a great blue heron, a large gray bird standing motionless on stiltlike legs with its large head tucked between its shoulders or erect on its long neck. Include a stop at the shore dimpled with tracks left by the area's frequent visitors: squirrels, skunks, foxes, and mule deer.

As your group walks the boardwalk through the cattail marsh, let them know this plant provided many types of food for Native Americans. In spring they gathered young cattail shoots to eat the way we eat asparagus. Later, the flower buds were eaten like corn on the cob, and the cattail roots were pounded into a flour to make breads. When the cigar-shaped seed head was mature and started to disperse its fluffy seed heads, they collected the down to soften their sleeping areas and cradleboards. Ask which part of the plant Native Americans would gather today and how they would use it.

When the boardwalk rejoins the Lake Loop Trail at 1.1 miles, turn left to return via its remaining 0.8 mile around the lake's east shore (or you can return as you came).

 BLUFF LAKE

BEFORE YOU GO
Map Self-guided booklet available at trailhead
Information For current conditions and more information, contact Bluff Lake Nature Center, www.blufflakenaturecenter.org or (303) 344-0031

ABOUT THE HIKE
Location Denver, Stapleton Redevelopment Site
Day hike; Easy
1-mile loop
Hikable Year-round
Starting elevation/High point 5300 feet/5300 feet
Accessibility Most of trail is wheelchair-accessible

GETTING THERE
From I-70, head south on the Havana exit, turning left at the light off the exit ramp. Go through the four-way stop at Smith Road, continuing through the light at Martin Luther King Boulevard. At the next light turn left (east) onto East 29th Drive. Go through the light at Iola Street and follow the road as it curves to the right. The entrance to Bluff Lake Nature Center is 0.5 mile down the curvy road, on the left (north) side. Ample parking is provided.

LOGISTICS

The nature center is open sunrise to sunset. Vault toilets are found at the visitor center and near station 4. There is no drinking water. School groups frequently visit here midweek, so plan accordingly. Bring binoculars. Dogs, bicycles, and swimming are not permitted.

ON THE TRAIL

Bluff Lake Nature Center is Denver's wildlife pocket, perfectly sized for kids to detect tracks, spy on birds, and discover the hidden habitats of animals and plants. The 123-acre oasis is also a source of solace for adults and a showcase of environmental remediation. The lake and adjacent Sand Creek, once polluted remnants of Stapleton Airport, were rescued in the 1990s by the Clean Water Act and an organization dedicated to preserving the area as a wildlife refuge. Your kids will be amazed when you tell them the bluff they are standing on is a human-made geologic formation; concrete from the old airport lies beneath their feet!

The trail begins on the bluff with grand views of Denver, the Front

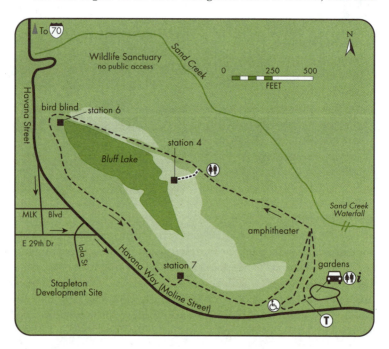

Range, and the basin where Bluff Lake lies quietly removed from the city. A guide to the center's nine stations is also available here. The signs posted at each site provide explanations, and, more importantly, fun insights on ways of looking and listening for nature's clues.

Take the broad, stepped walkway from the bluff down to the trail circling the lake. Veering to the right leads you to Sand Creek Waterfall, created as a means of adding oxygen to the water and to prevent flooding. Kids, however, like watching the ducks paddling in the eddies here.

Huge, grandfather-sized cottonwoods shade the walkway, offering a cool relief in summer, a gold canopy in the fall. Dozens more cottonwoods have been planted along the lake, some just "baby-sized," others perhaps "as old as mom," one young visitor commented.

Quiet hikers may be lucky enough to spot a snowy egret.

Encourage your crew to walk quietly as they approach station 4. The boardwalk here leads directly into head-high reeds, among which they might spot a great blue heron ("GBH!!" I heard a young birder call) or a snowy egret. The bird blind at station 6 provides another chance to see the lake's inhabitants.

The last portion of trail rises from the lake's wetlands to prairie grasses, with stops at a prairie dog town and a cliff pocked with nests of mud made by bank swallows.

The last station, Outfall (station 7), leads to a reminder of Bluff Lake's origin; a storm drain spills water from city streets into the cattail-edged marsh where it is filtered clean of litter.

The trail returns to the Bluff Lake Nature Center where you're asked to leave the brochure guide in the box on the post.

ROCKY MOUNTAIN ARSENAL NATIONAL WILDLIFE REFUGE

BEFORE YOU GO
Map RMA NWR brochure
Information For current conditions and more information, contact RMA NWR, www.fws.gov/rockymountainarsenal or (303) 289-0930

ABOUT THE HIKE
Location Commerce City
Day hike; Easy
0.5-mile loop, Lake Mary; up to 1.7 miles one way, Ladora Trail
Hikable Year-round
Starting elevation/High point 5217 feet/5217 feet
Accessibility Visitor center, learning lab, and parts of Lake Mary Trail are wheelchair-accessible

GETTING THERE

From Denver, take I-70 to Quebec Street north, and drive 2.8 miles to Prairie Parkway (64th turns into Prairie Parkway). Turn right at Prairie Parkway and travel 0.6 mile to Gateway Road. Turn left at Gateway Road and proceed to the parking area alongside the Rocky Mountain Arsenal NWR visitor center. Stop here to take in the exhibits before driving 3 more miles to the trailhed. To reach the trailhead, exit the visitor center parking lot and turn left on East 64th Avenue. At the 4-way intersection, turn left on Havana Street, drive past Lake Mary, then turn right into the Learning Lab parking lot, where the hike begins.

LOGISTICS

The refuge is closed on Mondays; open 6:00 AM–6:00 PM summers, 7:00 AM–5:00 PM winters; visitor center, 9:00 AM–4:00 PM. Call ahead for event information and reservations. Restrooms and drinking water are available at the visitor center and Discovery Learning Lab. Pets are prohibited. Binoculars and cameras are recommended.

ON THE TRAIL

The transformation of a chemical manufacturing complex into a wildlife refuge is a feat as amazing as the destination itself. Rocky Mountain Arsenal is now a 17,000-acre prairie habitat where families watch bison graze, prairie dogs perch, and eagles soar overhead. It's a destination where kids dissect owl pellets, hop on a hayride, and "walk on water"

A proud angler poses with the day's catch (and release) from Lake Mary.

to a fine fishing spot. Denver's nearest island of wildlife serves as a sanctuary for 330 animal species—and countless harried grown-ups.

The action starts at the visitor center, which opened in May 2011. At the headquarters for one of the largest urban wildlife refuges in the country, kids stand nose-to-nose with a stuffed bison, then explore such hands-on displays as a migration mapping puzzle and a Cold War–era "explosion-proof telephone." The center's engaging exhibits show how the one-time bison territory was homesteaded, then became a toxic site of chemical technologies. A roost of eagles spotted here in 1986 triggered the Environmental Protection Agency to begin the renewal that led to today's stewardship of the land by the U.S. Fish and Wildlife Service.

To get the best of your family's visit to the refuge, call ahead to reserve spots on a free, naturalist-guided tour. Birding, biking, and photo expeditions are among the featured outings. A popular spring

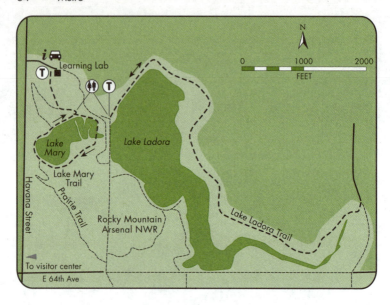

tour takes visitors to watch young burrowing owls emerge from their underground homes, the prairie dog tunnels their parents took over. Reservations are also needed to join the refuge's Wild Ride, a two-hour family-friendly wildlife-viewing tour featuring America's original breed of bison.

The 3-mile drive from the visitor center to Lake Mary passes an active prairie dog village before it reaches the parking lot and Learning Lab. Inside, there's a live beehive safely housed in a faux oak tree, designed for kids to search for the queen. Hikers on the 0.5-mile loop around Lake Mary begin the trail in the shade of cottonwoods outside of the Learning Lab, then follow the floating boardwalk to the stocked lake's prime fishing spots (catch-and-release only). During my July visit I watched a twelve-year-old pull out a pole-bending catfish. Nearby a young sibling trio snagged ten bluegills in less than an hour.

The Lake Mary Trail circles the lake, returning to the trailhead. Those continuing on to Lake Ladora bypass the Lake Mary loop and pick up the Ladora Trail. If time and temperature allow, head north for a 1.4-mile walk alongside the lake's north edge, then return via the same trail, circling Lake Mary. Another option is to make a clockwise loop along the southern Lake Ladora Trail, returning on the Prairie Trail to rejoin the Lake Mary Trail.

NIEDRACH NATURE TRAIL AND GAZEBO BOARDWALK

BEFORE YOU GO
Map Barr Lake State Park brochure
Information For current conditions and more information, contact Barr Lake State Park, www.parks.state.co.us/parks/barrlake or (303) 659-6005

ABOUT THE HIKE
Location Barr Lake State Park Day hike; Easy
0.25-mile loop, Niedrach Nature Trail; 3.25 miles round-trip
Hikable Year-round
Starting elevation/High point 5100 feet/5100 feet
Accessibility Wheelchair-accessible

GETTING THERE
From Denver, take I-76 northeast to Bromley Lane (exit 22); follow this for 1.8 miles to Picadilly Road and turn south. Proceed 1.9 miles to the park entrance, then continue 0.25 mile southwest to the nature center and parking lot.

LOGISTICS
Picnic and toilet facilities, drinking water, binoculars, and a map are available at Barr Lake Nature Center. Camping and swimming are not

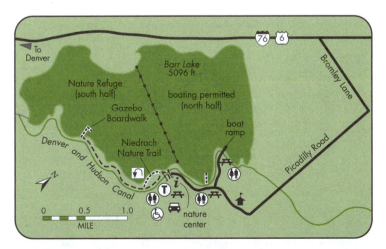

permitted; dogs and boats are prohibited from the southern half of the lake, where the nature refuge is located. (Barr Lake Nature Center is closed on Mondays and Tuesdays in winter.)

ON THE TRAIL

Home to one of the few nesting bald eagles on Colorado's Front Range, Barr Lake State Park offers a pleasant day hike along a prairie reservoir. A boardwalk and a gazebo situated in prime viewing areas provide opportunities for watching the hundreds of waterbirds that stop over, nest, or stay here. Kids love to use binoculars to watch the large birds take off and land on the water. Before beginning the hike, stop at the nature center. Throughout the week, free wildlife programs and guided walks begin here. The center's naturalist will tell of recent bird sightings.

From the parking lot at the nature center, walk across the bridge over the Denver and Hudson Canal and turn left, walk about 100 yards, then bear right onto the Niedrach Nature Trail. Named for Robert Niedrach, an ornithologist who studied the birds of Barr Lake, this 0.25-mile boardwalk meanders through a cottonwood and willow marsh along the lake's eastern shore. The nature refuge, which is on the lake's southern half, also begins here.

Along the nature trail boardwalk, kids like stopping at the viewing stand to watch the grebes, white pelicans, and great blue herons that frequent these waters. Grebes can be identified by their long, swanlike

The boardwalk at Barr Lake enters a cottonwood and willow marsh.

necks, which are white underneath. If you plan your Barr Lake visit for late May or early June, you may see the grebes performing their mating dance—a well-choreographed ritual of the male and female birds crossing their necks, then running across the water in synchrony with each other.

The Niedrach Nature Trail loops back to the trail along the canal. Opposite the canal trail, a meadow of tall grasses reaches the horizon. On windy days, point out how the grasses move like waves on water. Along the shore of the shallow bay are several park benches nestled under a cottonwood tree, perfect for viewing the ducks—mallards, pintails, teals—that patrol these waters. At the junction of the nature trail and canal trail, you can turn left to return to the bridge and parking lot; to continue, turn right.

If a chance to see bald eagles is a priority—January through March is the most likely time of year—continue your walk 1 mile farther to the Gazebo Boardwalk, which extends 950 feet out over the lake. Remind eager eagle watchers to approach the gazebo as quietly as possible. At this overlook, double-crested cormorants, white pelicans, and snowy egrets are among the birds dotting the waters of the surrounding heron rookery. Bald eagles raise their young here in the summer but are seen throughout the year in this region.

From the boardwalk, return along the canal trail to the nature center.

6 LICHEN LOOP TRAIL

BEFORE YOU GO
Maps Boulder County Parks and Open Space–Heil Valley Ranch; USGS Lyons
Information For current conditions and more information, contact Boulder County, www.bouldercounty.org or (303) 678-6200

ABOUT THE HIKE
Location Heil Valley Ranch
Day hike; Easy
1.3-mile loop
Hikable April through October
Starting elevation/High point 5895 feet/6050 feet
Accessibility None

GETTING THERE
From Boulder, take the Foothills Highway (US 36/CO-7) north 5 miles and turn left (west) onto Lefthand Canyon Drive. Travel 1 mile to Geer

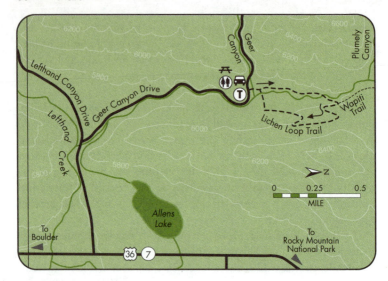

Canyon Drive, where you turn right; please respect private property when traveling through Geer Canyon. Continue 1.5 miles to the parking lot on the right.

LOGISTICS

Toilet facilities are provided at the trailhead. Groups of runners or mountain bikers use the adjacent 2.5-mile Wapiti Trail, which ends in the 2.6-mile Ponderosa Loop. Dogs are not permitted at Heil Valley Ranch.

ON THE TRAIL

Close to Boulder yet separate and serene, in the 5000-acre Heil Valley Ranch the Great Plains meet the southern Rocky Mountains. The pedestrian-only Lichen Trail loops around a rocky, pine-dotted foothill, giving hikers a sampling of the region's grasslands, shrublands, forests, and canyons. A gentle creek provides a cooling start and end to summer hikes here.

The Lichen Loop Trail begins at the west end of the parking lot at the footbridge over a small creek. When the trail forks, follow it to the left for a gentle ascent around the loop.

The trail's namesake shows off as bright green and gold crusts on the rocks and boulders here. Lichen, seemingly dry and lifeless, reigns among the oldest plants in the region, hundreds of years in most cases. Kids are surprised to learn that lichens actually break down rock. The crusts are composed of two plants, algae and fungi. The algae provide food for the plant, and fungi supply a protective covering. Meanwhile, rootlike hairs of the lichen probe into the rock surface emitting a mild acid. Water seeps into these tiny sites, where season after season of freezing and thawing eventually creates a break in the rock surface. Lichen erosion of rock is slow but continuous.

Deer browse on some lichen types in winter. Hummingbirds build their nests with lichen. Native Americans used lichens to dye wool for weavings, to brew medicinal teas, and to poison their arrow tips. Fine perfume has even been made from lichen! How many different types and colors of lichen does your group spot on this hike?

The trail climbs gently through stands of ponderosa pines with prickly pear and yucca at their feet as it loops back to the trailhead. During the feet-cooling stop at the creek, look for square-stemmed mint plants. Kids remember the plant after feeling it and smelling it.

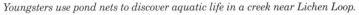

Youngsters use pond nets to discover aquatic life in a creek near Lichen Loop.

ANNE U. WHITE TRAIL

BEFORE YOU GO
Map Boulder County Parks and Open Space
Information For current conditions and more information, contact Boulder County, www.bouldercounty.org or (303) 678-6200

ABOUT THE HIKE
Location Boulder
Day hike; Easy
1.6 miles one way
Hikable Year-round
Starting elevation/High point 6040 feet/6530 feet
Accessibility None

GETTING THERE

In Boulder, take Broadway north to Lee Hill Drive and turn left (west). Drive 1.1 miles to Wagonwheel Gap Road; turn left (west). Travel 1.1 miles to Pinto Drive where parking is available on the right. Additional parking for three vehicles (including two handicapped sites) is available at the trailhead, 0.2 mile west on Pinto Drive. Remember to respect the rights of property owners in this residential area. Be aware that mountain lions have been spotted in this canyon—keep your crew together.

LOGISTICS

Leashed dogs are allowed on this trail; bicycles are prohibited. During summer weekends, plan to hike this popular trail in the early morning or evening hours.

ON THE TRAIL

The playful gurgle of Fourmile Canyon Creek greets visitors at their first steps into Boulder's secluded riparian corridor. Kids love stopping at trailside shaded pools, many edged by boulders seemingly arranged as chairs for their adult companions. The near-to-town Anne U. White Trail follows a narrow, wooded canyon, preserved from development thanks to the work led by Ann Underhill White in the 1980s.

A small grotto and pool at 0.3 mile marks the trail's first of many creek crossings, all easily negotiated by legs short and tall. The littlest of hikers may be content with pool play here, making it their day's destination. For those going on, encourage your hikers to keep track of each time they cross the creek; discovering the total crossings motivates them to reach the trail's length. (Spoiler alert: it's twenty-two times.)

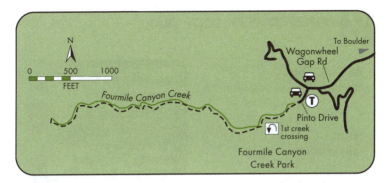

Add more fun to the hike with wow-stops at a wildflower blooming in someone's favorite color or to watch a butterfly dance through a tree branch. Mint, among the more abundant plants here, is detectable by smell and feel. Its scent will direct noses to a 10- to 24-inch-tall plant with finely toothed leaves attached to a square-shaped stem, easily felt between two fingers. Birdsong and chipmunk chatter are among the sounds worth tuning into in this natural oasis. The Anne U. White Trail checklist of mammals, birds, and wildflowers, available at the trailhead, may serve the budding naturalist in your group.

At crossing number sixteen, 1.3 miles, the stream spills down a 5-foot-tall rock ledge into a quiet pool. Few resist stopping at this lovely sanctuary. Others may be drawn to scramble up the false trail climbing steeply to the right. Instead, encourage the creek-crossing counter in your group to veer left over the creek, reaching the trail's terminus. Did anyone in the group guesstimate the correct number of crossings?

Return via the same trail.

Hikers assigned as "creek-crossing counters" explore the stream alongside a trail.

PINES-TO-PEAK LOOP TRAIL

BEFORE YOU GO
Maps Bald Mountain Scenic Area brochure; Boulder County Parks and Open Space; USGS Gold Hill
Information For current conditions and more information, contact Boulder County, www.bouldercounty.org or (303) 678-6200

ABOUT THE HIKE
Location Bald Mountain Scenic Area
Day hike; Easy
1.5-mile loop
Hikable Year-round
Starting elevation/High point 6960 feet/7160 feet
Accessibility None

GETTING THERE

From Boulder, take 9th Street west to Sunshine Canyon Drive. Turn west and proceed 5 miles to the parking lot for the Bald Mountain Scenic Area on the south side of the road.

LOGISTICS

Picnic tables and seasonal restrooms (April–October) are provided at the trailhead.

ON THE TRAIL

Requiring little effort, yet offering magnificent views, a hike up Bald Mountain can be the first "peak" attained by beginning mountain climbers. Hikers also get a chance to see the charred remnants of the September

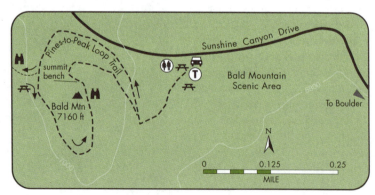

2010 Fourmile Canyon Wildland Fire that stopped at Bald Mountain Scenic Area.

The trail to this barren, windswept mountaintop begins in the friendly confines of a ponderosa pine forest adjacent to the parking lot. While walking through this forest, alert kids to the rhythmical tapping of a hairy woodpecker or the chatter of tassel-eared Abert's squirrels, both residents here. Your youngsters may see a stout gray bird climbing headfirst down the pine trees. This acrobat is a nuthatch, of either the pygmy or white-breasted variety.

Contouring the base of Bald Mountain, the trail heads west 0.3 mile into an open grassland where the wildflowers at your feet are as spectacular as the views of snow-covered mountaintops on the horizon. Equally important, though far less glamorous, are the grasses that blanket the slope. During the next rest stop, ask your companions to find two or three grass varieties. Unlike many wildflowers, grasses grow in tight clumps, holding the minimal soil here in place. For kids, however, grasses are better suited as tickling wands!

As the trail loops around and heads south, watch for the short spur trail on the right, at about 0.7 mile, that leads to a throne of rocks, a perfect seat for assessing the views. A ponderosa pine tree, securely rooted in the rubble, seems to like this spot also.

As the trail continues south, the Boulder valley, Denver, and beyond can be seen. To the west look for fire-blackened tree trunks, remnants of the 6181-acre Fourmile Canyon Wildland Fire. The trail heads north again for 0.3 mile, taking you to the summit with a bench—the perfect place to photograph the day's climb.

Few trees survive at the top of Bald Mountain, hence its name. Close inspection of the soil shows that it is composed of tiny rocks. Your children may point out other factors, such as steep terrain, hot summer sun, and cold winter winds that prevent trees from taking root on this mountaintop.

From the summit, follow the trail north then south down the opposite side of the mountain to return to the parking lot.

Even "cute" golden-mantled ground squirrels thrive without human food.

CANYON LOOP TRAIL

BEFORE YOU GO
Maps Betasso Preserve brochure; Boulder County Parks and Open Space
Information For current conditions and more information, contact Boulder County, www.bouldercounty.org or (303) 678-6200

ABOUT THE HIKE
Location Betasso Preserve
Day hike; Moderate
3.2-mile loop
Hikable May to October
Starting elevation/High point 6540 feet/7420 feet
Accessibility None

GETTING THERE

From Boulder, take Boulder Canyon Drive about 4 miles west, then turn right on Sugarloaf Road and watch for the sign for Betasso Preserve. Continue to the Betasso Preserve parking lot.

LOGISTICS

The preserve is open from sunrise to sunset. Toilet and picnic facilities are available at the parking lot. The best days to visit with kids are Wednesdays and Saturdays, when bikes are prohibited.

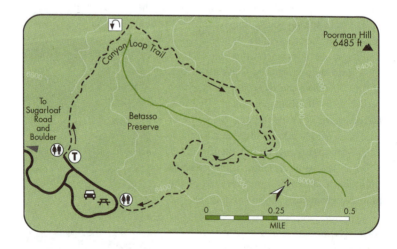

The youngest hiker gets a free ride!

ON THE TRAIL

This land 6 miles west of Boulder was not homesteaded until 1912, three years later becoming a cattle ranch operated by the Betasso family. Now operated by Boulder County Parks and Open Space, Betasso Preserve features deer instead of cows. The vigorous Canyon Loop Trail crosses flowered fields, a lush streambed, a dense forest, and a meadow as it loops around the junction of Boulder and Fourmile canyons. Families with little ones take the easy climb across a meadow at the trail's beginning, and older kids steam ahead to explore the changing terrain.

Begin the trek on the old farm road heading northwest from the parking lot. In 0.5 mile, you'll reach the narrow trail traversing a meadow. This is an ideal destination for very young hikers. To continue, turn right on the trail.

Timing your hike to take place in the early morning or evening increases your chance of seeing a small group of deer feed. Throughout the day, the area's bird choir gives a free concert, telling each other where food can be found or warning of human presence. Encourage your crew to listen for two birds communicating.

At 1 mile, the trail dips down the canyon ravine. Kids will notice chunks of pink and white quartz rocks sprinkling the ground. These are examples of the oldest rocks in Boulder County—Boulder Creek granodiorite. This 1.7-billion-year-old rock was formed from molten material. Your school-aged companions can tell you that the rocks are igneous.

Within a steep 0.5-mile descent, the trail meets a stream bordered by a thick stand of a variety of trees. This small area, considered a riparian zone, is an important source of food, water, and shelter for the area's birds and mammals. (Ninety percent of the state's wildlife depends on riparian zones, yet only three percent of the state is classified as such.) Enter this area quietly, asking youngsters to watch for animals using this habitat. Birds alighting on tree branches, water strider insects skimming across the creek, bees feeding on flowers, or a spider spinning a web may be among their finds. Enjoy a cool rest in the shade here—it's a serious climb up and out of the canyon.

Within 0.5 mile of climbing, the trail levels out as it crosses an open hilltop. Views of the surrounding slopes and canyons are excellent here. Continue hiking south another mile or so as the trail winds past a picnic site and returns to the parking lot.

 MUD LAKE OPEN SPACE

BEFORE YOU GO
Maps Boulder County Parks and Open Space; USGS Nederland
Information For current conditions and more information, contact Boulder County, www.bouldercounty.org or (303) 678-6200

ABOUT THE HIKE
Location Nederland
Day hike; Easy
0.8 mile, Tungsten Loop; 1.1 miles, Kinnickinnick Loop
Hikable Year-round
Starting elevation/High point 8373 feet/8550 feet
Accessibility None

GETTING THERE
From Boulder, head west on Canyon Drive/CO-119 up Boulder Canyon to the town of Nederland. Veer right (north) onto CO-72, continuing 1.9 miles to CO-126. Turn left (west) onto County Road 126 and continue 0.3 mile on the paved road, turning left after 0.1 mile at the sign for Mud Lake Open Space. Ample parking is provided.

Mud Lake is an easy-to-reach getaway edging the Indian Peaks Wilderness.

LOGISTICS

The area is open from sunrise to sunset. Toilet facilities are provided, but no drinking water. Dogs are permitted on leash only. Swimming, fishing, and boating are prohibited at Mud Lake.

ON THE TRAIL

Despite its name, Mud Lake charms its visitors. The easy-to-reach getaway, near Indian Peaks Wilderness Area, appeals to hikers hoping to spot a moose, elk, or long-tailed ermine. Equally alluring is the area's spring-through-summer wildflower pageant followed by the aspen fall color show. Few kids resist the fun of poking around the lake edge, skipping rocks, or discovering what lurks under a log.

Two trails, the Tungsten and Kinnickinnick, form a figure-eight path through the area. Checking out the lake may be the day's destination for some hikers. Others will want to look for signs of wildlife in the forests of pine, spruce, and aspen along the two looped trails.

Starting from the northwest end of the parking lot, near the restrooms, a short trail leads through the pines to the 0.8-mile Tungsten Loop. Since the lake is where kids want to be, head left at the trail junction to walk the pedestrian-only trail along Mud Lake's north shore. The trail edges along tall reeds and cattails, then drops to the lake in two places. The area surrounding the lake's southern half, a critical wildlife habitat, is not accessible. Among the wildlife protected here is Colorado's only salamander, the tiger (*Ambistoma tigrinum*). As an adult, the orange-and-black-patterned tiger salamander dwells beneath logs, and in its immature form, sometimes called "waterdog," lives underwater. Return to the start of the Tungsten Loop, then follow the trail as it loops west, with views of the nearby mountains and glaciers mirrored in Mud Lake.

Watch for and turn right onto the 100-foot connecting trail to the Kinnickinnick Loop, veering left as the trail rises gently through aspens and pines. In sunny, dry areas you'll see the trail's namesake, also called bearberry, an evergreen ground cover flowering pink in the spring

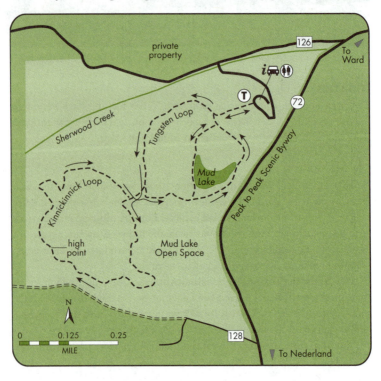

followed by dry red berries favored by birds. The high point of this loop features mountain views and a look at the entire trail. Along the way, encourage kids to watch for signs of wildlife, including various types of scat, tiny holes drilled in a tree trunk, teeth marks on bark, spiderwebs, an insect gall, a bird nest, an anthill. Include wildlife sounds as well; a frog's croak, red-tailed hawk's *kree-ee-ee,* and a woodpecker's rhythmic tapping are commonly heard here.

Return via the Tungsten Loop, turning right at the end of the connecting trail, heading back on the eastern portion of the Tungsten Loop.

RATTLESNAKE GULCH TRAIL

BEFORE YOU GO
Maps Eldorado Canyon State Park brochure; USGS Eldorado Springs
Information For current conditions and more information, contact Eldorado State Park, www.parks.state .co.us or (303) 494-3943

ABOUT THE HIKE
Location Eldorado Canyon State Park
Day hike; Moderate
1.4 miles one way; 0.8-mile loop to Continental Divide overlook
Hikable May to October; in winter
Starting elevation/High point 6050 feet/6760 feet
Accessibility Wheelchair-accessible on first 0.2 mile of Fowler Trail

GETTING THERE

From Denver, take I-25 north to CO-36 west toward Boulder. Exit at Louisville-Superior, heading west on CO-170. Drive 8 miles to the park entrance station. Continue 0.5 mile to the trailhead on the left. The visitor center is another 0.1 mile farther west.

LOGISTICS

Toilet facilities and drinking water are available at the visitor center. Binoculars are recommended. There is a state park entrance fee.

ON THE TRAIL

Exploring the remains of a luxury hotel perched on a canyon promontory is just one reason to walk this popular trail in Eldorado Canyon State

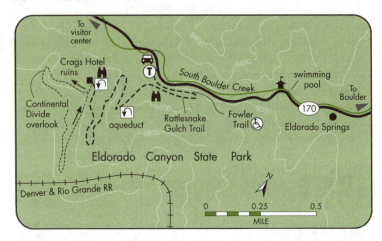

Park. Rock climbers clinging to 1000-foot sandstone walls, views of the Continental Divide, and a chance to see a still-in-use historic railroad line 500 feet overhead are among the attractions on the Rattlesnake Gulch Trail.

From the trailhead, follow the wheelchair-accessible Fowler Trail for the first 0.2 mile. From here, the Rattlesnake Gulch Trail traverses the canyon wall. The foaming white torrent slicing the narrow canyon below you is South Boulder Creek. Initially, the trail winds through a boulder-strewn path, then edges close to open cliff sides—youngsters who tend to wander need to be reined in here.

Following the canyon contours, at 0.4 mile the trail nears a 10-foot-wide cement aqueduct carrying water from South Boulder Creek to Denver. Have kids place their hands on the pipe to feel and hear the water

Climbers scale the cliffs of Eldorado Canyon.

rushing past. The meadow area around here could serve as a destination for younger hikers.

When you hear the rumble of a train, look up—the Denver & Rio Grande is riding the rails laid at the turn of the twentieth century for the Moffat Railroad line. As the trail continues climbing the canyon for another mile, the views of Eldorado Springs and the sheer rock walls of the park loom grandly. Binoculars are useful here for watching rock climbers scale the precipitous cliffs.

The remains of the Crags Hotel, a short-lived luxury resort, lie in stone and brick pieces on the grassy promontory at 1.4 miles. Beginning in 1908, guests arrived above here via the Moffat Railroad, then took a burro and buggy ride to the hotel. Young detectives in your group will enjoy finding what's left of the hotel's fireplaces, garden pools, and even fountains. Fire destroyed the hotel in 1912. From here, turn around and head back the way you came.

For another view of the canyon and the Continental Divide (looking west), as well as access to the same path the hotel guests once used, you could continue following the trail 0.3 mile through a forested hillside. The railroad line appears 250 feet above on the left just before the viewpoint. From here you can continue on the trail for another 0.5 mile, looping back to the hotel site, or return via the same trail.

HORSESHOE TRAIL TO FRAZER MEADOW

BEFORE YOU GO

Maps Golden Gate Canyon State Park (available at park); USGS Blackhawk

Information For current conditions and more information, contact Golden Gate Canyon State Park, www.parks.state.co.us or (303) 582-3707

ABOUT THE HIKE

Location Golden Gate Canyon State Park

Day hike or backpack; Moderate

2 miles one way

Hikable June to mid-October

Starting elevation/High point 8100 feet/9050 feet

Accessibility None

GETTING THERE

From downtown Golden, head northwest on CO-93 for 1.5 miles to Golden Gate Canyon Road and turn left. Proceed 13 miles to the visitor

Horseshoe Trail winds through Frazer Meadow.

center of Golden Gate Canyon State Park, then turn right onto County Road 57 and drive 0.3 mile northeast to the Frazer Meadow trailhead.

LOGISTICS

Toilet facilities and drinking water are located at the visitor center; a vault toilet is at the Frazer Meadow trailhead. Obtain required backcountry camping permits at the visitor center. No fires are allowed at backcountry campsites in the park. Check at the visitor center for information about nature walks and Saturday programs. There is a state park entrance fee.

ON THE TRAIL

Birdsong and a babbling brook accompany hikers along this pleasant journey through an aspen- and pine-fringed meadow that leads to a homesteader's cabin. Kids may see forgotten horse-drawn farm equipment in the tall grass surrounding the cabin.

At the Frazer Meadow trailhead, the trail begins its 850-foot gradual climb in an aspen-shaded forest paralleling a creek. Have kids watch for the horseshoe sign on markers along the trail. Tell them they will cross the creek four times before reaching Frazer Meadow.

At 1.2 miles, a spur trail on the right leads to primitive campsites in Greenfield Meadow, an area homesteaded by a family of that name. Beyond the junction, the trail crosses the creek and enters a lodgepole and ponderosa pine forest. Stop to compare the two pines: the differences in needle length, the smell and size of the trunk, and the shape of the cones. Ponderosa needles grow in bundles of two to three and are 3 to 9 inches long, whereas lodgepole needles come in pairs, 1 to 3 inches long.

The trail meets the Black Bear Trail on the left at 1.5 miles. Continue following the Horseshoe Trail to the right (northwest); the leaves of the young aspen trees seem to applaud your passage. The last creek crossing leads to the open meadow where John and Rufus Frazer built their log cabin and barn in the 1880s. The brothers raised cattle here, earning extra cash by cutting and hauling timber. Perhaps the cart used to carry the logs down the valley can be found among the homestead remnants. Visitors are asked not to climb or enter the historical structure. The meadow is the turnaround point for the featured 4-mile round trip. Those planning an extended hike can join one of three trails that intersect at the log cabin and barn.

During the return walk, listen for the whirring buzz of the broad-tailed hummingbird, identified by its iridescent green back and red throat. Frequently seen darting above meadows in the Rocky Mountains, this flying ace cannot walk or glide but will perch for a moment on the bare limb of an aspen. If a female hummer is in the vicinity, you may be able to watch the tiny male bird in its courtship dance, looping straight upward then down and around, as if riding an invisible roller-coaster.

GREAT GETAWAYS

For camping near Hike 12, head to Golden Gate Canyon State Park, 14 miles west of Denver on Golden Gate Canyon Rd., off CO-93. Go to www.reserveAmerica.com or call 303-470-1144 or 800-678-2267 to reserve campsites.

Within the park, the Raccoon Trail to Panorama Point is a 2.5-mile loop hike with a 100-mile view of the Continental Divide. And for kids who love to fish, check out Kriley Pond and Ranch Pond, two of the stocked ponds within the park.

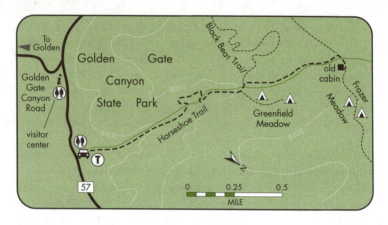

13 RED ROCKS TRAIL

BEFORE YOU GO
Maps Matthews-Winters Park; Jefferson County Open Space
Information For current conditions and more information, contact Jefferson County Open Space, www.jeffco.us/openspace or (303) 271-5925

ABOUT THE HIKE
Location Matthews-Winters Park
Day hike; Moderate
1.9 miles one way, with a longer option
Hikable Year-round
Starting elevation/High point 6360 feet/6680 feet
Accessibility None

GETTING THERE
From Denver, take I-70 west to exit 259 (Morrison) and head south under I-70 for 0.25 mile to County Road 93. Go approximately two blocks and turn right at the park entrance.

LOGISTICS
Picnic and toilet facilities, drinking water, and maps are available near the trailhead. Camping is not allowed. If possible, enjoy Matthews-Winters Park early in the day; mountain biking is popular here in the late afternoon and early evening.

ON THE TRAIL

A stroll through an historic town site, followed by flower-dappled meadows with panoramic views of the region's alluring geology, makes the Red Rocks Trail an ideal venture for the entire family.

The hike begins in Matthews-Winters Park on the 0.3-mile Village Walk, bypassing the bicyclists' 0.6-mile Village Ride, on the left. The two trails circle the original Mount Vernon, a gold-mining boomtown. A small path along the walkers' trail leads to a fenced area protecting the town's only remains, two gravestones. Ask your keen-eyed kids to read the dates here to calculate how many years ago Mount Vernon was a "real town." Point out the miners' route to the goldfields of

Among summer's first flowers, wild iris delights hikers in Matthews-Winters Park.

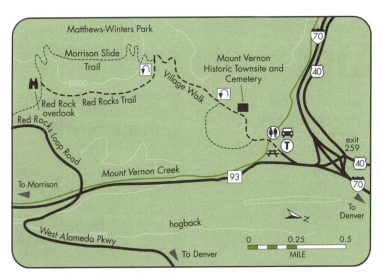

Central City, where County Road 93 now bisects the valley below.

The Village Walk joins the Red Rocks Trail as it spans a meadow and descends gently to the lush streambed of Cherry Gulch at 0.8 mile. The shade of chokecherry, wild plum, and willow trees creates a welcome snack stop along this sun-exposed trail. Summer hikers can have a field day learning about wildflowers; I identified more than twenty different bloomers during my late-June visit. Bring a flower guide, but realize that youngsters may have more fun finding their favorite blossom, the "teeniest," the biggest, or the prettiest-smelling rather than learning the names of different varieties.

Continue on the Red Rocks Trail as it ascends the streambed, passing the Morrison Slide trailhead. Look to the east at the ridge of yellow-white Dakota sandstone tilted on edge. This formation is called a hogback. Remind the football fan in your group that the Arkansas razorback is a fierce hog (boar) with armor-like plates along its spine, an image similar to the geologic barrier to the east.

Within 0.8 mile of the shaded gulch, hikers reach a red-rock overlook (and the other end of the Morrison Slide Trail). This rock formation, your budding geologist may like learning, was laid down millions of years ago by high-energy rivers flowing off a mountain range that existed before our Rocky Mountains. For a more expansive view of Red Rocks Park, climb a few switchbacks up the Morrison Slide Trail. Enjoy the views, then return via the same route.

 LAIR O' THE BEAR PARK

BEFORE YOU GO
Map Jefferson County Open Space
Information For current conditions and more information, contact Jefferson County Open Space, www.jeffco.us/openspace or (303) 271-5925

ABOUT THE HIKE
Location Morrison
Day hike; Easy to moderate
1 mile, Creekside Trail to Dipper Bridge; 1.9 miles, Bruin Bluff Trail
Hikable April through November
Starting elevation/High point 6400 feet/6700 feet
Accessibility Wheelchair-accessible fishing pier

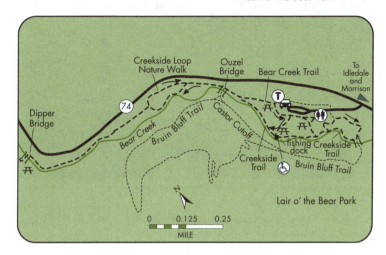

GETTING THERE

From the Denver area, take I-70 west to exit 259 (Morrison) and turn left at the bottom of the ramp onto CO-26. Take CO-26 through Morrison to Stone Street and turn right onto CO-74. Continue driving west 8 miles, passing through the town of Idledale, and then turn left 1 mile west of Idledale onto the park road. Ample parking is provided in the park's paved lots at the end of the short park road.

LOGISTICS

Toilet facilities and drinking water are available in the park. Though capacity is limited, weekend picnicking is popular here.

ON THE TRAIL

The trails at Lair o' the Bear Park weave around and above Bear Creek, encouraging hikers of all ages and abilities to discover the plant and animal bounty of this riparian zone. Numerous songbirds add a melodic background to the hiking, fishing, and picnicking opportunities in the park. The wheelchair-accessible fishing dock, located just 50 yards from the trailhead, overlooks a broad, clear span of water, perfect for spotting the creek's trout, minnows, suckers, and longnose dace.

Crossing a meadow of tall grasses, the short walk from the parking lot leads to the fishing dock, picnic area, and the Creekside Trail. Turning right, head west on the Creekside Trail toward the Creekside Loop. Within 0.1 mile Ouzel Bridge provides a dry-hands-and-knees

A beaver-chewed cottonwood trunk intrigues a young hiker.

look at the stream's inhabitants. Encourage your companions to watch for beaver-chewed tree stumps. Early mornings and evenings are the best times to view these industrious water engineers.

Continue walking west, as the trail edges Bear Creek, bearing left (creekside) on the Creekside Loop. Follow the creek and trail another 0.6 mile to the Dipper Bridge where picnic tables nestled in the shade of willow, cottonwood, and river birch trees provide a perfect setting for lunch. From the bridge a portion of the Bruin Bluff Trail spanning the bluffs can be seen. Discuss with your group why this park is named for a bear's den, a lair. Talk about what it's like to be a bear here. What food and shelter might a bear find?

 At most times of the day, the bridge's namesake, the dipper, can be spotted bobbing along the water's edge in search of its food: insects. Watch the dark gray bird appear to water-ski shallow areas, while in deeper water it dives in with its wings half-open. The dipper's loud, bubbly call is easily heard over the water's noise. Return via the Creekside Trail, bearing left on the Bear Creek Trail, which leads directly to the parking area.

The return trip also leads to the Bruin Bluff Trail, reached by crossing Ouzel Bridge and walking 0.2 mile east on (beaver-inspired) Castor Cutoff. The 1.3-mile loop gives ambitious hikers in your group a switchbacked climb through the bluffs above the creek, before descending to the river bottom. They return to the parking area via Ouzel Bridge or by completing the loop and walking 0.3 mile east on the Bruin Bluff Trail, which leads to a bridge over Bear Creek and returns to the parking area in 0.3 mile.

MEADOW-CASTLE LOOP

BEFORE YOU GO
Map Mount Falcon Park
Information For current
conditions and more
information, contact Jefferson
County Open Space,
www.jeffco.us/openspace or
(303) 271-5925

ABOUT THE HIKE
Location Mount Falcon Park
Day hike; Easy
1.8-mile loop; 4.9 miles one
way with shuttle
Hikable March to November
**Starting elevation/High
point** 7750 feet/7800 feet
Accessibility None

GETTING THERE

Take I-70 to CO-470 south, exit west onto US 285 (signed to Fairplay). Continue west on US 285 for approximately 2.3 miles. Turn right onto Parmalee Gulch Road. Stay on Parmalee Gulch Road for 2.5 miles, turning right on Picutis Road. Follow the signs to the parking area for the west trailhead. To extend the hike with a shuttled vehicle, park near Morrison Town Park, accessed via CO-8 south of Morrison, turning west on Forest Avenue and north on Vine Avenue.

LOGISTICS

Picnic and toilet facilities, a map, and drinking water are available at both trailheads.

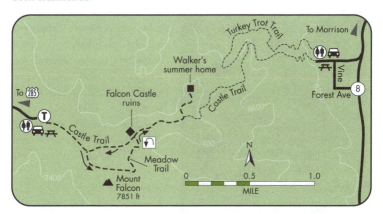

ON THE TRAIL

A peaceful walk through meadows to a mountaintop castle is what dreams are made of—and few hikers on the Castle and Meadow trails can resist dreaming of an equally grand palace to replace the remains of John B. Walker's palatial home that briefly crested Mount Falcon. The various trails in Mount Falcon Park provide options for easy day hikes and more demanding ventures. Start the Meadow-Castle Loop from Mount Falcon's west parking lot. From here, take the Castle Trail, which crosses a flower-speckled field for 0.4 mile before it meets the Meadow Trail. Turn right to follow this smooth, wide walkway as it contours the grassland's edge and dips into the trees for 0.5 mile. It then turns north for 0.3 mile, crossing an open meadow, before reconnecting with the Castle Trail. The crumbling remnants of Walker's dream are perched on a ridge just north of this intersection.

Although broken stone walls and charred fireplaces are all that remain of Walker's magnificent house, the views of the plains to the east and mountains to the west must have fueled his inspiration. Here, kids are prone to pretend. I watched three nine-year-olds stoically guard this mighty fortress, then capture it as reckless bandits. This destination is a good turnaround point for tired hikers, who can head west on the Castle Trail for 0.8 mile back to the trailhead.

For a look at another grandiose plan of this diversely talented entrepreneur, walk 0.8 mile east of this spot where the foundation of Walker's summer home for U.S. presidents sits on a ridge at 2 miles. Construction on the summer White House started in 1918, but when Walker's home was struck and destroyed by lightning, and then his beautiful young wife

A variety of hiking shoes serve a variety of feet, kids, and trail surfaces.

died suddenly and several business ventures failed, he dropped his plans. In 1931, he died penniless at the age of eighty-three. From the summer White House site, point out to your children one of Walker's dreams that did come true: Red Rocks Park.

To return to the parking lot and complete the 1.8-mile loop, head west from Walker's summer home on the Castle Trail.

Or, with a shuttled vehicle in the east parking lot, you can follow the Castle Trail east 1.2 miles, then pick up the hiker-only Turkey Trot Trail and hike 1.7 miles farther to the east parking lot.

 ## PINE VALLEY RANCH PARK

BEFORE YOU GO
Map Pine Valley Ranch Park
Information For current conditions and more information, contact Jefferson County Open Space, www.jeffco.us /openspace or (303) 271-5925 for picnic shelter reservations, (720) 497-7600 for Lookout Mountain Nature Center

ABOUT THE HIKE
Location Pine Valley Ranch Park
Day hike; Easy to moderate
0.6 mile, Pine Lake Loop; 0.5 mile, North Fork View, one way; 0.8 mile, Park View, one way
Hikable April to November
Starting elevation/High point 7000 feet/7430 feet
Accessibility Two fishing piers

GETTING THERE

From south Denver, take US 285 west approximately 6 miles past Conifer to Pine Junction. Turn left (southeast) onto Pine Valley Road (County Road 126). Continue 6 miles to the park access road, Crystal Lake Road, and turn right. Ample parking is provided in the paved, three-level parking lot.

LOGISTICS

Toilet and water facilities are available at the park. There are two wheelchair-accessible fishing piers along the park's Pine Lake. The park's sheltered picnic facilities, designed for large groups, can be reserved. Evening programs at the nearby observatory on Star View Road are provided throughout the year by the Lookout Mountain Nature Center, (720) 497-7600.

ON THE TRAIL

Pine Valley Ranch Park is an ideal destination for families wishing to picnic, fish, and explore the edges of Pike National Forest. Hikers, from those who are stroller-bound to those bound to explore, will discover the park's spruce-lined riparian areas via three hiker-only trails edging the North Fork of the South Platte River and rising above it.

Begin on the Pine Lake Loop by taking the short walk from the parking lot to the lake. The sheltered picnic area and fishing piers here serve as a pond-peering stop for your youngest hikers. The angler in your group will want to fish the lake's rainbow trout–stocked waters.

Following the trail to the left along the lake's south shore leads to the North Fork View Trail intersection. Turn right here to complete the lake-edging loop that returns along the north shore of the lake to the parking area. Turn left (west) to enjoy the wildflower meadows of the North Fork View Trail. The 0.5-mile trail ends at a footbridge across the river. Little ones who tend to wander may need extra supervision along this swift and strong river flow. Bigger brothers and sisters are surprised to learn that one-fourth of this river's water came from the other side of the mountains where it was stored in Dillon Reservoir. A tunnel under the Continental Divide brings the water into this river before before entering Denver's water supply system.

Look east from the bridge to the spruce-flanked hillside

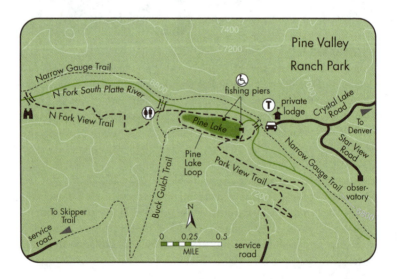

Newly formed cones of a ponderosa pine

above Pine Lake to see the private lodge built in 1925 for William Baehr, a wealthy businessman from Chicago. The "Baehrden of the Rockies" included an observatory where evening programs are currently conducted by Lookout Mountain Nature Center (see "Logistics" for details).

Return via the same trail, or cross the river and turn right (east), taking the multi-use 0.6-mile Narrow Gauge Trail to the parking area.

For a bird's-eye view of the valley, walk the Park View Trail by returning to the Pine Lake Loop where it begins near the picnic shelter. Four switchbacks along the Park View Trail's 430-foot climb can serve as breath-catching, bird-watching opportunities. Stop, look, and listen for the pygmy nuthatch, a small (3.5 to 4.5 inches) blue-gray bird that creeps head-first down trees in search of insects. The nuthatch leaves tiny 1-inch-deep holes in the tree bark, indicating the bird is helping to keep the forest healthy by eating insects. Several families of pygmy nuthatches will inhabit one tree. Your companions will like hearing its happy, high-pitched *peep-ee*. Continue up the Park View Trail as far as desired (it ends at a sign for the Strawberry Jack Trail) and return via the same route.

ALPINE GARDEN LOOP AND M. WALTER PESMAN TRAILS

BEFORE YOU GO
Maps Mount Evans Wilderness (brochure of area available at entrance station); USGS Clear Creek, USGS Mount Evans
Information For current conditions and more information, contact the Clear Creek Ranger District, www.fs.fed.us/wildflowers/regions/rockymountains or (303) 567-3000

ABOUT THE HIKE
Location Mount Evans Recreation Area
Day hike; Easy
0.5-mile loop, Alpine Garden Loop; 1.5 miles one way, M. Walter Pesman Trail
Hikable Late May to early October
Starting elevation/High point 12,152 feet/12,140 feet
Accessibility Wheelchair-accessible for 400 feet at nature center

GETTING THERE

From I-70 near Idaho Springs, take CO-103 south 13 miles to Echo Lake and its junction with the Mount Evans Scenic Byway (CO-5). Turn right here at the entrance station. The Mount Evans Scenic Byway officially opens on Memorial Day weekend and closes the first weekend in October. Drive 4.8 miles to the M. Walter Pesman upper trailhead sign. Parking is adjacent to the highway. The lower trailhead for shuttled vehicles is 1.5 miles east at Dos Chappell Nature Center.

LOGISTICS

Toilet facilities are available at the nature center. Discourage kids from venturing off the trail due to the extreme fragility of alpine plants. Chipmunks, ground squirrels, and even marmots may be seen here; remember that feeding them (or any wild animals on public land) is illegal.

ON THE TRAIL

A child's walk among tundra's treasures followed by a downhill hike through a wind-sculpted forest is what makes this combination of trails a delight. The trail flanks the new Dos Chappell Nature Center, perhaps the highest and best of its kind. It is named for the founder of Volunteers for Outdoor Colorado.

Easily accessible from the Mount Evans Scenic Byway, the Alpine Garden Loop starts at 12,152 feet. Views of Chicago Lakes Basin dominated by Mount Evans (14,264 feet) first capture everyone's interest at this windy summit. (An extra jacket, preferably hooded and windproof, is a must for this hike!) At the trailhead, point out the three peaks to the east: Chief Mountain, Squaw Peak, and Papoose Mountain. Ask your crew which is which.

The trail begins just off the highway adjacent to the trail sign. The field of rocks here is called a fell field, where in early summer hikers are likely to find alpine forget-me-nots, a mat of tiny sky-blue flowers with yellow centers. To demonstrate why flowers in this area are short, have the kids feel and compare the power of wind when standing tall and when crouched low, like the flowers. Please stay on the trail; plants may grow less than a quarter inch during the brief season. By midsummer, the yellow, sunflower-like plant sometimes called "old man of the mountain" will help you find east; it faces that direction throughout its brief flowering glory. Ask your companions to point to west, north, and south.

Circling around the rocky summit, the Alpine Garden Loop meets a trail post marking the M. Walter Pesman Trail at about 0.3 mile. Groups of two adults with hikers of mixed ability can separate here; while the

Alpine nooks are tundra treasure chests for hikers near Mount Evans.

Pesman Trail hikers continue their trek another mile or so, the adult with the loop trail hikers can, when finished, drive to the Pesman Trail's end, 1.5 miles northeast of the alpine loop parking lot. Here the group reunites at the Dos Chappell Nature Center, home to the highest man-made rock garden in the world.

Those who walk the M. Walter Pesman Trail are treated to un-obstructed vistas of the Mount Evans massif as they descend into a stand of bristlecone pines. Youngsters are often surprised to learn these trees are among the oldest living things on Earth today—1500 to 2000 years old! (The oldest bristlecone pine, found in Nevada, shows 4964 growth rings.) The relentless forces of timberline wind have twisted and gnarled the bristlecone pines and Engelmann spruce into bizarre, imagination-teasing shapes called *krummholz* (German for "crooked wood"). Do your kids see faces and creatures in these artfully scoured trees?

The last 0.3 mile of trail winds through a thick stand of conically shaped bristlecone pines growing in a relatively windless area. Point out how this same variety of tree grows full and symmetrical when not shaped by nature's forces. The 400-foot-long wheelchair-accessible trail into the bristlecones begins near here, leading to the Dos Chappell Nature Center.

GREAT GETAWAYS

Two campgrounds are located within easy reach of Hikes 17 and 18. On your approach to these hikes, you'll pass West Chicago Creek Campground 9.3 miles southwest of Idaho Springs on State Route 103, and you'll find Echo Lake Campground at or near the trailhead for both hikes. You can reserve sites at both campgrounds at www.reserveusa.com or (877) 444-6777. Echo Lake is stocked with rainbow and brook trout.

Just beyond Echo Lake Campground you'll find the Mount Evans Scenic Byway—the highest road in North America. (Be sure to bring binoculars for close-up views of mountain goats grazing slopes!) Stop in at Dos Chappell Nature Center to learn about the ways plants and animals thrive in harsh alpine conditions. Then head to the trailhead at the summit parking lot to take the shortest climb up a Colorado fourteener via the easy 0.25-mile Summit Trail to 14,264-foot Mount Evans (www.mtevans.com). At Summit Lake the 0.25-mile trail to Chicago Basin Overlook has more spectacular views.

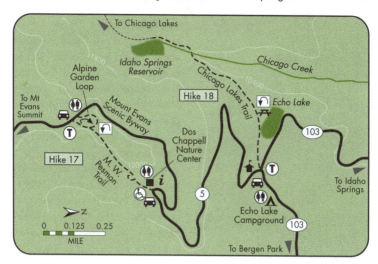

18 CHICAGO LAKES TRAIL TO IDAHO SPRINGS RESERVOIR

BEFORE YOU GO
Map USGS Idaho Springs
Information For current conditions and more information, contact the Clear Creek Ranger Distirct, www.fs.fed.us/r2/arnf/recreation/trails/index or (303) 567-3000

ABOUT THE HIKE
Location Arapaho National Forest;
Day hike; Moderate
1.7 miles one way
Hikable Mid-June to October
Starting elevation/High point 10,600 feet/10,800 feet
Accessibility None

GETTING THERE

From I-70 near Idaho Springs, take CO-103 south 13 miles to Echo Lake and its junction with the Mount Evans Scenic Byway (CO-5). Near this junction are Echo Lake, Echo Lake Campground, and the trailhead parking lot.

LOGISTICS

Drinking water and toilet facilities are available at Echo Lake Campground. Due to sheep and goat birthing, the trail is closed until mid-June.

It's okay, and fun for kids, to pick dandelions.

ON THE TRAIL

Hikers of all sizes and interests enjoy the Chicago Lakes Trail as it descends gently to Echo Lake and Idaho Springs Reservoir. Many hikers fish and picnic at the lakes, allowing plenty of time to investigate the shorelines' aquatic world.

From the parking lot, walk up the Mount Evans Scenic Byway 50 yards to where powerlines cross above the road; the trailhead is in the trees directly below the lines, on the right. Begin the walk on a level path through a spruce forest. Ask the kids to watch for trail markers or blazes on trees. In doing so, they'll notice "old man's beard," a gray-green hairlike growth hanging from tree branches. This lichen lives off dead matter on the tree but doesn't harm it. Within the first 100 yards, the trail reaches the south side of Echo Lake, paralleling it for another 0.2 mile to a picnic area, a fine destination for very young hikers.

From here, the trail jogs a bit to the left before it enters a boulder-dotted area and veers south. Watch for views of the mountains above Chicago Lakes from this point. Limber pines dominate the forest here. Introduce this tree to the kids by having them carefully bend its young, seemingly elastic branches. Also, ask them to count its needles, which grow in clumps of five.

From Echo Lake the trail descends 200 feet in 0.8 mile via shallow switchbacks through the forest. Encourage your companions to explain why the trail zigzigs. Remind them that good hikers don't shortcut the switchbacks. They know that staying on the trail is easier on their knees and, more importantly, prevents damage to the forest. The trail meets the dam over Chicago Creek that forms Idaho Springs Reservoir. Those with fishing gear (including a license!) have a good chance of catching supper.

Return via the same route.

SOUTH RIM LOOP TRAIL

BEFORE YOU GO
Map Roxborough State Park brochure (available at park)
Information For current conditions and more information, contact Roxborough State Park, www.parks.state.co.us or (303) 973-3959

ABOUT THE HIKE
Location Roxborough State Park
Day hike; Moderate
3.3-mile loop
Hikable Year-round
Starting elevation/High point 6200 feet/6500 feet
Accessibility None

GETTING THERE
From CO-470 in Denver, exit at CO-85/Santa Fe Road and travel south for 4.9 miles to Titan Parkway. Head west for 3.4 miles where the road bends south and continues as Rampart Range Road for 3.3 miles. Turn left onto Roxborough Road, then make a direct right into the park. Drive 2.25 miles to the parking area and visitor center.

LOGISTICS
Drinking water, toilet facilities, and naturalist-guided hikes are available at the George O'Malley Visitor Center. As a National Natural Landmark, this park protects its unparalleled scenery by prohibiting pets, camping, bicycling, and climbing on the rocks. There is a state park entrance fee.

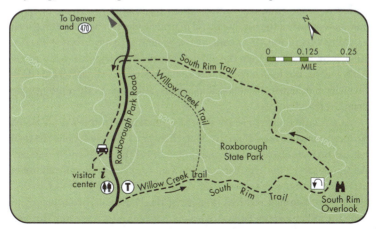

Wedges of the Fountain Formation stand tilted amidst dense brush in Roxborough State Park.

ON THE TRAIL

Less than an hour's drive south of Denver (and south of Chatfield Reservoir), Roxborough State Park offers visitors a look at more than 1.7 billion years of geologic time spread across a variety of natural habitats. Mule deer, coyotes, and squirrels are common sights here, and bobcats and elk make occasional appearances. Watchful visitors sometimes see a golden eagle circling overhead. The best way to sample this unspoiled enclave of nature is via the South Rim Trail, among the park's newest trails. For an informed walk through the park's geologic display and to learn the flora and fauna that frequent the trails, start at the visitor center, where numerous displays, movies, and lectures explaining these features are available. Naturalist-guided activities begin here as well.

Access to the South Rim Trail is from the Willow Creek Trail, located across the road from the visitor center. Walking in the shade of scrub oak, hikers notice the unique blend of prairie and mountain plants such as plains cactus and yucca sharing the ground with aspen and wild rose. Keep a safe distance from the patches of poison ivy that line a few of the park's trails, but take a moment to show children its characteristic dark green, shiny leaves. In late summer, poison ivy leaves turn temptingly bright red and orange.

At 0.5 mile continue south past the junction with the Willow Creek Trail, staying to the right on the South Rim Trail. Benches along the trail act as comfortable rest stops and protectors of the fragile environment. As the climb to the rim begins at 1.2 miles, your kids will pay more attention to the park's spectacular rock formations.

The iron-stained red-rock wedges of the Fountain Formation erupt from the valley's green foliage like a giant stegosaurus crawling through lush vegetation. The light-yellow ridge east of it is the Lyons Formation, once a series of stream deposits and sand dunes along ancient seas. The next rock formation, the Dakota Hogback Ridge, is composed of sandstone formed of beach deposits 140 million to 120 million years ago.

Stop at the South Rim Overlook at 1.5 miles for a look at the distinct colors of these rows of tilted boulders. As the Rocky Mountains rose 70 million years ago, these formations also tilted upward. The overlook is a good turnaround spot for an easier hike.

The views at your feet can be equally unforgettable here, especially if they include a prairie rattler, sometimes seen in this protected natural resource. If your group happens to spy a prairie rattler, keep a safe distance, 3 yards or more, and notice the snake's rattles at the end of its tail, a series of horny interlocking segments. A new rattle forms when the snake sheds its skin, two to four times a year. Though not aggressive, vipers rattle and assume a coiled, defensive position if approached. If left alone, they crawl away and hide.

From the rim, the trail descends 1.3 miles across an open slope to another junction with the Willow Trail shortly before crossing the park's access road. From here, the trail parallels the road through meadow grasses for 0.5 mile before returning to the visitor center parking lot.

INNER CANYON–LAKE GULCH LOOP

BEFORE YOU GO
Map Castlewood Canyon State Park brochure
Information For current conditions and more information, contact Castlewood Canyon State Park, www.parks.state .co.us/parks/castlewoodcanyon or (303) 688-5242

ABOUT THE HIKE
Location Castlewood Canyon State Park, Franktown
Day hike; Moderate
2 miles
Hikable Year-round
Starting elevation/High point 6375/6400 feet
Accessibility Canyon View Nature Trail at the Castlewood Canyon State Park visitor center

GETTING THERE
From Denver, head south on I-25 to CO-86/Founders Parkway (exit 184) and drive east 4 miles to Franktown. At the stoplight, turn south on CO-83, continuing 5 miles to the park entrance and visitor center.

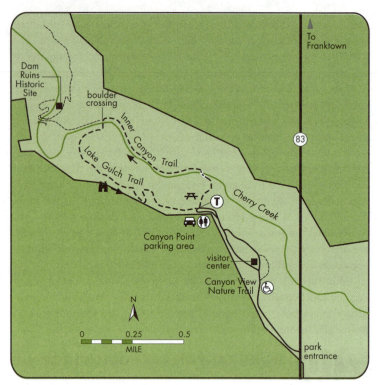

Proceed about 0.5 mile to park at the Canyon Point parking lot. Before doing so, stop at the park's visitor center for its interactive exhibits and a stroll on the accessible Canyon View Nature Trail.

LOGISTICS

Toilet facilities are provided at the trailhead. Drinking water is available at the visitor center. Castlewood Canyon State Park is open from 8:00 AM to sunset. Pets on a leash are allowed on the trails described.

ON THE TRAIL

Tucked in the rolling shortgrass prairies east of Denver, Castlewood Canyon State Park is a boulder-scrambling, pond-probing, surprisingly quiet getaway for the whole family. Birdsong highlights spring and summer hikes here, while winter visitors walk beside sun-warmed canyon walls, sometimes spotting a golden eagle or a red fox.

At the Canyon Point parking lot, start the loop on the Lake Gulch

Trail, heading north on the paved walkway to the canyon rim. Here the narrow dirt trail descends through Gambell oak. Stop at the sign, "LEAVES OF THREE, LET IT BE" to warn your kids of poison ivy. The small shrub or vine thrives in disturbed areas common to places kids like to explore.

Creek sounds, then a clearing in the trees lead to a boardwalk over Cherry Creek that joins the Inner Canyon Trail. Turn left (west), following the path as it threads Cherry Creek's boulders, suitable for scramblers of all sizes. Numerous spur trails lead directly to the creek, a shoe-shedding destination of sandy-bottomed pools swimming with crayfish and tadpoles. Creek play here tends to stretch a planned morning visit into the afternoon.

Spring visitors to the canyon bottom may hear a bleating chorus of *w-a-a-a-h* from a Woodhouse toad, the male's mating call. The adult toad is about 2 to 5 inches long, greenish-gray and covered in bumps (warts). These bumps do not cause warts; rather, they produce a poison that few predators like to ingest. Advise your waders to avoid disturbing the female toad's string of eggs covered in a gelatinous envelope. A cluster of eggs may be those of a leopard frog, another common creek inhabitant. Also, encourage curiosity along with caution when kids discover tadpoles, the next stage of both toad and frog development.

The last stretch of the Inner Canyon Trail leads to a span of boulders that serve as bridge over the creek to the hike's return route on the Lake Gulch Trail. Just before the creek crossing, the 0.35-mile Historic Dam spur leads to the remnants of the dam that burst in 1933, flooding downtown Denver with a 15-foot wave. More images of this dramatic event and other interactive exhibits can be seen at the park's visitor center.

From the crossing, the 0.8-mile Lake Gulch Trail ascends

Creek play in Cottonwood Canyon appeals to hikers of all sizes.

the canyon bottom through tall ponderosa pines before reaching the prairie and leading back to the parking lot. While the trail climbs to the prairie, ask your companions to keep watch for the group's first sighting of Pikes Peak.

 CENTRAL GARDEN TRAIL

BEFORE YOU GO
Map Garden of the Gods map, available at the visitor and nature center
Information For current conditions and more information, contact the Garden of the Gods Park, www.gardenofgods.com or (303) 634-6666

ABOUT THE HIKE
Location Garden of the Gods Park
Day hike; Easy
1.5-mile loop
Hikable Year-round
Starting elevation/High point 6450 feet/6475 feet
Accessibility Wheelchair-accessible

GETTING THERE

From south Colorado Springs, take I-25 north to US 24 (exit 141), head west to 31st Street, and turn right. Drive to Colorado Avenue, turn right, and proceed to 30th Street, then turn left. Drive about 2 miles to the visitor center on your right; turn left onto Gateway Road to Juniper Way, then turn right onto this one-way road and drive approximately 0.3 mile to the main parking area and trailhead. From north Colorado Springs, take I-25 south and turn right on Garden of the Gods Road (exit 146). Turn left on 30th Street and watch for the visitor and nature

A young climber rappels from a rock formation at Garden of the Gods.

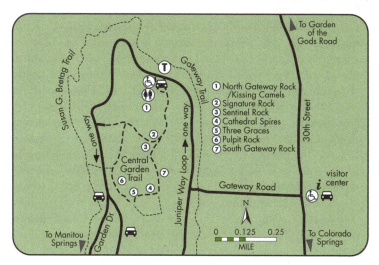

center on your left. Turn right onto Gateway Road to Juniper Way, then turn right onto this one-way road and drive approximately 0.3 mile to reach the main parking area and trailhead.

LOGISTICS

Toilet facilities, drinking water, and climbing permits are available at the visitor and nature center; all other rock scrambling and climbing is prohibited. Sandstone is easily eroded; please refrain from touching the rock.

ON THE TRAIL

A garden walk among Garden of the Gods Park's most stunning red rock spires is what you can expect from this paved, wheelchair-accessible trail. Although a *Theiophytalia kerri* skull was found here in 1878, the park's sandstone formations reflect geologic history eons before the dinosaurs arrived. Intriguing shapes and coloration throughout the park spark the imagination of all hikers. Before hiking, stop at the park's recently built visitor center to see the exhibits and the film *How Did Those Red Rocks Get There?*

From the trailhead parking lot, take the Central Garden Trail, heading south. You will see the "Kissing Camels" edging the horizon on the right and, no doubt, rock climbers scaling these walls.

At 0.2 mile you'll meet the loop portion of the Central Garden trail system. Look to the right at Signature Rock. In 1858 the first settlers of Colorado City (now called Old Colorado City, located within Colorado Springs) carved their names and initials in the rock. Unfortunately, the historic signatures have been lost to vandalism. Follow the Central Garden Trail, the paved pathway winding through the heart of the park, by heading left and soon stopping at Sentinel Rock, also called Twin Spires. The two formations are similar in shape and size, but compare the fine-grained sandstone of one spire with the coarse, conglomerate rock of the other. The coarser conglomerate rock and mixed sandstone began as rock from the Ancestral Rockies more than 300 million years ago. The other spire is composed of sand from the shallow seas that covered an area near here millions of years later. How might the Twin Spires look in another million years?

As the trail veers south, it loops around the formations named Cathedral Spires and Three Graces. Encourage your companions to see why the formations were named so. The name of Pulpit Rock, the rock standing alone in the grassy meadow, may be meaningless to some kids, but they'll have fun naming it themselves. Snowcapped Pike's Peak adds a grand backdrop to photographs taken here. At this point, look back to South Gateway Rock, the massive formation passed on your left just before reaching Cathedral Spires. Some hikers' imagination may need prompting to see the profile, formed by the lighter red rock, of a Native American woman weeping.

As the trail crosses the meadow, watch for rabbits posed statue-still. Overhead, white-throated swifts soar, feeding on insects.

Follow the loop trail to Signature Rock, then to the parking lot via the same trail you started on.

RED ROCK CANYON LOOP

BEFORE YOU GO
Map Red Rock Canyon brochure
Information For current conditions and more information, contact Colorado Springs Parks, Recreations and Cultural Services, www.springsgov.com /rrc or (719) 385-5940

ABOUT THE HIKE
Location Red Rock Canyon
Day hike; Moderate
1.7 miles with longer options
Hikable Year-round
Starting elevation/High point 6200 feet/6500 feet
Accessibility None

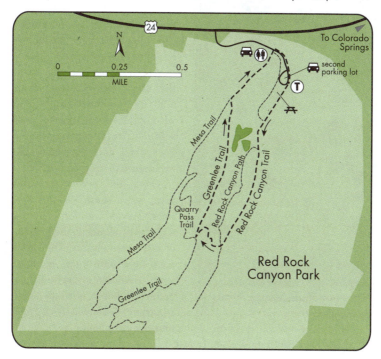

GETTING THERE

From US 24 (Cimarron Street) in Colorado Springs, drive west to Ridge Road, marked by a sign on the left for Red Rock Canyon. Turn left (south) into the park, turning left again, passing the first parking area continuing another 500 yards to the second parking spot.

LOGISTICS

Red Rock Canyon is open from dawn to dusk. Dogs must be on a leash. Climbing over 10 feet off the ground is prohibited. Remember, it's always easier to climb up than to climb down. Vault toilets are provided, but water and camping facilities are not available.

ON THE TRAIL

Massive stone slabs jutting from a slope draw countless climbers to Red Rock Canyon Park. Hikers, however, experience the amazing formations via easy to advanced trails that offer insights into the area's history, geology, and natural wonders. The network of trails here

A staircase of cleaved rock forms the Quarry Pass Trail.

allows for many combinations. The following is just one loop to consider for your crew.

At the heart of the park, the Red Rock Canyon Trail and Greenlee Trail form a loop with options for all members of a family. Including the Quarry Pass Trail adds a memorable experience to everyone's hike.

From the second parking area, start south on the Red Rock Canyon Trail for 0.15 mile as it gently climbs to the first set of interpretive signs. The small pond and dam here increase your chances of spotting a great blue heron, with its 4-foot wingspan, S-shaped neck, and blue-gray plumage.

At the next trail intersection, in just 0.1 mile, some members of your group may opt for walking the Red Rock Canyon Path as it edges a stone slab. They are likely to see climbers spidering their way up this nearly vertical wall. The Red Rock Canyon Path and the Red Rock Canyon Trail meet again at the start of the Quarry Pass Trail. Turn right and look up to see a staircase cut into the east face of a hogback. During the rock mining days of 1880s and '90s, miners cleaved slabs of rock for use in grand homes and buildings. Let your kids know that steel and concrete provide the strength needed for today's structures. Explain that a quarry is generally a place where materials like rock are mined for use in building. The 0.2-mile crossing through the quarry gives a close-up look at the straight-line cleaves of sandstone.

At the Greenlee Trail intersection, turn right (north), following the trail's easy 0.7-mile descent. Watch for views of Red Rock Canyon's sister park, Garden of the Gods (see Hike 21). The Greenlee Trail returns to the parking lot and the start of the hike. A large bird soaring overhead may be a Cooper's or red-tailed hawk. In summer, the buzz of hummingbirds is likely.

Hikers wanting more red-rock immersion can turn left at the

Greenlee and Quarry Pass trail intersection. Follow the Greenlee Trail south for 0.4 mile, then head right (west) at the Roundup Trail for 0.2 mile to the junction with the Mesa Trail. From here, head north on the Mesa Trail for a 1.15-mile return to the parking lot and trailhead.

 BEAR CREEK TRAILS

BEFORE YOU GO
Maps El Paso County Regional Parks and Trails brochure (available at nature center); USGS Manitou Springs
Information For current conditions and more information, contact El Paso County Regional Parks, www.elpasoco.com/parks or (719) 520-6375

ABOUT THE HIKE
Location Bear Creek Regional Park
Day hike; Easy to moderate 0.1- to 0.8-mile loop
Hikable Year-round
Starting elevation/High point 6350 feet/6440 feet
Accessibility Wheelchair-accessible on Songbird Trail

GETTING THERE
From I-25 in Colorado Springs, take exit 141 and head west on US 24 (toward Cimarron) 1.8 miles to 26th Street. Turn left (south) and drive 1.4 miles to the intersection with Gold Camp Road. From the stop sign, proceed northeast 0.1 mile to Bear Creek Road; turn right and in a short distance turn left at the Bear Creek Nature Center entrance and parking.

LOGISTICS
The hands-on nature center offers Discover programs as well as toilet facilities and drinking water. The park's trails are open from sunrise to dusk, allowing the best wildlife viewing for edge-of-the-day hikers, but the nature center is open only 9:00 AM–2:00 PM Wednesday through Friday and 9:00 AM–4:00 PM Saturday.

ON THE TRAIL
Visitors to Bear Creek Regional Park can enjoy an exploratory hike or an easy saunter through the variety of ecosystems blanketing the foothills of Pikes Peak. Four diverse trails wind through the park's

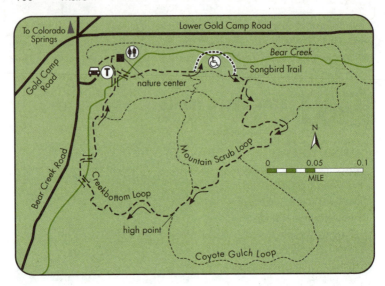

1235 acres, enabling almost every hiker to claim, "I saw a hawk!" (or deer, hummingbird, fox squirrel, or towhee . . .). Plan your hike to begin or end with a visit to the recently rebuilt and enlarged (9000 square feet) Bear Creek Nature Center, the first of its kind in Colorado. Kids scramble to see the center's wildlife diorama featuring a full-size black bear and cubs. Interactive computerized touchscreens teach visitors of all ages about the area's geology, weather, plants, and wildlife.

From the nature center, the music of birdcalls lures most hikers to the 0.1-mile Songbird Trail. This wheelchair-accessible boardwalk trail passes over Bear Creek before entering an oak thicket where interpretive signs describe the area's birds, their habits, and calls.

Turn left and then right to join the Mountain Scrub Loop, following the trail left (east) 0.1 mile through open meadows interspersed with scrub-oak thickets. At the junction, turn right (southwest) and follow the trail as it winds through stands of mountain mahogany shrubs, thriving on the dry, south-facing slopes. Show your kids the shrubs' midsummer seed: a 3-inch-long screwlike tail wearing a feathery coat. In 0.2 mile the Mountain Scrub Loop reaches its high point, where it meets the Creekbottom Loop; turn right on this trail. (To your left is the Coyote Gulch Loop, where coyotes, deer, and even black bears have been sighted. This less-traveled 0.5-mile loop wanders grassy meadows and edges deep ravines dotted with ponderosa pine and Douglas fir before rejoining the Mountain Scrub Loop at its south-facing slope.)

As the 0.2-mile Creekbottom Loop enters the wetland community of Bear Creek, point out the change in vegetation. Help your companions compare the broad-leafed plants growing near the stream with the narrow-leafed plants of the dry slopes—yucca, cactus, and Indian paintbrush—that they just walked through.

Mother and son try trailside bird-watching.

When your group crosses the bridges over the creek, look and listen for signs of wildlife, reminding your companions that most (90 percent) animals and insects living here or passing through need wet places like these, called riparian areas. Talk about what the area provides for wildlife. In a tree-shaded area near the creek, ask how the air temperature changed. Is it cooler or warmer? Look for animal tracks along the creek's shore.

Follow the trail to the bridge across Bear Creek back to the nature center.

GREAT GETAWAYS

For camping in the area of Hike 23, head to Mueller State Park, 33 miles west of Colorado Springs. Reserve sites at www.reserveAmerica .com or by calling (303) 470-1144 or (800) 678-2267. From the campground you can hike the 0.6-mile forested trail to Grouse Mountain Overlook, the 0.8-mile Wapiti Nature Trail, the 1.9-mile Homestead Trail, or the 0.8-mile trail to Lost Pond, which is a perfect spot for a picnic. The park's nature center offers hands-on learning and a variety of fun and interesting evening ranger talks.

A fun alternative hike in Bear Creek Regional Park is the 2.3 mile Outlook Ridge Trail, which features excellent views.

CATTAIL MARSH AND FOUNTAIN CREEK TRAILS

BEFORE YOU GO
Map El Paso County Regional Parks and Trails brochure (available at nature center)
Information For current conditions and more information, contact El Paso County Regional Parks, www.elpasoco.com/parks or (719) 520-6375

ABOUT THE HIKE
Location Fountain Creek Regional Park
Day hike; Easy
2.5 miles round-trip
Hikable Year-round
Starting elevation/High point 5500 feet/5530 feet
Accessibility Wheelchair-accessible on all trails

GETTING THERE

From Colorado Springs, drive south on I-25 to exit 132, then east on CO-16 for 0.5 mile to the Security exit to US 85/87; turn right (south). Continue south on US 85/87 for 0.6 mile to Cattail Marsh Road and turn right (west). In 0.5 mile, park at the Fountain Creek Nature Center.

LOGISTICS

Toilet facilities and drinking water are available at the nature center (open 9:00 AM–2:00 PM Wednesday through Friday and 9:00 AM–4:00 PM Saturday), adjacent to picnic facilities and a large playground. Toilet facilities and drinking water are also available at the Willow Springs Road Pavilion.

ON THE TRAIL

Turtles sunning on a log, cormorants airing their wings, and great blue herons mirrored in a pond's still waters are among the common wildlife sightings that hikers of all sizes and stamina enjoy at Fountain Creek Regional Park. The 2.5-mile-long park encompasses one of the region's few wetlands, featuring wildlife observation pavilions and informative kiosks around the spring-fed ponds. The nature center, a "must-see" interactive environment, offers a multi-sensory survey of the park's stream, cottonwood, pond, marsh, and meadow communities. The trails may be explored independently; however, kids on a park-sponsored interpretive hike have fun discovering new ways of listening and looking while walking in a natural setting. The volunteer-led hikes are offered year round.

Riparian wildlife flourishes at Fountain Creek Regional Park.

From the nature center, head south, then west to follow the Cattail Marsh Nature Trail clockwise. As you begin your walk, remind young wildlife watchers to approach the kiosks quietly; their reward may be the sighting of a white-tailed deer darting through the woods or a cluster of cattail leaves propelled by an underwater muskrat (however, muskrats are often nocturnal feeders).

As you descend the nature trail to pond level, the red-winged blackbird's call, a low *chuck* followed by a high *teeyee,* announces your presence. Found from subarctic Canada all the way to the tropical swamplands of Central America and Cuba, red-winged blackbirds thrive in cattail marshes. The tall, slender stems of the cattail provide still supports for the blackbird's nests. Encourage your companions to listen for calls from other wetland residents: a bullfrog's deep *jug o'rum*, the loud *quack* of a female mallard duck, or the quick *witchity-quitchety* of a yellow warbler. Even carp have been heard here splashing and sucking air on the water's surface.

Follow the nature trail as it enters an edge community of cottonwood, Russian olive, and tamarisk trees, then borders the pond again. Milkweed, with its umbels of pink star-shaped flowers that later fruit into large spiney pods, edges the sun-drenched portions of the trail. The large, grayish, velvety plant is host to monarch butterfly caterpillars in

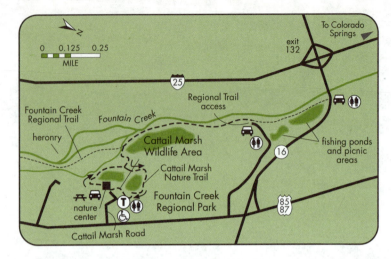

August. You may see the bright orange and black butterfly fluttering over the park before leaving on its 1000-mile flight south. Your companions will be surprised to learn that these fragile beauties migrate an average 60 miles a day.

In 0.3 mile, turn left onto the Fountain Creek Regional Trail. Viewing scopes in each of the wildlife observation pavilions along this portion of the trail offer close examination of the great blue heron, Fountain Creek's signature bird. The large (43 to 52 inches tall) blue-gray bird stands motionless in shallow water waiting to stab prey with its sharp beak. A heron rookery, visible from mid-March to mid-May, can be observed from portions of this trail.

Another wetland resident's trademark—beaver-chewed tree stumps—marks each of the viewing platforms. Encourage your kids to feel the scars left by the timber harvester. Remind them that beavers' teeth, unlike our own, continue to grow, and the process of gathering food and lodging materials keeps the animals' teeth trimmed. Your companions may spot one or more of the four lodges made by the resident beaver family here in the banks along the ponds.

Follow the regional trail north less than 0.5 mile to the Willow Springs Road access before turning around and retracing your steps back to the junction with the nature trail. Here turn left to complete the loop, discovering the sights and sounds of the final 0.3-mile section of the nature trail.

25 COLUMBINE TRAIL

BEFORE YOU GO

Maps North Cheyenne Cañon Park brochure (available at Starsmore Discovery Center in park); USGS Manitou Springs
Information For current conditions and more information, contact City of Colorado Springs, www.springsgov.com/ncc or (719) 633-5701

ABOUT THE HIKE

Location North Cheyenne Cañon Park
Day hike; Moderate
3 miles one way
Hikable March to November
Starting elevation/High point 6800 feet/7300 feet
Accessibility None

GETTING THERE

From the intersection of 21st Street/Cresta and US 24 in Colorado Springs, travel south 3 miles to Cheyenne Boulevard. Turning west, drive 1 mile through a suburban neighborhood to the North Cheyenne Cañon Park entrance; the turnoff to Seven Falls is on the left. Continue west 1 mile to a small parking area near a sign marking the midway point of the Columbine Trail; you can pick up one-way hikers here. For the upper Columbine trailhead, continue west 1.8 miles (2.8 miles west of the park entrance) to the trailhead 0.1 mile beyond the Helen Hunt Visitor Center.

LOGISTICS

Toilet facilities and drinking water are available near the upper Columbine trailhead.

Red rock sentinels similar to those at Garden of the Gods greet hikers on the Columbine Trail.

ON THE TRAIL

The Columbine Trail offers a perfect solution for groups of eager trailblazers mixed with not-so-certain toddlers: While one adult and the youngsters explore the Helen Hunt Falls area near the trailhead, another adult leads hikers down the Columbine Trail. At a prearranged time, say, in 1.5 hours, the adult with the waterfall explorers drives to Columbine Trail's midpoint parking area, where the group reunites.

From the upper trailhead, the Columbine Trail climbs the hillside via three short switchbacks before overlooking Helen Hunt and Silver Cascade Falls. Although the trail is well graded, hold on to youngsters quick to dart off—the trail runs along steep, open, and gravelly terrain. The promontory at 0.4 mile offers views of Colorado Springs and the plains beyond; this is a good destination for a shorter hike.

Following the canyon's contours, the trail descends through forests of pinyon, spruce, and Douglas fir until it crosses a dry creek and climbs to another viewpoint at 1.6 miles, a turnaround point if the one-way hike is not an option. Here I heard a hiker ask, "Is that Kansas out there?"

Stop to inspect those patches of bright green ivy called kinnikinnick that cling to the granite-laden soil of the canyon. Also called manzanita or bearberry, this ground cover produces red berries favored by bears, deer, and birds. Its leaves have medicinal value and were used by Native Americans as a tobacco. Alongside the trail, watch out for poison ivy's trio of dark green, pointed, and often red-stained oval leaves 1 to 3 inches long.

In this rocky terrain, stay on the switchbacks. Cutting across them strips away meager vegetation leaving a barren, vertical path.

Damage to delicate plant life such as this takes years to repair itself. Encourage slow, careful walking for the last mile; the loose gravel of this steep section is made up of pebbles, sometimes causing loose footing and skinned knees. After crossing a small creek, the trail continues to descend, reaching the midpoint at a massive red-rock formation similar to those in Garden of the Gods (see Hike 21). The parking area is near here.

 PAINT MINES INTERPRETIVE PARK

BEFORE YOU GO
Map El Paso County Regional Parks and Trails brochure
Information For current conditions and more information, contact El Paso County Parks, www.elpasoco .com/parks or (719) 520-6375

ABOUT THE HIKE
Location Calhan
Day hike; Easy
1.6 miles round-trip to hoodoos; 3.1-mile loop
Hikable Year-round
Starting elevation/High point 6760 feet/6760 feet
Accessibility None

GETTING THERE
From Colorado Springs, take US 24 east 28.8 miles to Calhan. At the east end of town, turn south (right) on Yoder Street (becomes Calhan Highway) for 0.6 mile. Turn east (left) onto Paint Mine Road and drive 1.4 miles, passing the park's first parking area and trailhead on the left. Continue an additional 1.1 miles southeast, veering left at the fork to the park's flagstone sign with 30550 Paint Mine Road. Parking and interpretive signs mark the trailhead.

LOGISTICS
Paint Mines Interpretive Park is open from dawn to dusk. Pets, horses, and bicycles of any kind are prohibited; there is no camping. Please stay on the trails; climbing the formations is prohibited. Drinking water is not provided, but there is a vault toilet at the first trailhead. Early mornings in spring are ideal times to be here.

ON THE TRAIL
Every visitor to the Paint Mines delights at the sight of what appears to be rainbow sherbet–colored rock formations melting into the prairie.

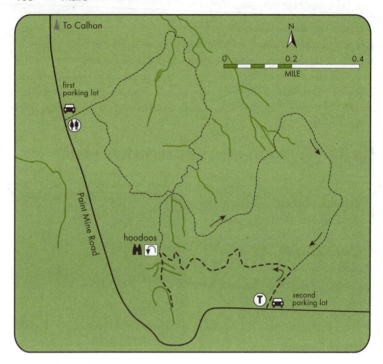

Their thrill continues as several paths lead them into the park's shallow canyon of spires streaked white, gold, pink, and lavender. Few forget their first sight of this rare prairie jewel.

A figure-eight network of gravel trails provides access to the 750-acre county park developed in 2005. The featured hike for those eager to enter nature's paint box begins at the southeast trailhead. Spiky grasses and yucca bristle the prairie where a pronghorn bounding in the distance may catch your eye. Along the way, tell your companions that people came here for thousands of years to gather clay to make colorful ceramics and paint. Even today there are buildings in Colorado Springs and Pueblo made of bricks formed from multi-hued clay mined here in the early 1900s.

From the southeast trailhead, the path gently slopes downhill about 0.1 to a trail junction; turn left and continue 0.6 mile to a viewpoint with an interpretive sign. The overview here of the prairie's paint box features the wildly shaped spires of clay, formed beneath a harder capstone, called "hoodoos." Composed of Dawson Arkose, the sedimentary layer formed 55 million years ago when a dense forest covered the region. On the right, just past the sign you won't miss the cluster of bright white hoodoos a fellow hiker dubbed the "Gathering of Ghosts."

The short walk to the canyon bottom leads to several pathways, each allowing a close-up look at the formations' vibrant bands of color formed from gypsum. Stop to feel the sand floor, sparkling with quartzitic crystals. Meanwhile, let the columns of spires and clusters of hoodoos provoke imaginations by encouraging your kids to describe what they "see." Also note the plant variety thriving in the natural drainages. Ask your crew to name and count the number of different colors they find flowering. Wands of white chokecherry blossoms along with pink wild rose, white evening primrose, chiming bluebells, and orange paintbrush are among the wildflowers greeting spring visitors to the Paint Mines. In summer months, yellow composites, like sunflower and prairie coneflower, dominate in the prairie while in the sandy bottoms white sand verbena and purple-flowering morning glory thrive.

After exploring the base of the formations, head back on the same trail. For a 1.5-mile return offering great views and interpretive signs featuring the area's history and geology, turn left (north) at the viewpoint. Watch and listen for Colorado's state bird, the lark bunting. The male's jet-black plumage with white wing patches is as distinct as its rich warbling song.

Hoodoos and spires in shades of sherbet appear to melt into the prairie at the Paint Mines Interpretive Park.

27 WALDO CANYON LOOP TRAIL

BEFORE YOU GO

Maps Waldo Canyon Trail booklet, Pike National Forest; USGS Cascade .

Information For current conditions and more information, contact the Pikes Peak Ranger District, www.fs.fed.us/r2/psicc or (719) 553-1400

ABOUT THE HIKE

Location Pike National Forest Day hike or backpack; Moderate to challenging 1.7 miles one way to loop, plus 3.6-mile loop, for 7 miles round-trip

Hikable April to November

Starting elevation/High point 7020 feet/8000 feet

Accessibility None

GETTING THERE

From Manitou Springs, take the US 24 bypass west for 2 miles. Watch for the parking area on the north (right) side of the highway.

LOGISTICS

A wood sign and stairway mark the beginning of the trail. Toilet and water facilities are not provided here. Bring plenty of water per hiker. Plan to hike this very popular trail midweek or in early morning or late afternoon.

ON THE TRAIL

A loop trail offering views of Pikes Peak, a meandering stream, boulders for climbing, flowering cactus, and a variety of forests—what more could one ask for? Waldo Canyon Loop Trail combines all of these, along with destinations that will suit the stature or time frame of any hiker.

The Waldo Canyon Trail No. 640 climbs a ridge with Pikes Peak dominating the vista along most of the trail. However, watch for the equally exquisite sights at your feet: spring-flowering barrel cactus or perhaps the tracks of a bighorn sheep. At 0.6 mile, the trail leads to a boulder-filled overlook; this shaded picnic destination or stop for young climbers to try their skills can also serve as a turnaround point for a shorter hike.

Kids may want to inspect the gray-green lichen that crusts these and other boulders in the region. (A magnifying glass is fun to use here.) They'll be fascinated to know that lichen is actually a combination of

Pikes Peak dominates the views from Waldo Canyon.

two microscopic plants that are dependent on each other for survival. One plant in the partnership is an alga that produces sugars. The other is a fungus that produces an acid that breaks down the rock, providing mineral nutrients for both plants. Encourage your hikers to discover different varieties of lichen by colors and textures.

From the overlook, the trail descends gradually into Waldo Canyon. At 1.6 miles, the trail enters a clearing, formerly the site of the Waldo

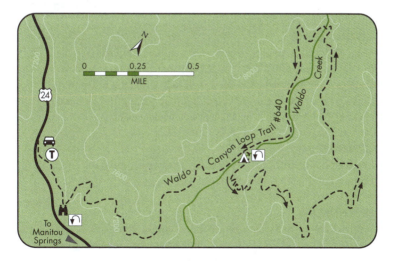

Hog Ranch. Hot, tired feet can cool off in Waldo Creek, which borders the trail. Numerous undeveloped campsites dot this area. Just 0.1 mile beyond is the junction for the 3.6-mile loop portion of the hike.

If you turn around at this trail intersection, first head north (left) a little way to enjoy the trail's streamside tranquility. To hike the loop counterclockwise (advised), turn right (east) to begin a steady climb up and around the canyon, with magnificent views of Pikes Peak as your reward. A casual descent takes you alongside forest-shaded Waldo Creek back to the junction that closes the loop. Return via the Waldo Canyon Trail No. 640.

28 THE CRAGS TRAIL

BEFORE YOU GO
Maps Pike National Forest; USGS Woodland Park, USGS Pikes Peak
Information For current conditions and more information, contact the Pikes Peak Ranger District, www.fs.fed.us/r2/psicc or (719) 553-1400

ABOUT THE HIKE
Location Pike National Forest
Day hike; Moderate to challenging
1.7 miles one way
Hikable Late May to mid-October
Starting elevation/High point 10,040 feet/10,680 feet
Accessibility None

GETTING THERE
From Colorado Springs, travel west on US 24 past Woodland Park to Divide. Turn left (south) on CO-67 and proceed 4 miles to County Road 62 (Forest Road 383), then turn left. Drive 3.6 miles to the Crags Campground; the trailhead is located just beyond the last campsite. A parking lot for hikers is on the left side of the road.

LOGISTICS
Picnic and toilet facilities and drinking water are available at the Crags Campground.

ON THE TRAIL
Children of all ages discover rocks to climb, pinnacles to reach, and streams to investigate on this intriguing trail leading to what my

then-twelve-year-old son called an awesome rock formation. Groups consisting of those with little legs and those with strong, eager ones will find a number of satisfying destinations along the way.

From the trailhead parking lot, the trail meanders through aspen meadows fringed with pines. Clear, shallow, gravel-bottomed Fourmile Creek accompanies hikers as they enter a marshy area at 0.3 mile. Look up here to see the trail's namesake crags, a group of rock pinnacles on the horizon. Entering a meadow at about 0.5 mile, point out the tangles of gray, fallen aspen trees on the left. Ask kids what kind of tree is growing in place of the aspens (pine trees and spruces).

Continue walking another 0.7 mile northeast, where boulders rimming meadows on both sides of the trail increase in size and take on imagination-teasing shapes. Looking directly north, a horizon-high rock formation appears to be the crenellated walls of a castle, and nearby is a giant palace of rocks. Ask the kids to describe what they see.

Along this boulder-studded region, a number of spur trails lead to rock walls. Climbers, new and seasoned, like trying their finger- and toehold techniques on the cracks and fissures. At the base of these formations, enjoy a snack stop near the babbling creek. This can be a turnaround spot for some hikers.

While resting, point out the erosion of waist-high rocks. When kids

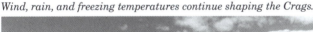

Wind, rain, and freezing temperatures continue shaping the Crags.

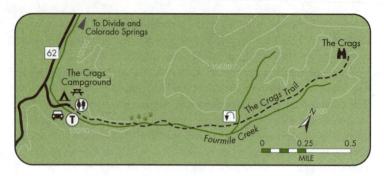

merely touch these boulders, quarter-inch pebbles crumble off, like snakes shedding skin. Perhaps they can estimate how long it will take these rocks to naturally erode into a pile of rubble. Please allow nature, not human fingers, to erode the rocks.

At 1.5 miles, the trail reenters a forested area and then climbs to an overlook of the area's reservoirs and forests. From here, the trail's last 0.2 mile to the Crags' promontory gets a bit hard to follow as it traverses a granite base. Keep heading west and uphill. In this timberline region, twisted limber pines cling to life between the boulders. Steady winds carrying snow and rain have stunted these trees into unusual shapes. When kids discover the bendable nature of the tree's thin branches, they'll know why the tree is called "limber."

At the promontory, you'll have 360-degree views of mountains and valleys silhouetted by towering rock pinnacles that rival those seen from Pikes Peak. A jacket may be needed for this windy summit. Return via the same route.

BEST RIVERSIDE WALKS

Denver

See Hike 1, Highline Canal Trail.

Boulder

The Bobolink Trail is a cottonwood-shaded, paved pathway where you can watch for bobolinks, dressed tuxedo-like, and large blue-gray kingfishers darting from the adjacent prairie into South Boulder Creek. The 1.5-mile path is maintained by the City of Boulder Open Space and Mountain Parks. The trailhead and parking are found near the intersection of Cherryvale and Baseline roads in east Boulder. Bicycles are not permitted on the trail. Drinking water and toilet facilities are available at the East Boulder Community Center, located about one-third of the way along this walk.

www.ci.boulder.co.us/openspace   (303) 441-3440

Colorado Springs/Fountain

Walk any length of the 10-mile Fountain Creek Regional Trail, and your crew is sure to spot at dozen or more of the 250 bird species along the trail's ponds, marshes, creek, and meadows. Many families start at the Fountain Creek Nature Center where parking, restrooms, and seasonal water are available. (The center's network of trails is described in Hike 24, Cattail Marsh and Fountain Creek Trails.) Walking north on the regional trail leads to Willow Springs Pond, popular with young anglers. Those heading south go to Fountain Creek Regional Park, a playground for sports enthusiasts of all ages. For nature center events, call (719) 520-6745. The Fountain Creek Nature Center is located at the junction of US 85/87 and Cattail Marsh Road. Dogs are not allowed at the nature center.

www.elpasocountyparks.com   (719) 520-7529

Pueblo

The Historic Arkansas Riverwalk of Pueblo treats visitors to a 32-acre urban waterfront experience featuring the renovated canal that returned the river to its historic downtown location. The 1.5-mile path, enhanced with stone fountains, hand-carved benches, and bronze animals embedded in the landscape, loops around the canal, passing plazas and family-fare restaurants. The riverwalk leads to Lake Elizabeth where kids explore the lake by foot-powering a pedal boat, available for rent May through September. Access the riverwalk from I-25, exit 98B, west on 5th Street, South on Union Avenue, where parking is available on either side of the street.

www.pueblohorp.com   (719) 595-0242

Golden

Clear Creek Trail's 1-mile section, located between the 6th Avenue underpass and Ford Street's Vanover Park, links downtown with the city's premier Clear Creek Whitewater Park. Parking is available at Lions Park on 10th Street, adjacent to the whitewater park, or in the downtown parking garage on Jackson Street, between 11th and 12th streets. Seasonal drinking fountains and year-round restrooms are provided.

http://ci.golden.co.us/ (303) 384-8100

Cañon City

The Arkansas Riverwalk, a 1.25-mile section of Cañon City's 7-mile riverside trail between South 9th Street and Reynolds Avenue, offers expansive views of the river and bluff with great birding and an adjacent ropes course. Parking access is at John Griffin Park, on Sell Avenue, three blocks east of South 9th. Toilet and picnic facilities are provided, but no drinking water. When completed, the town's Whitewater Kayak and Recreation Park will connect with this section of the Riverwalk.

tourism@canoncity.com (719) 275-2331

Opposite: Triple cascades mist a hiking duo at Rifle Falls State Park.

CENTRAL

GREAT SAND DUNES NATIONAL PARK, CENTRAL COLORADO, ASPEN, VAIL, AND SUMMIT COUNTY

ZAPATA FALLS

BEFORE YOU GO
Map USGS Twin Peaks
Information For current conditions and more information, contact the Bureau of Land Management, www .blm.gov/co/st/en/BLM /zapatafalls or (719) 852-6212

ABOUT THE HIKE
Location Blanca, south of Great Sand Dunes National Park and Preserve
Day hike; Easy to moderate
0.5 mile one way
Hikable Year-round
Starting elevation/High point 9000 feet/9100 feet
Accessibility None

GETTING THERE

From the Great Sand Dunes National Park and Preserve entrance, drive south 8 miles on CO-150 to the "Zapata Falls Recreation Area" sign and turn left. Continue 3.5 miles on this gravel road to the parking lot. From Alamosa, travel east on US 160 for 14 miles to CO-150. Turn left and travel about 11 miles. Turn right at the sign for Zapata Falls and proceed 3.5 miles to the trailhead.

LOGISTICS

There is a vault toilet, but no water facilities. Those wanting to creek-scramble to the waterfall should bring or wear amphibious walking

The viewpoint at Zapata Falls trailhead spans the area's dunefields and the San Luis Valley.

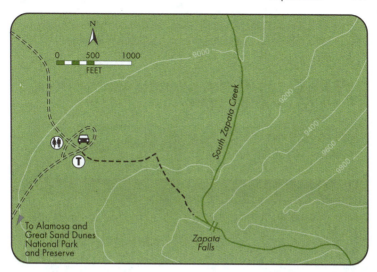

shoes. However, be aware that wet rocks are slick. The creek is often deep and swift in the early summer or after a heavy rainstorm. In winter, ice and snow make the hike very slippery.

ON THE TRAIL

A stop at Zapata Falls caps the trip for many visitors to Great Sand Dunes National Park and Preserve. After a morning of cavorting in the sand, the short hike to Zapata Falls leads to a cool retreat for creek play and exploration. Simply driving to the trailhead offers grand views of the dunefield and San Luis valley. Interpretive signs near the parking lot orient visitors to the valley, lakes, and mountains of the region.

The trail begins across the road from the parking lot. Pinyon and juniper trees flank the broad, rocky route to the falls. Careful stepping may be needed on this slightly steep, rock-hobbled trail.

The sound of water tumbling and a waft of cool air greets hikers nearing the creek at 0.5 mile. Tall cottonwoods shade the waterway where little hikers linger to explore. Their bigger companions will continue splashing another 100 yards through the ice-cold water over slippery boulders to reach the waterfall itself, tucked in a rock crevasse. Over millennia, South Zapata Creek has carved a narrow slot in the crystalline bedrock of the Sierra Blanca massif, forming a 30-foot waterfall. "It's like being inside a refrigerator in here!" claimed a young creek scrambler upon seeing the waterfall. Indeed, on hot summer afternoons Zapata Falls is "really cool." Winter and spring hikers here discover the falls as an ice sculpture enclosed in a rock shrine.

Return via the same trail.

 DUNES EXPLORATION AND MONTVILLE NATURE TRAIL

BEFORE YOU GO
Map Great Sand Dunes National Park and Preserve brochure (available at visitor center)
Information For current conditions and more information, contact Great Sand Dunes National Park and Preserve, www.nps.gov/grsa or (719) 378-6399

ABOUT THE HIKE
Location Great Sand Dunes National Park and Preserve
Day hike; Easy
0.3–4 miles one-way; 0.5-mile loop
Hikable Year-round
Starting elevation/High point 8040 feet/8790 feet
Accessibility Wheelchair-accessible picnic area and backcountry campsite. Dunes-accessible wheelchair available, (719) 378-6399

GETTING THERE

From I-25 south of Pueblo, take US 160 west 60 miles. Turn north onto CO-150 and travel 19 miles to the park visitor center. From Denver take US 285 south to CO-17 to County Lane 6N. Drive 0.3 mile farther north; on the right is parking for the Montville Nature Trail. Another 0.2 mile north is a turnoff on the left that leads 0.5 mile to the sand dunes picnic area.

LOGISTICS

Toilet facilities and drinking water are available at the visitor center; toilet facilities are also available at the picnic area. Although the average high temperature in July is 80°F, sand surface can get quite hot by midday. During hot summer months, plan your dune exploration for the cooler hours of morning or evening, and heed the sign warning that "SHOES SHOULD BE WORN AT ALL TIMES ON THE DUNES." The surface temperature of the dunes can reach 140°F on summer afternoons. For information on sand sledding in the park and Medano Creek's predicted flow, check the website above.

Hiking is a cartwheeling event at the Great Sand Dunes National Park and Preserve.

ON THE TRAIL

At Colorado's Great Sand Dunes National Park and Preserve, 30 square miles of sand sculpted by the wind into myriad hills and valleys invite climbing to the crest of a dune, then rolling and jumping down the hill—again and again. The day's destination may be the first knoll of sand or a trek to the top of the highest hill for leaping, sliding, even cartwheeling and somersaulting. Stop at the visitor center for information and interactive exhibits. Summer temperatures here average in the 80s, but by afternoon the surface temperature of the sand can get burning hot.

From the dunes parking lot, start by splashing across ankle-deep Medano Creek. In the spring or early summer, the creek flow is about 25 yards wide, washing the sand in peculiar wavelike pulses called "surge flow." After kids have fun at the crossing, point out how the creek flows in rhythms like the ocean's waves. Sand granules carried in the shallow current cause this motion.

No need to watch for trail signs; simply aim for a mountain of sand on which to play. Some hills are several cartwheels away, while the first

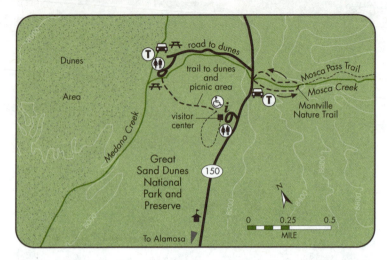

ridge, called "High Dune," takes about an hour for young hikers. Do bring a camera; the nearby snowcapped Sangre de Cristo Mountains add a stunning background to photographs of kids cavorting on sand. (Be sure to bring a case to protect your camera from sand.)

With no ocean or lake nearby, the dunes may seem misplaced, but the ingredients for making them—wind, sand, and water—are here. After pointing out the San Juan Mountains to the west and the Sangre de Cristo range to the east, explain to your companions that a huge lake once covered the valley between the mountains. Over many years the lake drained and sand remained. Winds from the San Juans in the west blew sand easterly to the Sangres. During storms, winds moved the sand back west, depositing it in the valley. In addition, two creeks in the Sangres, Medano and Sand, continue to capture and carry sand down to the valley floor. The balance of winds from the east and the west, along with creek deposits, has resulted in the highest dune in the park, measuring 750 feet. An 1874 photograph of a main dunefield compared to one taken in 1999 shows little change in size or location.

The dunes are a tough environment, but some plants and animals have their niche here. Found nowhere else on Earth, the Great Sand Dunes tiger beetle and six other insects unique to the dunes may leave their tiny tracks along your path. Youngsters discover how insects survive life on the hot sand by feeling the temperature difference of surface sand and the layer just below.

For a cool sampling of Great Sand Dunes National Park and Preserve, drive back out to CO-150 and the Montville Nature Trail parking lot. The 0.5-mile trail loops around Mosca Creek, which flows year-round, pooling in several places suitable for little feet.

GREAT GETAWAYS

Camp out close to Hike 30 at Great Sand Dunes National Park and Preserve. Offering first-come, first-served campsites, the park is 75 miles west of Pueblo and 35 miles northeast of Alamosa. Check www.nps.gov /grsa or call (719) 378-2312 for information. You'll find plenty of hikes that start at the Sand Dunes Visitor Center.

In Hooper, 25 miles west of the park, don't miss the Sand Dunes swimming pool (719-378-2807) for swimming. For stargazing magic or out-of-this world wacky fun check out the UFO watchtower.

Colorado 'Gators Alligator Farm (719-378-2612), which also has emus, ostriches, snakes, lizards, and more, is 3 miles north of the Mosca turnoff to Great Sand Dunes National Park and Preserve.

 NEWLIN CREEK TRAIL

BEFORE YOU GO
Map USGS Rockvale
Information For current conditions and more information, contact San Carlos Ranger District, www.fs.fed.us /r2/psicc or (719) 553-1400

ABOUT THE HIKE
Location Florence
Day hike; Easy to moderate
2.7 miles one-way
Hikable Mid-May to early November
Starting elevation/High point 6900 feet/8350 feet
Accessibility None

GETTING THERE

From downtown Florence and the intersection of CO-115 and CO-67, head south on CO-67 for 4.6 miles to County Road 15 and turn right. In 2.6 miles take the right fork. The pavement ends in 0.9 mile, making for slippery mud conditions when wet. Continue 0.8 mile, following the right fork and the sign for Florence Mountain Park. Pass the entrance to the park in 1.2 miles and continue past the next intersection at 0.2 mile, following the signs for Newlin Creek trailhead. Continue 0.1 mile to a private residence on the left. Please respect private property. Parking is available along this rough road just beyond the national forest sign boundary, in 0.2 mile. Or continue another 0.2 mile to the trailhead located near a small dam and pond and a small parking area.

LOGISTICS
Water and toilet facilities are not available here.

ON THE TRAIL
Little waterfalls and fern-laced cliffs disguise the logging-road origins of this pleasant hike to an old steam boiler rusting in a meadow. Kids enjoy the rock-hopping or balancing skills required at each of the many stream crossings. They are thrilled when they discover the historic treasure at the trail's destination.

 Newlin Creek is centered in a historic oil-, coal-, and silver-mining area of the Wet Mountains. Members of the Gunnison Expedition of 1853–54 named this range, located in south-central Colorado, after their rainy encounters there. Lumber was needed to fuel these industries of the late 1800s, which inspired Canadian entrepreneur Nathaniel F. Herrick to build a road up Newlin Creek. He then hauled a huge steam boiler and flywheel on his hand-built 5-foot-wide road. Water from Newlin Creek powered the boiler that ran the flywheel and saw. Unfortunately, Herrick's untimely death shortly after he established his site led to its abandonment. Today, lunch in the meadow at the trail's terminus serves as an effective motivation for hikers.

Beginning near the upper parking lot, the trail heads west in a mixed forest with the creek on your left. This portion of the trail up

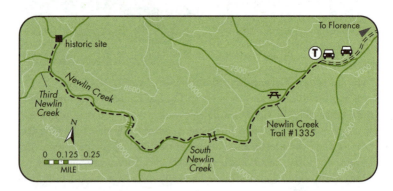

A hiker explores the rusted remains of logging-era steam relics on the Newlin Creek Trail.

to the bridge follows the 1880s wagon road Herrick built, supported in places with rock walls. Numerous floods and rock slides have eliminated its form, but your companions may find evidence of the historic road.

Watch out for poison ivy at 0.4 mile and a picnic table with fire pit shortly beyond it. The trail winds between steep rock walls, spanning the creek at 0.7 mile via a picturesque wooden bridge.

Assign a member of your group to be the Creek Crossing Accountant, a task that requires vigilance and balancing skills. (Spoiler alert! From here on the hike includes crossing either Newlin or a side creek seventeen times.) The climber(s) in your group will want to explore the boulder conglomeration beside the trail at 1 mile. The biggest of the waterfalls (almost 4 feet) is at 1.6 miles, to the right of the creek crossing. The next creek crossing is steep; look upstream a bit for an easier crossing spot.

When the trail enters a meadow at 2.5 miles, look to the right for the steam boiler and flywheel in a backdrop of aspens. Encourage your companions to look for other historic remnants, hopefully the chimney. It's another 0.2 mile west on the trail and then to the left of the trail. Kids love to climb on and around the old boiler. Remind them to respect it as a historical item not housed in a museum. The boiler and related artifacts in the area are protected under the American Antiquities Act. Encourage your hikers to examine the boiler for gargoyle-like facets and other curious markings.

Return via the same trail.

BISHOP'S CASTLE

BEFORE YOU GO
Map None
Information For current conditions and more information, contact Bishop's Castle, www.bishopcastle.org

ABOUT THE HIKE
Location Near Beulah
Day hike; Easy
0.1 mile or more
Hikable Year-round
Starting elevation/High point 9000 feet/9100 feet
Accessibility None

GETTING THERE

From I-25 south of Pueblo, take exit 74 onto CO-165 west and follow it 27 miles to Bishop's Castle. From Cañon City on US 50, take CO-67 south 25 miles to CO-165; turn left (south) and continue 12 miles. Parking is available alongside the road.

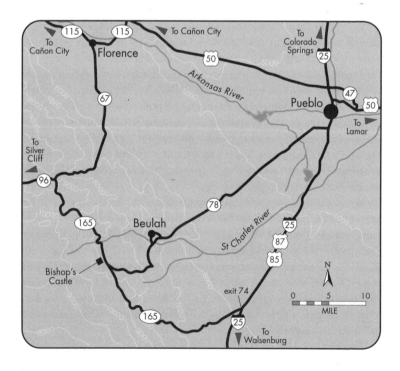

LOGISTICS

Toilet facilities and drinking water are available near the parking area. The castle is open daily May through October, weekends November through April.

ON THE TRAIL

A visit to Bishop's Castle is long remembered, whether as an acrophobe's nightmare or a kid's dream playground. (Though hiking here means climbing a rickety skeleton of a castle set next to the natural forest, I couldn't resist including it as a fun best hike.) Jim Bishop began building his dream of a "real castle in the woods" in 1969. Since then, he has hoisted and placed more than 1000 tons of rock from the San Isabel National Forest to

A steep staircase into Bishop's Castle leads hikers to a royal fantasyland.

create his stone and cement fortress. His ornamental ironwork (Bishop's "real" work in Pueblo, Colorado) flanks the castle's spiral staircases and suspended walkways. Weekend visitors often see Bishop busy welding, unloading rock from his truck, or holding court in his Gift Shoppe as he signs his latest CD, *Rant & Rave*. Visitors of all ages love checking out the costumes, fairies, dragons, and fantasy weaponry on sale in the Gift Shoppe, located in a small structure adjacent to the castle.

The 160-foot-tall castle, claimed as "America's biggest one-man construction project," thrills children as they explore its towers and dungeon, while grown-ups stand amazed as they consider the energy of its builder. A steep, tall concrete staircase in front of the castle leads to the grand ballroom. Breath-catchers stop to admire the stained-glass windows here, but kids race off to one of several staircases leading to the castle's balconies and towers. Little ones or those with questionable balance may need hand holding to negotiate some of the castle's near-vertical or spiraling stairwells. The fire-breathing dragon, Bishop's metallurgic work of art, wows all castle explorers. Other thrills include climbing to the highest point in a tower and waving to family members in the courtyard below or crossing a suspended walkway to a balcony.

With each visit, expect something new at Bishop's Castle. Intent on seeing "how much one man can build in a single lifetime," Bishop plans to build a moat and drawbridge to his castle, a roller-coaster mounted on the castle's outer walls, an orchestra-size balcony, and another castle for his wife, Phoebe.

 JUDD FALLS TRAIL

BEFORE YOU GO
Maps Gunnison National Forest; USGS Gothic
Information For current conditions and more information, contact the Gunnison Ranger District, www.fs.fed.us/r2/gmug or (970) 641-0471

ABOUT THE HIKE
Location Gunnison National Forest
Day hike or backpack; Easy to moderate
0.5 mile one way
Hikable June to October
Starting elevation/High point 9700 feet/9800 feet
Accessibility None

GETTING THERE

In Crested Butte, on CO-135, at the four-way stop continue northeast (straight) on Gothic Road past the Crested Butte Ski Area for 8 miles. At the Rocky Mountain Biological Laboratory's General Store, travel 0.5 mile farther and turn right. Go 0.5 mile to the Judd Falls parking lot.

LOGISTICS

The nearest toilet and water facilities are at the ski area. Plan to hike this very popular trail midweek or early morning or late afternoon.

ON THE TRAIL

In this short walk through an aspen forest, the reward comes easily and early. The sight of Copper Creek crashing through a dark, twisted, rocky chasm delights hikers of all ages. Along the way, day hikers and backpackers en route to the Elk Mountains can't resist stopping to examine the wildflowers that splash pinks, reds, blues, and yellows across the deep green terrain.

From the trailhead at the parking lot's east end, the Copper Lake Trail stays in a friendly, flower-studded forest accompanied by a quietly babbling brook. This constant moisture enables such towering beauties as cow parsnip, a leafy, stout plant topped by an umbrella of tiny white flowers, to thrive. Elk eat the succulent stems of this member of the parsley family and, although Native Americans used the plant's young shoots as food, don't let the kids sample it. Carefully point out the "hairs" from the plant stem. These can cause blisters on lips if the plant is put in the mouth. Another trail shader is the monument plant, especially attractive to elk and deer. Its cone-shaped columns of green and white flowers lure summer visitors of all sizes. Kids remember the plant by its other name, "deer's ears," when you show them its leaves, shaped just like the animal's ears.

Look to the trail's right for grand, aspen-framed views of Gothic Peak cradled in the lush

A trio of hikers steps carefully while descending a steep, rocky trail.

East River valley. Observant hikers will remember seeing this valley during the drive from Crested Butte to Gothic. After the trail descends 0.1 mile on an unforested hill, turn right on the no-longer-in-use Copper Creek four-wheel-drive road. The Judd Falls overlook is only 40 feet from here on the left, at 0.5 mile. Eager amblers need careful watching at this overlook; there are no guardrails along this 100-foot drop-off. This is the turnaround point for day hikers.

Backpackers continue from here, following the Copper Creek Trail. This popular trek gradually ascends the creek valley with a number of beautiful meadow destinations along the way. Copper Lake, at 11,321 feet, sits at the tree line, just east of East Maroon Pass, 5 miles from the trailhead.

GREAT GETAWAYS

The beautiful Lake Irwin Campground is 9 miles west of Crested Butte on Kebler Pass Road and is the ideal base near Hike 33. To reserve sites, go to www.reserveusa.com or call (877) 444-6777. Explore the many trails around the lake (be careful to avoid the private mining claims beyond the trails) or fish for rainbow and brook trout in the lake or in neighboring Anthracite Creek.

The Crested Butte Mountain Heritage Museum (970-349-1880) features the Mountain Bike Hall of Fame plus cool old-time ski equipment and a spooky mining exhibit. You can also head to Mount Crested Butte ski area (www.skicb.com, 970-349-2333) for hiking, biking, and even Frisbee golf!

 HANGING LAKE TRAIL

BEFORE YOU GO
Maps White River National Forest; USGS Shoshone
Information For current conditions and more information, contact the Eagle Ranger District, www.fs.fed .us/r2/whiteriver or (970) 328-6388

ABOUT THE HIKE
Location White River National Forest
Day hike; Challenging
1.2 miles one way
Hikable Year-round
Starting elevation/High point 6110 feet/7160 feet
Accessibility None

A sea of mountains fills the views north from Mount Sherman.

GETTING THERE

From Eagle head west on I-70, passing Hanging Lake (while in the tunnel), and exit at the Grizzly Creek rest area and trailhead. At Grizzly Creek turn left and immediately turn left again, returning to I-70, traveling eastbound. Pass the Shoshone exit, driving several miles to exit 125, Hanging Lake, which leads directly to ample parking. From Glenwood Springs, travel east on I-70 for 9 miles to exit 125, Hanging Lake.

LOGISTICS

Picnic and toilet facilities and drinking water, located near the parking area, are maintained during the summer. The area is closed to fishing, swimming, wading, and camping; no dogs are allowed. During summer, avoid crowds and heat by hiking midweek in early morning or late afternoon. Bring a camera on this hike.

ON THE TRAIL

It is little wonder that Hanging Lake, unforgettably beautiful and located just off I-70, is one of Colorado's most popular hiking destinations. The trail climbs 1000 feet along a geologic fault line to reach the turquoise lake and waterfalls. Frequent rest stops (benches are provided) to examine the changing terrain make the hike less strenuous. The fragile environment here, coupled with its heavy use, means hikers should take extra care to leave no trace.

From the parking lot, walk about 0.25 mile east. Here the trail begins, steadily climbing Dead Horse Canyon and crossing Dead Horse Creek several times. During spring and summer the creek runs full; however, later in the season portions of it flow underground. Have kids count

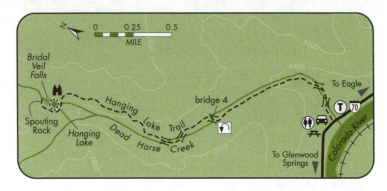

each time a footbridge spans the creek bed. The light-colored stone high above the second bridge, at 0.2 mile, is considered fossiliferous, but you can get a close-up look at prehistoric plant and animal life merely by examining the fossil-scarred rock in the middle of the trail.

While resting at the fourth bridge, at 0.6 mile—you're halfway there!—youngsters like searching for Smoky Bear's cave in the rock wall, about 200 feet up. A small log cabin shelter sits on the trail's left side just 20 yards beyond. This makes a good turnaround for a shorter hike.

The steepest leg of the trip begins at the fifth bridge, at 0.7 mile. Take it slow enough to point out the old horse stables near the sixth bridge, at 0.8 mile. In 1910, visitors at Hanging Lake Resort, located near the Colorado River, rode horses up this canyon trail. Metal pipe guardrails add a measure of safety to the final staircase-like pathway leading to Hanging Lake. Still, little ones need a helping hand here.

At the top of the climb, follow the boardwalk to the right, circling around Hanging Lake. A geologic fault caused the lakebed to drop away from the valley floor above, hence its name. You'll want to stop and feast your eyes on Bridal Veil Falls spilling into the lake's crystal blue waters. Kids, however, like to run ahead to climb the boulders near the waterfall. Remind your companions to stay on the path; the shoreline is fragile. It is composed of dissolved carbonates, deposited as the water flows over the edge.

Don't miss Spouting Rock and the lake below it; to get there, double back over the boardwalk, turn right, and walk 0.2 mile. An underground stream pushing through a hole in the cliff caused the waterspout. In midsummer, butterflies of many colors and sizes alight on the shore, seemingly teasing kids to catch them.

Return via the same trail.

MAROON LAKE TRAIL

BEFORE YOU GO
Maps USFS Guide to the Maroon Bells Recreation Area; USGS Maroon Bells
Information For current conditions and more information, contact Aspen-Sopris Ranger District, www.fs.fed.us/r2/whiteriver or (970) 925-3445

ABOUT THE HIKE
Location Aspen
Day hike; Easy
1 mile round-trip
Hikable Mid-June through September
Starting elevation/High point 9580 feet/9680 feet
Accessibility None

GETTING THERE

In Aspen, from the junction of Main Street (CO-82) with Mill Street, follow Main Street 1.2 miles west. Turn left on Maroon Creek Road, staying right, and drive 9.8 miles to the Maroon Creek parking lot in the day-use area. See Hike 36, Maroon Creek Trail, for vehicle restrictions and shuttle buses.

The Maroon Bells form a dramatic backdrop to hikes 35 and 36.

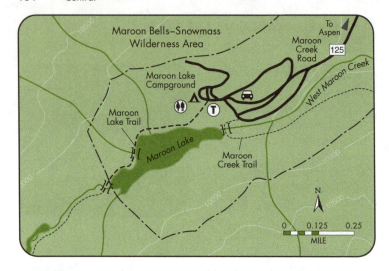

LOGISTICS

Toilet facilities are provided in the Maroon Creek parking lot. Dogs must be leashed here.

ON THE TRAIL

Few can resist this easy lakeside stroll with beautiful Maroon Bells providing a dramatic backdrop. Kids love spotting the lake's beaver lodge and examining the shoreline's aquatic life. Also, the Maroon Creek Trail (Hike 36) begins here, allowing families with mixed ages to take the youngest hikers on this lakeside hike while the older ones follow the more ambitious creekside trail downstream. The creek hikers can time their return on the shuttle bus to coincide with the lake hikers.

A short trail from the parking lot or bus stop leads to a signboard featuring a map of the area and information about the area's flora and fauna; the Maroon Lake Trail begins just left of the signboard. At 0.25 mile, you'll see the Deadly Bells Kiosk, which describes the climbing hazards these mountains pose.

Look up at the Maroon Bells and ask your companions how tall the two mountains stand. They are among Colorado's fifty-four tallest peaks. On your right is North Maroon Peak (14,101 feet); to your left, South Maroon Peak (14,156 feet). An iron-bearing mineral called hematite gave the mountains their red color. Geologic uplift caused their height. During the last ice age, glaciers carved the mountains and sculpted a basin for the lake. Today wind, rain, and snow continue to shape the Maroon Bells and everything around them. Early explorers named the peaks for their maroon color and distinctive bell shape. Ask, "What would you name these almost identical peaks?"

Continue to the left of the kiosk and on to the lake's edge, where kids are compelled to toss in a pebble. The beaver lodge, perched near the south end of the lake at about 0.3 mile, will attract everyone's attention. Chances of seeing the mostly nocturnal animals are slim, though in early evening, a large V moving across the lake signals a beaver en route. Does the lodge appear to have an entrance? Probably not. Beavers enter their homes from below the water's surface to store their food of aspen and cottonwood twigs. Talk about how this behavior helps the beaver survival rate. Discerning eyes may see small beaver trails leading from the lakeshore into trees opposite the lake.

Just beyond the beaver dam, cross a stream on a small footbridge and continue on the wide path, ignoring the trail to the right. At 0.5 mile, the trail enters Maroon Bells–Snowmass Wilderness Area and crosses another footbridge, over the creek feeding into the lake. Just beyond here, pass the trail to the right, which is steep and not well marked. About another 20 yards beyond is a large rockfall in the pine—a fine destination and turnaround point

 MAROON CREEK TRAIL

BEFORE YOU GO
Maps USFS Guide to Maroon Bells Recreation Area; USGS Maroon Bells, USGS Highland Peak
Information For current conditions and more information, contact Aspen-Sopris Ranger District, www.fs.fed.us/r2 /whiteriver or (970) 925-3445

ABOUT THE HIKE
Location Aspen
Day hike; Moderate
3.2 miles one way
Hikable Mid-June through September
Starting elevation/Low point: 9580 feet/8709 feet
Accessibility None

GETTING THERE

In Aspen, from the junction of Main Street (CO-82) with Mill Street, follow Main Street 1.2 miles west. Turn left on Maroon Creek Road,

The red, freckled tops of the poisonous Amanita muscaria *mushroom decorate forest floors in late summer.*

staying right, and drive 9.8 miles to the Maroon Creek parking lot in the day-use area. During summer, vehicle restrictions on Maroon Creek Road are enforced 8:30 AM–5:00 PM daily, but you are free to drive to Maroon Creek trailhead before 8:30 AM and can return at any time during the day. During restricted hours, shuttle buses provide transportation to Maroon Valley from the Aspen Highlands Village base area (located 2 miles up Maroon Creek Road), every twenty minutes 9:00 AM–5:00 PM. To purchase the moderately priced tickets, follow signs at the village parking lot to the Pro Sports shop. There is also parking at the lower trailhead at the East Maroon Wilderness Portal, about 2 miles from Aspen.

LOGISTICS

Toilet facilities are provided in the Maroon Creek parking lot; picnic facilities are provided at the East Maroon Wilderness Portal parking area and shuttle bus stop. Sturdy walking shoes are recommended for this trail. Dogs must be leashed here.

ON THE TRAIL

This creekside trail takes hikers on a quiet, sometimes roaring passage through the varied ecosystems of Maroon Bells. Less hiked than its trailhead partner, Maroon Lake Trail (Hike 35), the Maroon Creek Trail heads downvalley through dense conifer forest, rocky slopes, wildflower meadows, and aspen glens and over several streams. Before heading out, check the bus schedule to time your arrival either here or at the trail's end, East Maroon Wilderness Portal.

Beginning at the outlet of West Maroon Creek from Maroon Lake, take

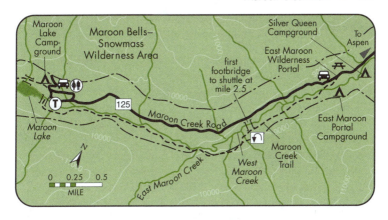

in the view of Colorado's signature mountains, North Maroon Peak and South Maroon Peak. Turn left to cross the footbridge and bear left into a dense conifer forest. Bright green patches of moss blanket the forest floor here, forming a velvety crazy quilt your companions will want to feel.

During my late-August hike here, a variety of mushrooms flocked the forest floor. Let kids know that mushrooms are the fruits of mycelium, a vast underground network of tiny white threads called hyphae. Just like an apple bears seeds, a mushroom bears reproductive spores. Mycologists examine spores to help identity a mushroom from some 50,000 different species. A brown or whitish powder you may see at the base of a mushroom or on its gills is a dusting of spores. Let hikers know that wild mushrooms are not harmful to touch, but they should never be eaten unless collected by people who have studied fungi for many years.

As the trail heads into a clearing at 0.5 mile, watch for a wide pool in the creek spanned by a beaver dam. Attention, however, is soon required for maintaining solid footing on the talus slope, a feat many kids skip through while parents step carefully.

At 1.2 miles the trail reenters a quiet, dense forest punctuated by the chattering of chipmunks. At about 2 miles the sound of water flowing signals the approach of East Maroon Creek. Within 0.5 mile a spur trail on your left leads to a bridge over Maroon Creek with access to a shuttle bus heading downvalley. Continue on the trail's remaining 0.7 mile as it ascends a ridge of aspens, then descends gradually to the creek, ending at the East Maroon Wilderness Portal. The large beaver pond here captures the attention of hikers waiting for the shuttle bus.

GREAT GETAWAYS

There are several camping options near Hikes 35, 36, and 37. Silver Bar, Silver Bell, or Silver Queen campgrounds are 5 to 6 miles west of Aspen (tents or pickup and pop-up campers only). Reserve sites at www.reserveusa.com or by calling (877) 444-6777. Fishing is plentiful in Maroon Creek, which runs through all three campgrounds, and at nearby Maroon Lake.

Snowmass Ski Area (www.aspensnowmass.com) is a great destination for some family fun. Ride the Silver Queen gondola up 3000 feet over 2.5 miles for panoramic views of Elk Mountains and to reach several short hikes, or ride the Burlingame chairlift to reach the family-friendly Village Bound bike trail. The area offers a lot of other hiking and biking options as well.

 HALLAM LAKE LOOP TRAIL

BEFORE YOU GO
Map ACES Hallam Lake Loop trail guide
Information For current conditions and more information, contact Aspen Center for Environmental Sciences, www.aspennature.org or (970) 925-5756

ABOUT THE HIKE
Location Aspen
Day hike; Easy
0.1-mile loop
Hikable Year-round
Starting elevation/High point 7970 feet/7970 feet
Accessibility Wheelchair-accessible

GETTING THERE

In Aspen, at the intersection of Main and Mill streets, drive north on Mill Street two blocks to Puppy Smith Street. Turn left (west) and drive one block past the U.S. Post Office to where Aspen Center for Environmental Studies (ACES) parking is provided.

LOGISTICS

Toilet facilities and drinking water are available at the ACES nature center.

ON THE TRAIL

ACES, located in the heart of Aspen, offers visitors a close-up look at wild and permanently injured animals housed in a natural setting. Summer visitors to the 26-acre wildlife sanctuary plan their outing for the daily "Bird of Prey" program, often featuring the resident golden eagle. Call ahead for other scheduled events. In winter, the preserve is fun to explore on snowshoes. Before starting your hike, stop

Dad and daughter stand eye to eye with a golden eagle at the Aspen Center for Environmental Studies.

inside the center to scan the nature displays or learn about regularly scheduled naturalist walks here and in the Aspen area. View a cross section of a mountain stream, home to local cutthroat trout. Borrow a Hallam Lake Loop trail guide and binoculars to assist you along the trail.

Access to the trail is via the cottonwood-shaded lane just outside the ACES nature center. A wheelchair-accessible boardwalk takes hikers approximately 90 feet from the nature center across a marshy area and alongside Hallam Lake and several beaver ponds. Here, kids like using binoculars (available at the nature center) to scan the waters in search of beavers or swans. Canada geese are likely to honk their annoyance at your presence. At about 100 feet a spur trail to the right leads to the path to the Bird of Prey House; stay left. Assistance with wheelchair use is recommended for the rest of the main loop beyond this junction.

Refer to the trail guide for interesting interpretations of the lush vegetation this trail winds through. Take time to scale the viewing platform, located at signpost 23 at about 300 feet, on the left side of the trail. From here your crew has a bird's-eye view of a riparian zone. Encourage them to keep their eyes open for jays, magpies, red-winged blackbirds, woodpeckers, or even a great blue heron fishing in the Roaring Fork River below.

At about 450 feet, you'll reach the other end of the spur trail to the Bird of Prey House, where nonreleasable birds are kept. Stay left and

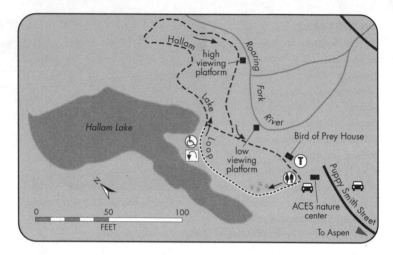

reach the house at about 500 feet. Hawks and great horned owls are among the recovered residents here. Remind kids that these animals are permanently injured; if released into the wild, they would not survive.

When you arrive back at the nature center, return the Hallam Lake Loop trail guide and binoculars.

 THE GROTTOS LOOP TRAIL

BEFORE YOU GO
Map USGS New York Peak
Information For current
conditions and more
information, contact Aspen-
Sopris Ranger District,
www.fs.fed.us/r2/whiteriver
or (970) 925-3445

ABOUT THE HIKE
Location Aspen
Day hike; Easy
0.25 mile one way
Hikable June to October
**Starting elevation/High
point** 10,000 feet/10,020 feet
Accessibility Wheelchair-
accessible (30 yards) to
picnic area

GETTING THERE
From Aspen, travel 10.2 miles east on CO-82 to a Forest Service sign on the right for Weller Campground. Continue 0.9 mile farther, just beyond the speed limit sign, and turn right on the gravel roadway.

The Roaring Fork River captivates every hiker, but keep a safe distance here.

LOGISTICS

Toilet facilities are available at the parking area. Recent improvements have made the trail easier to follow and safer for children, but adult supervision is required at all times here because there are no guardrails to prevent falls into the boulders or the roaring river. Plan to visit this popular site midweek, and be aware that high water during spring runoff can be very dangerous.

ON THE TRAIL

Just 10 miles south of Aspen, the Roaring Fork River takes a playful route. At the Grottos, it pools and spills over smoothly sculpted boulders, forming ice caves, quiet wading waters (in late summer), and a beach for building sand castles.

For a look at what's to come, take the accessible trail, starting at the parking lot's west side, and turn left onto the boardwalk. The smooth gravel path stays north of the river as it enters a pine forest and within 0.1 mile leads to views of the waterfall. Return via the same trail.

The slightly longer walking trail begins at the footbridge spanning the Roaring Fork River. After crossing, turn left, following the rocky path marked by a sign for the ice caves.

While passing the smooth granite boulders on your left, watch for the two erratics—rocks seemingly out of place here. At the base of the boulders, look carefully for scars left by the wagon wheels of miners and travelers hauling their loads on this path, once known as the Old Stage Road. In late summer a small section of the river near here forms a shallow wading pool beside a sandy beach. Boulders piled on the shore make this a mini-playground few kids want to leave.

Continuing on the foot trail, climb a slight hill, following the

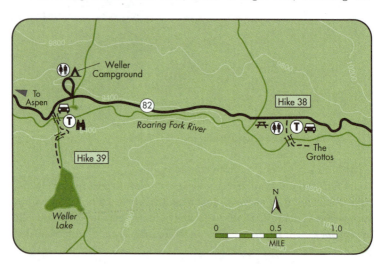

directional signs leading to the ice caves. While walking over the hollowed boulders, point out the ice formations inside the rocks. Why hasn't the ice melted? There are a few places here where kids can reach into the hollows to feel the cool temperature inside them. Do not encourage anyone to climb inside the caverns.

Continue walking in the direction of the river's roar along the trail's polished granite surface. In less than 0.1 mile you'll reach the raging river and boulder display. Hold little ones' hands as you approach and explore the waterfall site. Return via the same trail.

 WELLER LAKE TRAIL

BEFORE YOU GO
Maps Ute Scout Mountain Guide for Hiking and Biking (available at Aspen Visitor Center); USGS New York Peak
Information For current conditions and more information, contact Aspen-Sopris Ranger District, www.fs.fed.us/r2/whiteriver or (970) 925-3445

ABOUT THE HIKE
Location Aspen
Day hike; Moderate
0.6 mile one way
Hikable Mid-June to mid-October
Starting elevation/High point 9300 feet/9600 feet
Accessibility None

GETTING THERE

From Aspen, drive east on CO-82 approximately 10 miles. Turn right into the small paved parking area just before Weller Campground.

LOGISTICS

Toilet facilities and drinking water are at Weller Campground. As with all high-altitude hikes, plan this one for early in the day—prior to the sometimes-daily thunderstorms.

ON THE TRAIL

This shady, melodic climb through the forest winds past diversions kids love: creeks to poke, rocks to climb, and a lakeshore to explore. Better yet, almost every hiker on the Weller Lake Trail returns with an elated,

Alpine lakes reward hikers with clear, cold reflections.

"I made it to the top!" feeling.

The trail begins at the parking area's east end, where it descends into the lush river bottom. In midsummer, look for flowering cow parsnip to shade the shoulders of some hikers with its white, umbrella-like cluster of flowers. Your fellow hikers may think of a more descriptive name for the cow parsnip after you point out its regal companion, monkshood, wearing purple hoods along 4- and 5-foot-tall stalks.

Before 0.2 mile, the trail meets the Roaring Fork River, spanned by a wooden footbridge. In its clear, shallow waters, kids watch for fish darting in the shadows. Just beyond the river crossing, the Weller Lake Trail sign directs you to the right. Listen for a gurgling creek that appears to spill from a trailside boulder. The moss that graces this wet attraction invites little hands to feel it. Another sound that may delight your ears is the long, warbled song of the Townsend's solitaire. The large (8 to 9.5 inches) gray-brown bird with a white eye ring and whitish feathers edging its tail summers in mountain forests.

As the trail switchbacks up the slope, ask your kids if they hear the creek sound coming from behind, in front, below, or above them. Near the top of the switchbacks, have them feel the source of these sounds from the wooden footbridge that spans the creek. The last portion of the trail enters a forest of aspen and spruce in which the competition for sunlight has left many downed trees. Your hikers may notice that the spruce trees have won the battle for light, a common theme in forest regeneration.

Boulders and a steeply forested edge around Weller Lake inhibit lakeside exploration. However, most kids enjoy climbing the boulders that block the entrance to the lake. Opposite the lake's entrance, on the eastern slope, point out the dead trees: fire victims in the mid-1970s. Look to see how forest regeneration has begun.

Return via the same trail, perhaps playing "Rocks and Roots Only," a game in which hikers try to place each footstep on either of these common trail components. At the Weller Lake trail sign, follow the trail to the right for about 25 feet to the Roaring Fork overlook. Two wooden footbridges and a trail that leads to the creek edge allow all hikers one more chance to explore the water's edge.

 LINKINS LAKE TRAIL

BEFORE YOU GO
Map Ute Scout Mountain Guide for Hiking and Biking (available at Aspen Visitor Center)
Information For current conditions and more information, contact Aspen-Sopris Ranger District, www.fs.fed.us/r2/whiteriver or (970) 925-3445

ABOUT THE HIKE
Location Hunter-Fryingpan Wilderness Area
Day hike; Moderate to challenging
0.6 mile one way
Hikable Late June to mid-October (depending on snow)
Starting elevation/High point 11,506 feet/12,008 feet
Accessibility None

GETTING THERE
From Aspen, drive east on CO-82 for 18.5 miles to the last switchback before Independence Pass. The trailhead and limited parking is on the left (north) side of the highway.

LOGISTICS
Plan this hike for early in the day before the often-severe afternoon thunderstorms. Raingear is recommended on all hikes above timberline, where weather conditions change rapidly. Camping is not recommended due to the area's fragile tundra and the risks of high alpine exposure. Dogs must be on leash at all times in the Hunter-Fryingpan Wilderness.

ON THE TRAIL
This short but steep climb to an alpine lake is breathtaking, both visually and physically. Close-up looks at the flowers that jewel the tundra, as well

Alpine wildflowers lace the Linkins Lake shoreline.

as sweeping views of the Continental Divide, make this huff-'n'-puff hike a memory worth recording on film.

The trailhead begins at the parking area, left (west) of the Roaring Fork River. Within 200 yards, turn left at the trail sign for Linkins Lake (the righthand trail is the Lost Man Trail). Extra hands may be needed to help keep little feet dry during the creek crossing here.

The trail ascends immediately while the floral parade at your feet provides a delightful, breath-catching diversion. When passing marshy creek areas, warn your young companions to watch out for hordes of "little red elephants." Smiles replace fears when you show them the 10- to 28-inch-tall stalks covered with pink-purple flowers, each shaped like an elephant's head. Kids like meeting the floral rulers of these parts: red-topped king's crown and rose-topped queen's crown. And some hikers enjoy spotting flowers of every color of the rainbow. (Remember, picking wildflowers is prohibited in this and all wilderness areas.)

During breaks explain that Linkins Lake sits in a glacial cirque, formed over the last two million years. Glaciers once packed the area with rock, then began melting, scooping and scraping the mountains, leaving U-shaped valleys and high alpine lakes in their crunching passage backward. The lake's water—the temperature of recently melted snow (40° to 50°F)—supports a few plants and the seasonal

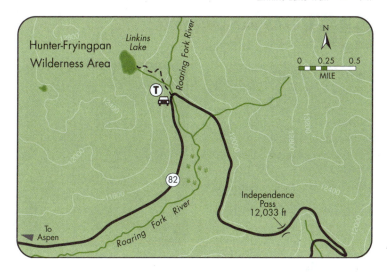

population of stocked fish. Plans for a refreshing dip in the lake will be vetoed after learning of the lake's cold conditions and the delicate state of natural balance it supports.

As the trail rises above timberline, be aware that the few remaining trees, though short in stature, may be long in age—some are 200 years and older. These trees have adapted to the short growing season, fierce winds, and bitter cold of the alpine climate. Their stunted appearance is called *krummholz,* a German word meaning "crooked wood." Those stopping at the uppermost cluster of krummholz beside the trail may guess the oldest tree's age by knowing that a tree with a 3-inch diameter growing at 11,500 feet in Rocky Mountain National Park was measured at 328 years old! Please protect the area's fragile plants near this area by stepping carefully.

After Continental Divide views wow your group, check out the survival scene at your feet. Notice the plants' small size advantage; growing snug to the ground keeps them out of the worst weather and requires less energy for plant production. Your hikers may find a red coloring edging many alpine plants. The pigment, called anthocyanin, acts like antifreeze by converting light to heat, thus warming the plant. Examine leaf size and the tiny hairlike covering protecting many plants. During this and any other alpine exploration, remind hikers to step on rock when possible; the plants here face enough challenges to survive.

Return via the same trail.

LILY PAD LAKE TRAIL

BEFORE YOU GO
Maps White River National Forest; USGS Frisco
Information For current conditions and more information, contact Dillon Ranger District, www.fs.fed.us/r2/whiteriver or (970) 468-5400

ABOUT THE HIKE
Location Eagles Nest Wilderness near Silverthorne
Day hike; Moderate
3 miles round-trip to Lily Pad Lake, or 2.5 miles one way to Meadow Creek trailhead
Hikable June to October
Starting elevation/High point 9800 feet/10,000 feet
Accessibility None

GETTING THERE

From I-70 at Silverthorne, take exit 205 onto CO-9 north, and at the 7 Eleven turn west (left) onto Ryan Gulch Road to the Wildernest subdivision. Continue through the subdivision 2.4 miles, parking at the end of the road. To shuttle a vehicle to the Meadow Creek trailhead: From I-70 near Silverthorne, take exit 203 west. Turn right at the end of the exit ramp, then west onto a gravel road, continuing 0.5 mile to the trailhead parking lot.

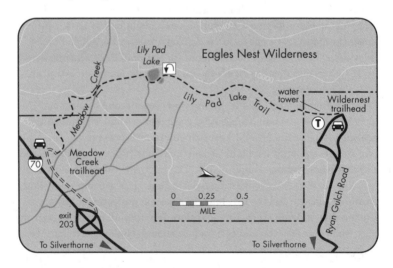

Lily pads provide essential shelter and shade for a pond's aquatic life.

LOGISTICS

Bicycles are not permitted in the Eagles Nest Wilderness, and dogs must be on leash at all times.

ON THE TRAIL

Whether you walk the Lily Pad Lake Trail in its entirety, with a car shuttle at the other end, or simply as a lake destination, returning via the same route, this is a delightful day hike for every hiker.

From the Wildernest road end, climb 100 yards up the access road; don't let this discourage little hikers. The trail begins just beyond the recently constructed water tower on the hillside. At the water tower, the trail enters a level lodgepole pine forest. Typically, lodgepoles thrive in dry, well-drained soils, forming dense stands with little vegetation beneath them. A pleasing difference here is the array of brooks gurgling across the forest floor. Lodgepoles are one of the first trees to reclaim a forest destroyed by fire. Examine a cone from these trees and let kids discover its tightly closed individual scales. A lodgepole seed is attached to each scale. Lodgepole cones remain this way for many years until opened by the heat of a forest fire, spilling the seeds on bare ground. Can your hikers find evidence of a fire? Why or why not? Are lodgepole seedlings growing here?

Within 1 mile, the trail enters an aspen-pine stand where a beaver pond necessitates a 25-foot-long footbridge constructed of lodgepole pine trunks. Native Americans used the slender trunks of these trees as poles for their teepees. Discuss how this use explains the tree's name.

Another 0.5 mile of subtle climbing leads to a lily pad–blanketed lake on the left. Adjacent to it is the larger, less flower-quilted Lily Pad Lake at 1.5 miles. Neither lake is suitable for swimming. The lakes are a good destination for a lunch stop or a satisfying turnaround for those who wish to head back to the same trailhead.

The trail follows a narrow passage between the lakes, then gradually descends, passing through several lovely aspen stands. In clearings between the trees, enjoy the views of Dillon Reservoir and the surrounding mountains. About 0.5 mile from the lakes, the trail switchbacks to a footbridge that spans Meadow Creek at 2 miles. The aspen background here makes for a great photo of kids crossing the bridge.

After the bridge, tell the hike leader to watch for the remains of a log cabin clinging to an aspen hillside on the right. Perhaps hikers will recognize that the structure's logs are those of a lodgepole pine. The cabin marks the trail's last 0.3 mile, reaching the Meadow Creek trailhead at 2.5 miles.

 ROCK CREEK TRAIL

BEFORE YOU GO
Maps White River National Forest; USGS Willow Lakes
Information For current conditions and more information, contact Dillon Ranger District, www.fs.fed.us/r2/whiteriver or (970) 468-5400

ABOUT THE HIKE
Location Eagles Nest Wilderness near Silverthorne
Day hike or backpack; Moderate
1.8 miles one way
Hikable June to September
Starting elevation/High point 9500 feet/10,200 feet
Accessibility None

GETTING THERE

From I-70 at Silverthorne, take exit 205 onto CO-9 north for 8.2 miles to a dirt road opposite the Blue River Campground. Turn west (left) and drive 1.4 miles to a road on the left directing you to Rock Creek. Continue 1.6 miles to the parking area.

LOGISTICS

Bicycles are not allowed in Eagles Nest Wilderness, and dogs must be on leash.

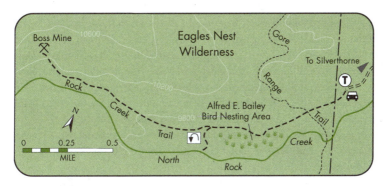

ON THE TRAIL

Hike through the Alfred E. Bailey Bird Nesting Area to the abandoned Boss Mine surrounded by magnificent mountain vistas. Access to the Eagles Nest Wilderness in the Gore Range is another attraction of this trail.

From the parking lot, walk west on the old mining road before reaching the wilderness boundary. The trail maintains a steady, gradual route up the Rock Creek valley, crossing the Gore Range Trail within the first 0.5 mile. (Several backpacking destinations are available on this trail.)

In 0.1 mile after the trail junction, enter the bird nesting area. Alert

A beaver lodge stands alone in an alpine lake.

your companions to walk quietly and watch for yellow-streaked birds. Pine siskins and yellow-rumped warblers, both common here, wear yellow. The siskin's coloring is drab compared to the vibrant gold throat, cap, rump, and flanks of the warbler. However, if a yellow-colored bird is sighted hanging upside down plucking seeds from pinecones, the acrobat is a siskin. A bird here wearing an aluminum leg band has been tagged for a study on the species that visit and breed in this zone. Even youngsters who don't see any birds are guaranteed to hear a musical concert by the winged forest dwellers. Encourage the kids to notice different birdcalls and try to imitate them.

At 0.7 mile, the forest on the left gives way to views of a meadow soggy with beaver ponds. Stop to lift your littlest ones high enough to see the beaver workings. At 0.9 mile, reach a fork (the left path leads 0.1 mile to North Rock Creek, a shorter destination for tired little legs); continue straight.

The main trail now begins its short (0.4-mile), steep climb along a scree-covered slope of Keller Mountain. Those who continue the additional 0.5 mile to Boss Mine—an 1880s silver strike, now a swath of tailings—enjoy superb views of the snowy Gore Range atop a lush green valley bisected by roaring Rock Creek. Watch on the right side of the trail for the few remains of Boss Mine's barracks—the old stove top, rusty bed frames, and cabin logs are fun to investigate. Remind hikers that these and other historic structures in the forest are fragile and should be treated with respect. Return via the same trail.

SURPRISE TRAIL

BEFORE YOU GO
Maps White River National Forest; USGS Mount Powell
Information For current conditions and more information, contact Dillon Ranger District, www.fs.fed.us/r2/whiteriver or (970) 468-5400

ABOUT THE HIKE
Location Eagles Nest Wilderness near Silverthorne
Day hike; Moderate to challenging
2.6 miles one way
Hikable Mid-June to October
Starting elevation/High point 8600 feet/10,000 feet
Accessibility None

GETTING THERE

From I-70 at Silverthorne, take exit 205 onto CO-9 north for 17.6 miles. At Heeney Road (Summit County Road 30), turn left and continue 5.7 miles to CR-1725 (Cataract Creek Road). Turn left (west) and drive 2.4 miles, passing Cataract Creek Campground, to the parking lot on the right.

LOGISTICS

Toilet facilities are available at the campground. In Eagles Nest Wilderness, bicycles are not allowed, and dogs must be on a leash at all times.

ON THE TRAIL

Pleasant Surprise Trail follows a staircase pattern, climbing then

Aspens are no surprise along this trail.

leveling off in forests of aspen, lodgepole, and spruce, ending at Surprise Lake. Meadows, colorfully peppered with wildflowers, make a perfect destination for little hikers willing to walk 1 mile.

The wooden footbridge directly south of the parking lot marks the trail's beginning. From here, hikers enter the wilderness area, gradually ascending a stand of mature aspen trees followed by a lodgepole pine forest. Just beyond 0.7 mile, youngsters may need a hand crossing the log bridge spanning the creek. This can serve as a destination for beginning hikers

The meadow at 1 mile, another good turnaround, is blanketed in a cornucopia of flowers in July and August. Purple lupines and lavender asters complement yellow daisylike flowers; towering over your shortest hiker is false hellebore. Its large pleated leaves protrude from stalks 3 to 6 feet high topped by a branched cluster of yellow-green flowers. Youngsters enjoy playing hide-and-seek in these tall stands of plant life. Bigger kids are interested in learning how Native Americans once used the leaves of the big plant to lower blood pressure and slow the heartbeat. But don't try such a treatment—eating false hellebore can be fatal.

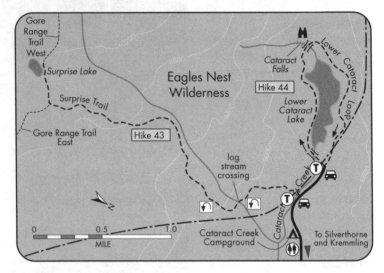

Climbing another stairstep, the Surprise Trail enters a lodgepole-edged aspen grove. At 1.7 miles, the trail levels, then winds through a dense pine forest. Encourage hikers to walk softly here; perhaps they'll hear the forest "ghosts": the creaking sound of partially fallen lodgepoles moved by the wind.

Within 0.5 mile, the trail forks at 2.2 miles. The Gore Range Trail East is on the left; turn right to reach Surprise Lake in 0.4 mile. At the creek just before the lake, turn left on the path that leads to the lakeshore. (The trail beyond the lake is the Gore Range Trail West.)

Return via the way you came.

 LOWER CATARACT LOOP TRAIL

BEFORE YOU GO
Maps White River National Forest; USGS Mount Powell
Information For current conditions and more information, contact Dillon Ranger District, www.fs.fed.us/r2/whiteriver or (970) 468-5400

ABOUT THE HIKE
Location Eagles Nest Wilderness near Silverthorne
Day hike; Easy
2-mile loop
Hikable June to October
Starting elevation/High point 8652 feet/8660 feet
Accessibility None

GETTING THERE

From I-70 at Silverthorne, take exit 205 onto CO-9 north for 17.6 miles. At Heeney Road (Summit County Road 30), turn left and continue 5.7 miles to CR-1725 (Cataract Creek Road). Turn left and drive 2.7 miles, passing Cataract Creek Campground, to the parking lot at the road end.

LOGISTICS

Toilet facilities are available at the campground. Weekday use of this popular walk is recommended. Camping is not permitted within 0.25 mile of the lake or along the trail. Bicycles are prohibited in Eagles Nest Wilderness, and dogs must be on leash at all times.

ON THE TRAIL

Cataract Falls, visible from the trailhead, lures hikers around mountain-fed Lower Cataract Lake and through sun-drenched meadows to pass into the cool, dark corridors of an old-growth forest. The lake's beautiful serenity, especially in the morning, sets the tone for quiet discoveries in the brooks, brush, and shore along the trail.

At the Lower Cataract Loop trailhead, located just west of the parking lot, take the 0.25-mile middle path, which leads directly to the lake. Just before reaching the lakeshore, turn left, crossing the footbridge spanning a creek draining from the lake. As the trail climbs a bit above the lake, it meanders past several springs percolating the rich, dark soil. Riparian zones such as these attract a wide array of wildlife. Encourage your crew to watch for birds, insects, and animal tracks along waterways.

Don't let the numerous spur trails leading in the direction of the falls confuse you; rocks or logs have blocked most of them. Before reaching the spurs, watch on the trail's right side for a four-hug-wide ponderosa pine snag. The dead tree provides homes and food for birds, rodents, and insects. Those lingering here watch forest animals using the tree. (A squirrel may scamper into a cavity in the limb. A woodpecker may alight on the trunk to drill a hole in search of insects. A hummingbird may perch on a thin branch.)

Just past the ponderosa snag, the tiny, grass-covered island adjacent to the lake makes a Lilliputian-style lunch break. However, the thundering of waterfalls draws hikers onward into the old-growth forest. A boardwalk bridge spans the widest section of the creek, providing a full view of the foaming falls. Remind hikers to stay on the trail to prevent damage to the riparian area.

Several "best hikes" begin near Summit County's recreation centerpiece —
Dillon Reservoir.

After a photography stop on the bridge, follow the trail to the right.
Within 25 yards of the bridge, the trail edges a calm section of the creek,
another ideal lunch stop. Remind young hikers that stream wading is
not encouraged in the Eagles Nest Wilderness. Beyond here, the trail
circles the lake's southwest edge, passing through tall-grass meadows,
then climbing slightly into an aspen glade.

At 1.5 miles, the trail meets the wilderness boundary fence. Follow
the trail through the spruce-aspen forest for 0.4 mile. Watch for the
chickaree squirrels' middens under the spruce trees on the left. The thick
mat of spruce cone pieces stores the squirrels' winter food stash. Does
anyone in your group see squirrel-size entry holes into the midden? The
trail then leaves the forest to meet the roadway back to the parking lot.

GREAT GETAWAYS

Near Hikes 41, 42, 43, 44, and 47 you'll find camping at Dillon
Reservoir, which is 2 miles northeast of Frisco. Reserve a site at Heaton
Bay Campground or Peak One Campground at www.reserveusa.com
or by calling (877) 444-6777.

From a trailhead on Dillon Dam Road, hike the easy 1-mile trail to
Old Dillon reservoir. At the campgrounds, take your kids for a spin
on the paved Dillon-to-Frisco mountain-bike path or play a round of
Frisbee golf at Frisco Disc Golf Course. You can also find a single-track
mountain bike trail at the nearby Peninsula Recreation Area.

45 MOUNT SHERMAN

GETTING THERE

From CO-9 and US 285 at Fairplay, take US 285 south 1.2 miles to Four Mile Creek Road (County Road 18). Turn west (right) and continue 10.5 miles. Parking sites are available at the old Leavick townsite on the north side of the road. Beyond here, the road offers limited accessibility for two-wheel-drive vehicles. Four-wheel-drive vehicles continue another 1.5 miles.

LOGISTICS

This hike is "open" after July 1; before then, snowfields may block the route. Ninety-eight percent of the trail crosses private property; please respect property owners' rights. **Only kids acclimatized to high altitude conditions accompanied by adults experi- enced in alpine hiking should attempt this or any mountain.** Hikers must be well rested and properly equipped with sturdy hiking shoes, raingear, a warm sweater, a hat, sunscreen, high- energy food, and at least one

Watch for herds of "little red elephants" in alpine marsh areas.

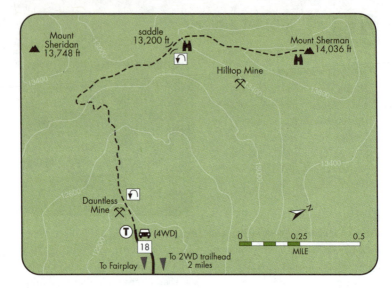

quart of water per person. Start the hike very early in the morning and watch for weather changes. **Warn your companions that you all must head back should clouds start blanketing the sky; weather changes can be sudden and severe above tree line.** Regardless of weather, be prepared to turn around when your crew becomes tired and irritable. See the introduction for ideas on keeping the hike fun and well-paced.

ON THE TRAIL

Climbing a "fourteener" is perhaps the ultimate goal of many hikers in Colorado. And because nearly all of the state's fifty-four mountains higher than 14,000 feet challenge even experienced hikers, youngsters often miss out on this experience. However, healthy, prepared kids relish the climb up Mount Sherman (14,036 feet). Plus, if clear skies prevail after summiting Sherman, hikers can continue their alpine ascent up the neighboring peak, Mount Sheridan, just 252 feet shy of fourteener status. The pair of peaks are named for Civil War generals.

From the road where most two-wheel-drive cars park, Mount Sherman is visible though no trailhead marks the route up the peak. It's a 2-mile walk to the four-wheel-drive road. Simply continue following the rocky, four-wheel-drive road 0.2 mile to the abandoned buildings of the Dauntless Mine. Do not enter the rather dilapidated mine. Point out the support timbers, called "deadmen," on the left between the two buildings, which reinforce the loose rock around the mine entrance. Near the mine entrance is a small rail line and its ore carts. The mine makes a good turnaround point for a short hike.

After the last building of the Dauntless Mine, bear right. Notice the spongy soil supporting tiny alpine flowers. Beyond here, rocks dominate the landscape to the summit. After hiking 0.8 mile from the mine, bear left toward a small log structure, then continue around it to the right. The trail becomes more visible as it approaches the 13,200-foot saddle, a pass between Sherman and Sheridan mountains. At the saddle turn right, following the cairns, piles of rocks marking the route. Within 0.2 mile of the saddle, the trail passes buildings of the Hilltop Mine. To the west is Leadville; to the east, South Park and Pikes Peak.

Notice the snow accumulation on the leeward (downwind) side of the ridge. Explain that these cornices build up as the wind blows from the windward (upwind) side. Cornices sometimes break off in spring, causing an avalanche. Also notice the electricity lines crossing the saddle. These lines supply power to Fairplay from Leadville.

The last 800-foot, 1-mile ascent to the summit is slow going. Look for cairns that basically head straight up the ridge of Mount Sherman. At one point, the trail is only 4 to 6 feet wide for nearly 75 yards, with steep dropoffs on both sides. Take extra care here.

As the trail nears the peak, the grade eases and you pass a false summit. Continue walking approximately 0.1 mile north to reach the real summit of Mount Sherman, a broad, nearly football-field-sized plateau. The views are good in all directions. The Collegiate Range is to the west past Leadville. Mount Massive and Mount Elbert, the state's two highest peaks, are visible. Have kids look to the east to spot their car. It may be just a speck of light reflecting the sun.

Some kids are surprised to find plant and animal life at 14,000 feet. Marmots and pikas whistle from the rocks, and small birds get moisture from the old snowfields. Tiny flowers blossom beside the rocks all the way up to the summit.

Return via the same route. If the group's energy and weather allow, continue the 600-foot climb up Mount Sheridan from the saddle, heading in the opposite direction of Mount Sherman.

MISSOURI LAKES TRAIL

BEFORE YOU GO
Maps USGS Mount of the Holy Cross, USGS Mount Jackson
Information For current conditions and more information, contact Holy Cross Ranger District, www.fs.fed.us/r2/whiteriver or (970) 827-5715

ABOUT THE HIKE
Location Holy Cross Wilderness
Day hike; Moderate to challenging
3.5 miles one way to main lake
Hikable Late June to September
Starting elevation/High point 10,000 feet/11,380 feet
Accessibility None

GETTING THERE

From Vail, take I-70 west to Minturn, taking exit 171 onto US 24 south. Drive 13 miles to Homestake Road 703 (Forest Road 203). Turn right and continue 8.5 miles, passing the Gold Park Campground, and turn right onto Missouri Creek Road 704. In 2.3 miles, at large aqueduct pipes of the Homestake I water project, the rough road turns sharply to the right; the roadside parking area and trailhead bordering the Holy Cross Wilderness are on the left.

LOGISTICS

One Forest Service campground and numerous primitive campsites edge the road to the trailhead; toilet facilities and drinking water are available at the Forest Service campground on FR 703. This trail begins in the Holy Cross Wilderness; mountain bikes are not permitted. Campfires are prohibited. Weekday use is recommended for this popular trail. Please self-register at the trailhead; doing so provides visitor use data that helps the Forest Service continue wilderness protection.

ON THE TRAIL

Missouri Creek's alluring waterfalls and flower-rimmed cascades draw you to its exquisite source: an alpine basin jeweled by a dozen pristine lakes. Even tired little ones resist turning back before reaching the lakes at the top.

From the parking lot, the Missouri Lakes Trail starts in a deciduous-coniferous forest, passing close to the remnants of a log cabin on the left at 0.2 mile. Stop to let youngsters examine how the logs were notched, then stacked.

Spotlighting the forest undergrowth here are crimson columbines, rare compared to the large blue-and-white state flower more commonly seen in mountain meadows and aspen groves. A hummingbird may frequent the red flowers, a stop that provides nectar for the bird and results in pollination. Kids who understand how each species is dependent on another leave the crimson columbines unpicked, available for the next hummingbird or hiker. (Picking blue columbines is prohibited in Colorado, as is picking any wildflowers within wilderness areas.)

Within 1 mile, the scene changes abruptly to the scars of a water development project. Pass the cement aqueducts and diversion dam above the hill to the right. (This water is diverted and stored for residents of Colorado's Front Range cities.) Back in the forest, the trail climbs a steep, rocky slope while edging the creek in full torrent.

A footbridge spans almost every crossing (count them!) of Missouri Creek. Stop at these crossings to feel the cool breeze spewing from the raging creek. At 1.8 miles, just past one of these coolers, have kids look to the left, through the trees, for an unforgettable view of the creek pounding through a miniature canyon. Meet the creek in a calm state just 0.2 mile farther. Here, at 2 miles, the creek spills into a quiet, shallow pool mirroring the surrounding peaks. A few may prefer to turn around at this soothing spot.

To continue, follow the trail around the alpine marsh and into the forest where the creek resumes its cascading style. At 2.7 miles a spur

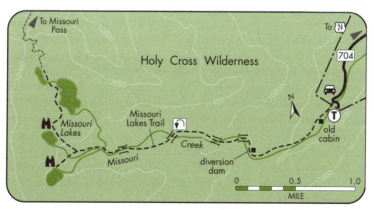

Summer thaws the alpine beauty of Missouri Lake.

trail on the left leads 0.3 mile to a small lake (an optional, though flowery, destination for some ·hikers). Looking south, you see Savage Peak looming above this lake. Continue on the main trail as it veers right, climbing 100 feet to another small lake on the left. The trail reaches the main lake at 3.5 miles, where it cradles an alpine basin near timberline. The islands of wind-deformed trees here are called *krummholz*, German for "crooked wood." Note how the trees capitalize on the effects of safety in numbers to cope with the conditions. Remind your companions that people, like trees, tend to stand close together for wind protection. Tree islands at high elevations also create higher humidity and alleviate temperature extremes. The few flowers your crew will find here thrive in wind-free nooks between rocks or by growing low to the ground.

After exploring the lake area, return via the same trail.

Hikers interested in exploring more alpine terrain can follow the trail 1 mile past the main lake and 900 feet up the switchbacks to Missouri Pass (11,986 feet).

47 SPRUCE CREEK TRAIL

BEFORE YOU GO

Maps White River National Forest; USGS Breckenridge
Information For current conditions and more information, contact Dillon Ranger District, www.fs.fed.us/r2/whiteriver or (970) 468-5400

ABOUT THE HIKE

Location Near Breckenridge Day hike or backpack; Moderate to challenging 3 miles one way from 2WD trailhead; 1.6 miles one way from 4WD trailhead
Hikable June to October
Starting elevation/High point 10,400 feet at 2WD trailhead; 11,080 feet at 4WD trailhead/12,200 feet
Accessibility None

GETTING THERE

From Breckenridge, on CO-9 south of I-70, travel 2.4 miles south, turning right (west) at County Road 800 at the Crown subdivision. Stay on this gravel road for 1.2 miles; bear left at the first fork. Turn left at the next fork to the second trailhead parking area on the left. Four-wheelers can continue another 1.5 miles to the next trailhead.

LOGISTICS

Backpackers should camp at least 200 feet from the lakes. Plan to hike Spruce Creek before the afternoon thunderstorms.

ON THE TRAIL

Cascading waterfalls and abandoned mining cabins set in an exquisite alpine cirque make this hike popular. Although the trail ends after a very steep climb to Upper and Lower Mohawk lakes, 0.5 mile before the lakes is an easier, very worthwhile destination: Continental Falls, spilling from a wildflower-blanketed hillside scattered with the rusty remnants of a bygone mining era.

From the two-wheel-drive parking lot, the trail winds through an aspen-wooded area for 0.5 mile before it crosses Spruce Creek via a two-log bridge. Mosquito repellent is a must for the next 0.8-mile walk through an old-growth spruce forest. While passing under the stately trees, point out the holes woodpeckers drilled in search of insects.

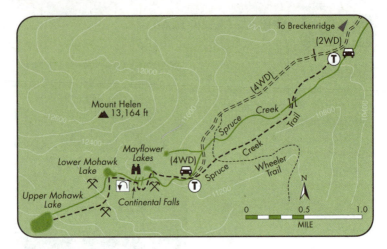

Explain that the tree-climbing bird removes an insect by spearing it with its long, flexible tongue. Woodpeckers also declare boundaries by dimpling dead trees.

At 1.3 miles you intersect the Wheeler Trail, which leads to the Gore Range; continue walking west 0.1 mile to the four-wheel-drive access road trailhead.

Beyond here, the trail climbs in earnest. However, as the trees thin, glimpses of waterfalls in 0.2 mile lure young hikers uphill. The mining cabins (some of which can be entered) at the crest of another 0.2-mile

Mining tram relics near Mohawk Lakes along the Spruce Creek Trail

climb are a good breath-catching spot. Remind youngsters to respect the delicate nature of these and other historic structures. To view Continental Falls, follow the trail another 0.2 mile northwest. The bald peak to the north of the mining area is Mount Helen (13,164 feet).

Eager hikers like to scramble the very steep 0.5-mile path alongside and above the falls to Lower Mohawk Lake. In doing so, they pass the top station of an old mining tramway. Notice the cart's big bull wheel and wooden brakes. Another 0.5 mile farther is Upper Mohawk Lake, surrounded by steep, scree-laden mountains.

Return via the same trail.

 EAGLES LOOP TRAIL

BEFORE YOU GO
Map Vail Summer Adventure guide (available at gondola ticket window)
Information For current conditions and more information, contact Vail Activities Desk, www.vail.snow.com or (970) 476-9090

ABOUT THE HIKE
Location Vail Mountain/Lionshead ski village
Day hike; Easy
1-mile loop
Hikable Mid-May to September
Starting elevation/High point 8156 feet/10,350 feet
Accessibility None

GETTING THERE
At Vail on I-70, drive to the Lionshead ski village office area and park at the base of the Lionshead Gondola.

LOGISTICS
Toilet facilities and drinking water are available at the base of the gondola in the ski village area. A sweater and raingear are recommended for this timberline destination where weather changes are often swift and unsuspected. Afternoon showers are common here, so take your walk in the morning. Everyone, especially fair-skinned folks, should use sunscreen; sun exposure at this altitude is 40 percent greater than it is at sea level.

A pika, also called a "haymaker," gathers grasses to dry in bundles on mountain slopes.

ON THE TRAIL

This hike provides a magnificent 360-degree view of the mountains around Vail, plus a close-up look at the plants and animals of alpine terrains. Better yet, the fourteen-minute gondola ride to the Eagles Loop trailhead makes the experience fun and effortless.

Once out of the gondola, kids automatically scamper to the ridgetop straight ahead. The trail starts here, 0.1 mile to the right, but do stop to find the legendary cross of snow spread across the face of the Holy Cross Range. For some, the cross is difficult to discern because the right arm was destroyed in a rock slide, but a keen-eyed young hiker advised me to look at the biggest mountain in the group, where the cross lies at an angle to the gondola lift. A photograph of the cross, taken by pioneer photographer William Henry Jackson in 1873, accompanies the interpretive sign here.

To walk the Eagles Loop Trail, go to the right. Top-of-the-world views of the Holy Cross Range to the south and the Gore Range to the west

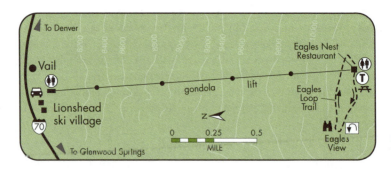

are among the attractions along this trail. Skiers enjoy seeing a green version of Vail's most popular runs. Little ones, however, may be drawn to such smaller spectacles as tiny wildflowers peeking between rocks or a patch of winter's snow lingering in the shade of a boulder.

The high-pitched whistle of a pika may lure youngsters across the meadow in futile pursuit. More often heard than seen, the small rabbitlike creature collects and dries grasses in miniature haystacks, hence its nickname: haymaker. If a storm approaches, the pika moves the food under a rock. By summer's end it can boast almost fifty pounds of greenery to live on during the winter. Watch for the pika's bundles drying on rocks in the sun.

The Eagles Loop Trail crosses under the gondola lift and at about 0.9 mile turns right, heading west about 0.1 mile back to the gondola lift.

 BROWNS LOOP

BEFORE YOU GO
Map USGS Fulford
Information For current conditions and more information, contact the Eagle–Holy Cross Ranger District, www.fs.usda.gov/wps/portal /fsinternet or (970) 827-5715; Sylvan Lake State Park, www.parks.state.co.us/parks /sylvanlake or (970) 827-5715

ABOUT THE HIKE
Location Eagle
Day hike; Easy
1.6-mile loop
Hikable June to October
Starting elevation/High point 9050 feet/9075 feet
Accessibility Fishing pier at campground

GETTING THERE

From the I-70 exit 147 for Eagle, turn south on Eby Creek Road to the Route 6 roundabout. Turn right (west) onto Route 6/Grand Avenue, driving 0.8 mile to the next roundabout. Follow the roundabout, turning at the third right onto Sylvan Lake Road. Continue 1.6 miles, turning right onto Brush Creek Road. Follow Brush Creek Road roughly 9 miles to the fork of East Brush Creek and West Brush Creek roads. (Sylvan Lake State Park visitor center is on your left, about 0.25 mile before this road fork.) Turn left (southeast) onto unpaved East Brush Creek Road (Forest Road 415) and drive 7 miles to Yeoman Park Campground. Day

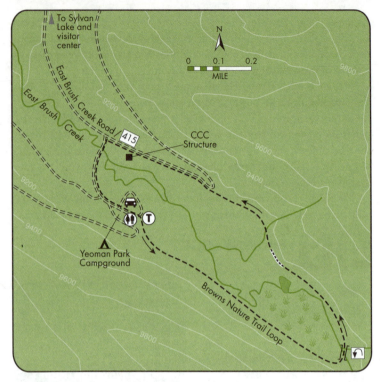

use parking is to the left of the campground entrance. The trailhead is located in the campground at the end of loop B.

LOGISTICS

Toilet facilities are available in Yeoman Park Campground, with the nearest drinking water at the Sylvan Lake State Park visitor center (see above for location). Before the hike, check the park's website for information on free family and kid activities in the area. Plan to stop at Sylvan Lake State Park's visitor center for updates on the latest wildlife sightings along with engaging exhibits and guidebooks.

ON THE TRAIL

Browns Loop ties it all together. The easy-to-follow trail threads a deep, dark forest, crossing brooks, then edging mountain-mirroring beaver ponds before it ends in a meadow of wildflowers. This lovely end-of-road

Aspens flank the slopes rising above the marsh near Browns Loop.

destination also appeals to hikers hoping to catch a fish or the sight of a moose. Yes, this is moose country!

The trailhead sign, Browns Loop Fishing Nature Trail, stands at the end of campground loop B. The hike begins on a softly padded forest floor, crossing quiet brooks that spill into East Brush Creek, a sometimes raging waterway. Numerous tree trunks lay sawed and cleared from the path, adding ease to walking this well-maintained trail.

At 0.5 mile the trail ascends out of the forest shade, then crosses a hillside of wildflowers. Veering left, the trail descends into the forested East Brush Creek. A tree trunk, sliced into two planks, serves as your bridge over the creek. An interpretive sign here describes the importance of woody debris for stream health. Those choosing the bridge as a turnaround point miss seeing beaver lodges, several "choice" fishing spots, and possibly getting their boots muddy!

The loop leaves the forest, passing a marshy area, then a few ponds marked by the woody mound of a beaver lodge. Your best chances of spotting a beaver skimming the water are by silently approaching the area during edge-of-light hours, sunrise and sunset. At 1 mile a long boardwalk spans a cattail-filled marsh before it crosses a meadow. Moose grazing willows are sometimes spotted here.

Where the trail returns to the campground road, you'll pass a 1940s-era structure built for housing members of the Civilian Conservation Corp—folks who planted trees and built roads in the area, creating this camping getaway.

COYOTE TRAIL

BEFORE YOU GO
Map Rifle Falls State Park map
Information For current conditions and more information, contact Rifle Falls State Park, parks.state.co.us /riflefalls or (970) 625-1607

ABOUT THE HIKE
Location Rifle Falls State Park
Day hike; Moderate
1.5-mile loop
Hikable Year-round
Starting elevation/High point 6500 feet/6570 feet
Accessibility Wheelchair-accessible for first 0.1 mile to the waterfalls

GETTING THERE

Rifle Falls State Park is located off I-70, exit 90, midway between Eagle and Grand Junction. Head north on CO-13 for 4 miles through the town of Rifle on Railroad Avenue. Turn right onto CO-325 and drive 9.8 miles to the park entrance. Ample parking is provided about 0.5 mile from the entrance, adjacent to the shaded picnic area and trailhead.

LOGISTICS

Toilets and drinking water are available at the trailhead. Bring headlamps or flashlights for touring the caves. Dogs on a leash are permitted in Rifle Falls State Park. There is a state park entrance fee.

ON THE TRAIL

The Coyote Trail has hikers coming back for more. First, there's standing in the mist of a 60-foot waterfall trio. Then, there's exploring cool, dark caves. And literally topping the hike is the thrill of stepping onto the trail's viewpoints suspended out over the falls. Equally pleasing is the state park's campground where shaded sites tucked into the canyon provide private settings alongside a babbling stream. Camping at this popular state park often requires reservations. Check the park's website for the summer schedule of fun interpretive activities held at Mountain Mist Amphitheatre.

The roar of three waterfalls calls kids of all ages from the parking lot to the Coyote Trail. Head north 0.1 mile on this broad, paved pathway for a grand view of the falls, and on sunny days, its rainbow shimmering mist. Walk closer to sample Colorado's only touch of tropics. The leafy,

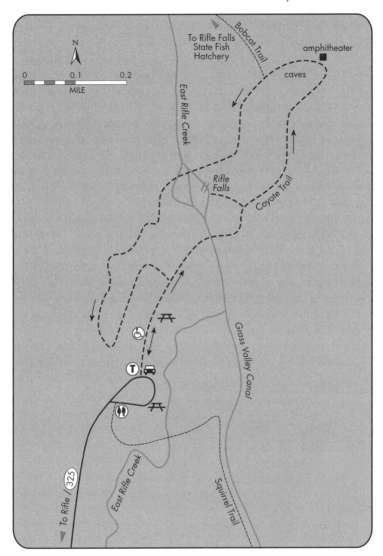

water-drenched setting suggests warm, steamy jungles, regardless of the temperature. Rifle Falls was one white cascade until 1908 when the town's power and light companies built Colorado's first hydroelectric plant here. A pipe installed to divert part of the falls also divided the water into two flows. The pipe has since been removed, turning the fall into three flumes of water. Return to the waterfalls viewing site, veering left while passing the park's amphitheater and group activity site.

Your companions will be surprised to learn that the falls spill over a limestone cliff started by beavers long ago. Geologists think water from a huge beaver dam became saturated with minerals, which eventually created the cliff formation East Rifle Creek spills over today. Continue another 0.1 mile as the trail edges the same limestone form-ation where pockets and caves of many sizes invite beginning and latent spelunkers to walk, then crawl into coolness and darkness. Headlamp-wearing hikers tend to extend their explorations here, so plan accordingly and with caution; avoid hurting heads while exploring the caves, and don't harm any hanging formations discovered.

Leaving the cave area, the Coyote Trail follows the base of the lime-stone cliff, veering left, passing the Bobcat Trail, the 1-mile link to the Rifle Falls State Fish Hatchery. Rainbow, brown, and cutthroat trout raised at this hatchery, the state's largest, often end up in the nets of anglers fishing East Rifle Creek in the park. Continue on the Coyote Trail, ascending to the grassland above the falls. Prevent anyone from leaning or sitting on the wood rail fence along the cliff edge; it's not designed for even a moment's photograph. For a bird's-eye view of the falls, turn left on the spur trails leading to the cliff edge. For some it's an adrenaline rush to

walk out over the falls on narrow observation decks. Maintain supervision of little hikers on these fenced viewpoints.

The remaining 0.4 mile of the trail heads down steeply to the waterfall area via steps built into the path, easing the descent. Returning to the trailhead with your crew, check out the information kiosk, where watercolor images artfully describe wetland vitality.

Hikers see outstanding views of Rifle Falls from suspended viewpoints.

To explore more of the park check out the 0.8-mile Squirrel Trail loop. It takes you through a cool oak forest, over a creek on a swinging bridge, up a steep canyon, down a ladder, and through a tunnel. To reach its trailhead from the parking lot, walk south 0.2 mile on the paved road.

BEST RIVERSIDE WALKS

Glenwood Springs

The Rio Grande Trail links Glenwood Springs with Aspen via the former rail corridor for the Denver & Rio Grande Western Railroad (D&RGW). Many sections of the 41-mile asphalt trail feature kid-friendly terrain where leafy riverside nooks outnumber speedy teams of cyclists. One such area in Glenwood Springs begins at Two Rivers Park and extends to Glenwood Springs Elementary School. The playground-to-playground 0.7-mile path edges the Roaring Fork River through sun and shade with numerous picnic spots along the way. Parking and seasonal restrooms are at Two Rivers Park, accessed from downtown Glenwood Springs, via US 24/6, south on Devereux Road.

www.visitglenwood.com   (970) 945-6589

Glenwood Springs

Atkinson Canal, the newest (October 2011) trail in town, features 1.4 miles of easy walking with spectacular views of the Roaring Fork River and Mount Sopris. The path's design highlights native riverside plants and the river's "Gold Medal" waters. The trail extends from the Glenwood Park Area to the 27th Street Bridge, and links to the Glenwood Springs River Trail. Free parking is available at the Three Mile Road lot, just off Midland Avenue.

www.ci.glenwood-springs.co.us   (970) 384-6301

Aspen

A family-friendly 2-mile section of the Rio Grande Trail begins at the trailhead behind the Aspen Post Office, heading west to Stein Park. The heavily shaded trail crosses the Roaring Fork River, then Hunter Creek before paralleling the Colorado River. The trail splits in sections, allowing separate getaways for bicyclists and families with little ones. Trail parking is not provided at the post office, but a small lot at Stein Park provides parking at the trail's west end.

www.riograndetrail.com   (970) 384-4975

Aspen

The 3.1-mile East of Aspen Trail takes walkers on a scenic path along the Roaring Fork River to the North Star Nature Preserve. Interpretive viewing stands along the trail describe the 175-acre preserve's unique biological diversity, including a rare high-elevation (8000 feet) wetland hosting a great blue heron colony. Unlike most heron colonies found in cottonwood and other deciduous trees, the GBHs (as in great big herons) here build their nests in blue spruce trees. Access the trail at several points along CO-82 and at the North Star Nature Preserve.

www.aspenpitkin.com   (970) 920-5120

Gunnison

Just 5 miles west of Gunnison begins the Neversink Trail's 1.5 miles of riparian splendor along the Gunnison River. A streamside variety of wildflowers and grasses landscapes the flat terrain, with cottonwood and willow bringing cooling shade in summer and spectacular color in the fall. Bird-watching begins at the Great Blue Heron Rookery adjacent to the trailhead at Neversink, a National Park Service (NPS) picnic, restroom, and parking site, located on the south side of US 550, 5 miles west of Gunnison. The Neversink Trail connects with Coopers Ranch, another NPS site, suitable for those wishing to walk 1.5 miles east along the river.

www.nps.gov/cure/   (970) 641-2337

Salida

The 0.5-mile sections of the Downtown Riverside Park and Trail follow the Arkansas River, with easy access to restaurants, shops, and views of the town's premier whitewater park, a year-round attraction for paddlers and kayaking wannabes. Salida is home to a large number of artists whose galleries offer an equally appealing diversion along the trail. Access the trail via F Street (Salida's only stoplight) over the bridge, turning right into Riverside Park where parking is provided. No restrooms or drinking water are provided along the trail.

www.info@salidachamber.org   (877) 772-5432

Opposite: Father and son cap the day's hike with an afternoon of fishing.

STEAMBOAT SPRINGS, ROCKY MOUNTAIN NATIONAL PARK, AND FORT COLLINS AREA

FISH CREEK FALLS

BEFORE YOU GO
Maps Routt National Forest;
USGS Steamboat Springs
Information For current
conditions and more
information, contact Hahn's
Peak–Bears Ears Ranger
District, www.fs.fed.us/r2/mbr
or (970) 870-2299

ABOUT THE HIKE
Location Routt National
Forest
Day hike; Easy
0.3 mile or more one way
Hikable Year-round
**Starting elevation/Low
point** 7440 feet/7340 feet
Accessibility Wheelchair-
accessible on upper trail

GETTING THERE

From US 40 in Steamboat Springs, travel north on Third Street one block to Fish Creek Road. Turn right and travel east to the road's end. Parking is available in the upper and lower lots.

LOGISTICS

New toilet facilities and a pavilion are at the upper parking lot. A parking fee is charged in both lots.

Kids play around boulders below Fish Creek Falls.

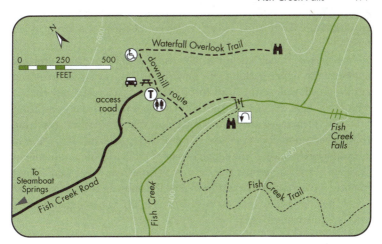

ON THE TRAIL

Waterfalls such as Fish Creek Falls are irresistible. Two trails lead to this spectacular water cascade. One takes a downhill route to the rock-strewn creek below the falls, where kids climb and explore for hours. The other, a paved, wheelchair-accessible trail, weaves through forest fineries, ending at the waterfall overlook.

The reconstructed downhill route to the falls begins at the upper parking lot's east end, to the right of the access road. After a brief, steep descent, the trail levels off, edging Fish Creek. The roar of water thundering 283 feet down a rock-choked cliff just 0.1 mile farther spurs youngsters to run ahead. Keep an eye on them; the large bridge spanning Fish Creek looks like a jungle gym to little climbers. Photographs taken here of kids and the waterfall may need to wait until after your explorers have scouted the site.

This is a destination few want to leave. The falls spill over what is called a hanging valley. During an ice age more than a million years ago, a small glacier and a huge glacier joined here. Over thousands of years, the glaciers melted. In doing so, the large one eroded great amounts of rock material under it. The little glacier scoured out a shallow valley, high above the larger one. The cliff under the waterfall marks the place where the glaciers met.

From the bridge, the Fish Creek Trail continues heading east for a total of 6 miles, ending at Long Lake. The farther you hike this trail, the fewer the people you'll see. Some hikers may want to turn around at the bridge and return the way they came. Those who continue walking east on Fish Creek Trail climb steeply for about 1.6 miles to a lovely aspen forest.

The paved wheelchair-accessible path to the waterfall overlook starts at the upper parking lot's north side. The variety of trees and shrubs growing along this 1500-foot path suggest a forest dweller's deli. Encourage kids to watch for the different foods animals may eat. Their finds may include acorns of the scrub oak, a wild rose's flower and fruit, thimbleberry (similar to raspberry), serviceberry (the fruit of a tree with round, serrated leaves), the winged seeds of the Rocky Mountain maple, the blue berry of a juniper tree, or even a dandelion. What food is most plentiful? What animal eats it? When do the animals come to eat here?

At the approach to the overlook, hold on to little ones' hands. Return via the same trail.

 MAD CREEK TRAIL

BEFORE YOU GO
Maps Routt National Forest; USGS Mad Creek, USGS Rocky Peak
Information For current conditions and more information, contact Hahn's Peak–Bears Ears Ranger District, www.fs.fed.us/r2/mbr or (970) 870-2299

ABOUT THE HIKE
Location Routt National Forest
Day hike or backpack; Moderate
1.7 miles one way
Hikable Mid-May to October
Starting elevation/High point 6763 feet/7140 feet
Accessibility None

GETTING THERE
From Steamboat Springs, turn north on the Elk River Road (County Road 129) and drive 5.7 miles to the bridge over Mad Creek. A fence surrounds the parking lot on the right.

LOGISTICS
A vault toilet is available at the trailhead.

ON THE TRAIL
This diversely forested trail gently climbs above Mad Creek's fuming torrent until it meets the stream in a calm meadow. Here, kids delight

A hiking family practices reading a topographic map in a familiar location.

in boulder-hopping across the creek or teasing its waters with a fishing pole. The Mad Creek Trail, sometimes called the Swamp Park Trail, is popular with cyclists and eager hikers when winter's snow lingers on most trails. However, use caution during periods of high melt-off.

Access the trailhead from the parking lot's north side, just across from a private drive. Mad Creek rumbles in the darkly vegetated crevice to the right. As the trail edges the south-facing slope and rises above private property, it enters dry, gravelly terrain where the occasional rattlesnake startles a hiker. Advise kids to keep their distance and walk slowly around any snake thicker than their thumb. Rock climbers know to place their hands and feet only in places they can see; no one wants to surprise a rattler.

A much more pleasant and common sight here is the large, white- petaled evening primrose. Watch for the ground-hugging flower in closed-bud stage. Then let a child feel the plant respond to his or her hands held carefully cupped around the unopened flower. Under the best of conditions (warm hands held for at least five minutes), the flower petals open. The sensation makes the hike unforgettable.

Within 0.5 mile, the trail veers north, topping a steep canyon of spruce and fir trees. Point out the exposed roots of mighty conifers towering overhead on the left side. Ask kids why the trees tip sideways. Will the trees stay like this? What happened to the soil around the roots? Numerous one-hiker-size spots on the right provide views of Mad Creek spilling white and fast 200 feet below. However, use caution in selecting these viewpoints; there are several sheer dropoffs along the way.

At 1.2 miles, the trail enters another oak-and-sage area and then

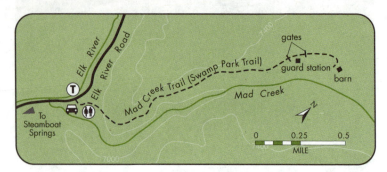

descends gradually into a lovely aspen-fringed meadow. Pass through the Forest Service gate, staying to the left of the buck-and-pole fence (constructed to protect the streambank vegetation from grazing animals). Follow the main trail around the Mad Creek Forest Guard station complex, staying north of the fence.

At 1.5 miles, turn right at the second gate and sign for the guard station (remember to close the gate). Follow the wide path through the meadow before it meets an old road leading to the creek. A picnic lunch in the tranquil grassland surrounding the creek is a pleasant highlight of this hike. Fishing is reportedly good at Mad Creek.

The nearby barn, built in 1905 by homesteader James Ratliff, was refurbished in 2001. Ratliff initially protested Forest Service restrictions on lands adjacent to his. Later he became the Forest Guard, supporting conservation of federal lands and grazing restriction. Nowadays, kids love unrestricted wandering in the meadow before returning via the same trail.

GREAT GETAWAYS

Steamboat Lake State Park, 28 miles northwest of Steamboat Springs, is the best camping option near Hikes 51, 52, and 53. To reserve sites go to www.reserveAmerica.com or call (303) 470-1144 or (800) 678-2267.

Steamboat Lake is loaded with terrific options for families. Cool off at the swimming beach or rent fishing boats, kayaks, canoes, and paddleboats at Steamboat Lake Marina (719-879-7019). When you're ready for more hiking, don't miss the Tombstone Nature Trail, a 1-mile interpreted loop described as "one of Colorado's best short trails," or the Pearl Lake Connection, an easy 0.6-mile hike to the dam.

RABBIT EARS PEAK

BEFORE YOU GO
Maps Routt National Forest;
USGS Rabbit Ears
Information For current
conditions and more
information, contact Hahn's
Peak–Bears Ears Ranger
District, www.fs.fed.us/r2/mbr
or (970) 870-2299

ABOUT THE HIKE
Location East of Steamboat
Springs
Day hike; Moderate to
challenging
2.5 miles one way
Hikable Mid-June to
September
**Starting elevation/High
point** 9590 feet/10,654 feet
Accessibility None

GETTING THERE

From Steamboat Springs, drive US 40 south and east 21 miles to the
turnoff for Dumont Lake Campground, FR 315 (1 mile west of Rabbit
Ears Pass). Proceed 1.6 miles, passing the campground, to a large
boulder on the left. Here turn left on FR 311 and travel 0.3 mile farther,
turning right onto FR 291, to a parking area.

LOGISTICS

Drinking water, toilet facilities, and picnic grounds are at the nearby
Dumont Lake Campground on FR 315.

Columbines thrive in Rabbit Ears Peak country.

ON THE TRAIL

The hike to Rabbit Ears Peak, named for its twin rock pillars visible from the highway, begins as a casual walk through a spectacular flowerland. For some hikers, the last 0.25 mile to the "ears" poses a challenge; to others, it's a fun rock scramble. Either way, the views near the summit are grand.

The trail begins on an old jeep road, following an easy grade through what appears to be a carefully orchestrated explosion of colors. Wildflowers of scarlet, pink, yellow, and lavender brighten the field throughout the summer. Locals say they peak in mid-July. However, the flower show during my early-August trek to Rabbit Ears was my summer's best.

A flower guide is useful for such walks, but kids have more fun finding their favorite color, the oddest-shaped, tallest, shortest, best smelling, and so on. Remind your crew to leave the flowers for other hikers and bees to enjoy.

For 1.5 miles, a steady sprinkling of lodgepole pines, spruce, and aspen dots the meadow as the trail makes a wide arc to the left of Rabbit Ears. From this angle, the rock pair no longer looks like a rabbit's ears. The trail then enters a spruce forest before reaching the steep, rocky climb to the peaks. This may be a delightful destination for little ones.

The road ends at the base of Rabbit Ears. Scramble straight up and over the rocks for about 30 feet. Check each handhold; the rocks are not secure. A faint trail on the right loops around a large block of rock (not an "ear"). A causeway between the block and two ears can be walked. The views from this point on the Continental Divide include Walton

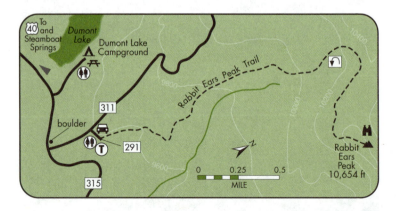

Peak in the southwest, Indian Pass to the southeast, followed by Carter Mountain and Grannys Nipple. To the north are Round Mountain and the ripple of peaks in the Continental Divide range.

To some, the mounds of lava rock at their feet are more fascinating than the views. Explain that long ago, lava erupted from deep within the Earth as a hot, liquid rock. Have kids hold a piece of lava and decide if it feels lighter than most rocks its size. What makes it feel light?

Return via the same trail.

 BLUE LAKE TRAIL

BEFORE YOU GO
Maps Roosevelt National Forest; USGS Ward
Information For current conditions and more information, contact the Boulder Ranger District, www.fs.usda.gov/arp or (303) 541-2500

ABOUT THE HIKE
Location Indian Peaks Wilderness
Day hike; Easy to moderate
1 mile one way to Mitchell Lake; 2.4 miles one way to Blue Lake
Hikable Late June to September
Starting elevation/High point 10,470 feet/10,720 feet at Mitchell Lake; 11,320 feet at Blue Lake
Accessibility None

GETTING THERE
From Boulder, travel 20 miles west on CO-119 to CO-72 near Nederland. Turn right, heading north on CO-72 to Ward. Turn left at the road for Brainard Lake, driving 5.7 miles to the trailhead parking area.

LOGISTICS
Toilet and picnic facilities and drinking water are available at the parking lot.

ON THE TRAIL
The walk to Mitchell Lake is a tranquil meander through a stately subalpine forest. Children find it fairy-tale charming as they discover rock gnomes and flower angels along the way. The brisk trek to Blue Lake edges a year-round snowbank before reaching the waterfall-fed lake, which remains frozen until midsummer.

Feel the spiky, square-shaped needles of a spruce "hand."

From the Blue Lake trailhead on the southwest (left) side of the parking lot, the wide path enters a cathedral-quiet stand of senior subalpine firs. Have kids feel the flat, flexible fingers (needles) of this grandfather tree. Compare them to the square and spiky needles of the Engelmann spruce, the firs' frequent companion.

At 0.4 mile, a footbridge spans the raging Mitchell Creek, before the trail enters the Indian Peaks Wilderness. Although roots and rocks make for good gnome-

hunting territory, they rubble the trail, requiring careful footing. Point out how the silent forest inhabitants have painted their rock homes with lichen. Encourage youngsters to find different colors and textures of lichen. Kids of all ages remember how this half-algae, half-fungus plant is formed when the following story is told: When Alice Algae met Freddy Fungus, they decided they had a lichen for each other. The two married, but now their relationship is on the rocks! The real story—that the algae portion of lichen produces food for the plant, while the fungus part serves as a rock-attaching, water-holding structure—appeals more to hikers than to little gnome hunters.

At 1 mile, flower fairies abound where the trail reaches the creek

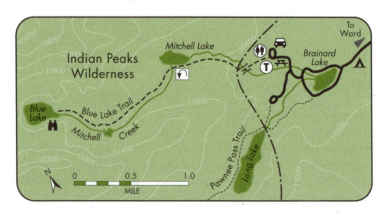

draining into Mitchell Lake. Take time to meet some of the subalpine forest's prettiest flower maidens. Tall (12 to 18 inches) and slender, Parry's primrose wears a cluster of pink-red blossoms atop its lean stem. Rose crown, also in pink, shows rows of fleshy leaves. Little red elephant is actually a chorus line of flower heads, each raising its "trunk" high. A wallflower, white marsh marigold blooms close to banks of snow. Some hikers find Mitchell Lake a perfect destination.

Hikers continuing to Blue Lake climb the steep Mitchell Creek drainage for 1 mile before reaching a snowbank at tree line. In early summer, the trail hides under winter's blanket; by mid-July it skirts to the right of the snow. Blue Lake wears a winter coat through most of the summer. However, the lake's waterfall cascading into the northwest shore with Mount Toll soaring 1600 feet above is a worthy summer destination. Watch and listen for yellow-bellied marmots among the boulders.

Return via the same trail.

LILY MOUNTAIN TRAIL

BEFORE YOU GO
Maps Roosevelt National Forest; USGS Longs Peak
Information For current conditions and more information, contact the Boulder Ranger District, www.fs.fed.us/r2/arnf or (303) 541-2515

ABOUT THE HIKE
Location Roosevelt National Forest
Day hike; Moderate
2 miles one way
Hikable Mid-April to October
Starting elevation/High point 8800 feet/9786 feet
Accessibility None

GETTING THERE
From Estes Park on US 34, go south on CO-7 about 6 miles. Watch for the Marys Lake Power Plant sign and continue past it 2.4 miles. A small parking area is available on the shoulder of the road, on the west side where the trail begins. Additional parking is located at the Lily Lake Visitor Center, 0.25 mile south on CO-7.

LOGISTICS
Toilet facilities and drinking water are available at the visitor center.

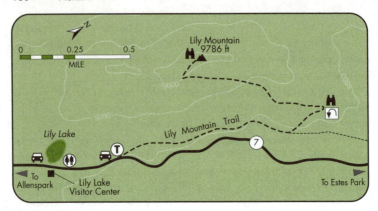

ON THE TRAIL

Lily Mountain is an ideal first ascent for beginning climbers and their parents. This 1000-foot climb requires some huffing 'n' puffing, followed by a short but fun rock scramble to the summit. As in every good climb, views from the top are most rewarding. Predawn hikers may view a spectacular sunrise from the summit, plus enjoy a cool, solitary hike. A stop at the Lily Lake Visitor Center adds to everyone's understanding of the terrain bordering the east side of Rocky Mountain National Park.

 The climb begins directly at the trailhead at the small parking area. The first 0.7 mile parallels the highway and ascends the ridge. Limber pines interspersed with imposing rock groups decorate the slope. Stop at the pines to let kids carefully bend the trees' branches. Explain that "limber" is another word for "flexible." Have them count the number of needles in a bundle. Limber pines are the only Colorado tree that bears five-needle bundles. Farther up the trail, they will find a similar tree with needles that grow in groups of two—the lodgepole.

 The trail continues heading north, reaching a trail junction at 1 mile; here stay left and follow a gently rolling grade as it reaches an overlook of the Estes valley at 1.2 miles. This boulder-shaded spot is an ideal destination for very young mountaineers.

From here the trail traverses south, climbing steadily through a gallery of lodgepole pines. Note the yellow, flowering, fleshy plants splashed like drops of sunshine across an otherwise dry and dull forest. Examine (but don't pick) the leaves of this plant, called stonecrop. If a leaf were squeezed, water would ooze out. This is the plant's method of conserving water for life in a very dry home.

The challenge of routefinding comes into practice as the trail nears

Long Peak dominates the view from Lily Mountain.

the summit. Look to the right to see Lily Mountain's peak, which consists of a rock pile. Cairns mark the route to the top. Following the cairns is a fun exercise for almost any hiker who comes this far. The view from the top includes Twin Sisters to the south. Turning to the right, you'll see Meadow and St. Vrain mountains and Longs Peak and to the northwest, the Mummy Range.

Return via the same route.

 ## ADAMS FALLS AND EAST INLET TRAIL

BEFORE YOU GO
Maps Rocky Mountain National Park brochure; USGS Shadow Mountain
Information For current conditions and more information, contact the Kawuneeche Visitor Center, www.nps.gov/romo or (970) 627-3471

ABOUT THE HIKE
Location Rocky Mountain National Park
Day hike or backpack; Easy to moderate
0.3 mile one way to Adams Falls; 5.5 miles one way to Lone Pine Lake
Hikable Mid-June to September
Starting elevation/High point 8400 feet/9885 feet at Lone Pine Lake
Accessibility None

GETTING THERE

From US 34 in Grand Lake, turn east on CO-278. At 0.3 mile, the road divides. Take the left fork, which bypasses the town and leads directly to Adams Tunnel. Continue on this paved road 2.1 miles, passing the West Portal. Turn left on the gravel road to the trailhead parking lot.

LOGISTICS

Toilet facilities are available at the trailhead.

ON THE TRAIL

The East Inlet Trail offers a short stroll to Adams Falls or a longer meander through the lush valley spilling into Grand Lake. Beyond the falls, hikers follow a gently rolling grade to several worthy destinations: a beaver-worked meadow, mountain vistas, a flower-fringed stream, and a lake with an island.

Before reaching Adams Falls, hold on to little ones' hands; there are no guardrails and the surrounding smooth rocks tend to be wet and slippery. On sunny mornings, point out the rainbow arched over the waterfall's spray. The falls are a destination for some hikers.

Beyond the falls, the trail edges the river, then enters a marshy area—a favorite home for mosquitoes. Everyone's pace naturally quickens here. Within 0.3 mile the river roar retreats as the trail veers from the waterway, threading aspen and areas recently cleared of beetle-killed lodgepole pines. At 1.2 miles the trail brings you to the first of two lovely

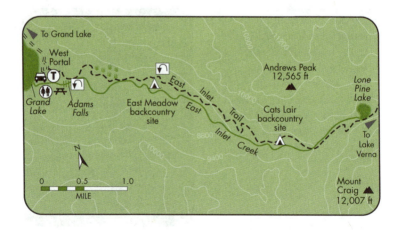

meadows. The view to the east includes Mount Craig (12,007 feet), locally called Mount Baldy for its treeless summit. Several spur trails lead to the river's edge, where wildflowers thrive. This small meadow can serve as a destination, or you can continue on to Lone Pine Lake.

Ask kids how the land and stream flow here looks changed. Look for recent signs of beaver activity. Aspen stumps in a chiseled conical shape are the classic sign of beavers, but young naturalists may find beaver tracks in the muddy shore. In the early evening hours, quiet observers occasionally see beavers swimming across still waters. Musk-rats have been spotted here as well.

At the far end of the meadow, at 2 miles, the trail begins its up-and-down climb to Lone Pine Lake. After rising and falling, the trail edges the river at 3 miles. Colorful clusters of pink Parry's primrose, blue chiming bells, and white marsh marigold thrive here. As the trail continues switchbacking through the subalpine forest, stop during breath-catching breaks for fine views of Mount Craig to the east and Andrews Peak (12,565 feet) to the west.

From here the trail continues climbing, then at 5 miles circles a forested hill before reaching Lone Pine Lake. The lake's namesake, a singular lodgepole pine rooted in the rock island, has surrendered to weather's forces. However, a group of brave young pines and an Engelmann spruce have replaced it.

Return via the same trail.

Adams Falls tumbles through the boulders of East Inlet Creek.

HOLZWARTH HISTORIC SITE

BEFORE YOU GO

Map Rocky Mountain National Park brochure

Information For current conditions and more information, contact the Kawuneeche Visitor Center, www.nps.gov/romo or (970) 627-3471

ABOUT THE HIKE

Location Rocky Mountain National Park

Day hike; Easy

0.5 mile one way

Hikable Mid-June to October

Starting elevation/High point 9000 feet/9010 feet

Accessibility Accessible for most wheelchairs

GETTING THERE

From Kawuneeche Visitor Center at Rocky Mountain National Park's Grand Lake entrance, travel north on US 34 for 7.9 miles. Turn left on the gravel road to the parking lot for Holzwarth Historic Site.

LOGISTICS

Tours are offered regularly in summer. There is a national park entrance fee.

ON THE TRAIL

Holzwarth Historic Site's landscape and original homestead—the family's cabins, taxidermy shop, icehouse, and woodshed—tell the story of early dude ranching in Colorado. For kids, a visit here means imagining how they'd set the rusted trap to catch a bear, washing clothes in the hand-cranked wringer machine, and powering a sewing

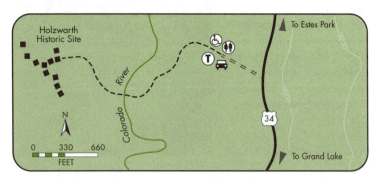

Aged farm implements grace the field surrounding Holzwarth Historic Site.

machine with their foot. It's an encounter with turn-of-the-twentieth-century ranch life.

The 0.5-mile guided walk, to the cabins and lodge of Holzwarth Historic Site begins at the parking lot. This level, smooth gravel path is accessible for most wheelchairs. The interpreter describes the natural history of Kawuneeche Valley and the challenges homesteaders faced in this mountain frontier. (*Kawuneeche* is an Arapaho word meaning "valley of the coyote.") Interpreters remain on hand to answer questions and prompt kids on how the surrounding farm tools were used.

Halfway to the site, the trail crosses a "creek," the Colorado River, a babe here compared to the raging giant it becomes 500 miles south in the Grand Canyon. Johnny Holzwarth was one of the first homesteaders to irrigate his fields with Colorado River water. Today's kids use the ankle-deep stream for wading.

The short, wide path leads to the Holzwarths' cluster of cabins and outbuildings. A walk through the Mama cabin, built in 1917, provides a look at how Sophie (Mama) prepared multi-course meals for her guests using a woodstove and a water pump. Her aprons and bonnets hang from a kitchen hook. At the icehouse, point out the sod roof. Ask, "Why wasn't a wood roof used? Where did the ice come from?" (The Never Summer Range, with its perennial snow patches, was a good source.)

The adjacent taxidermy shop is a popular place to take photographs of children dressed in a buffalo robe and top hat or a lady's bonnet. Trapping apparatus and a stuffed deer are remnants of Papa's taxidermy trade, after a tractor accident kept him from farmwork.

Allow time for kids to investigate the farm's implements before returning to the parking area.

GREAT GETAWAYS

Grab one of the first-come, first-served sites at Timber Creek Campground if Hikes 56, 57, and 59 are in your plans. The campground is 10 miles north of Grand Lake in Rocky Mountain National Park (www.nps.gov/romo).

Activities in the area include the Coyote Valley Trail, a 1-mile wheelchair-accessible path through wildflower meadows to the Colorado River. The trailhead is 2.5 miles south of Timber Creek on CO-34. Take advantage of the educational activities at the Alpine Visitor Center, located near Hike 59, or encourage your kids to earn a Junior Ranger badge at Kawuneeche Visitor Center near Grand Lake.

 ## NORTH FORK TRAIL TO DESERTED VILLAGE

BEFORE YOU GO
Maps Roosevelt National Forest; USGS Glen Haven
Information For current conditions and more information, contact the Canyon Lakes Ranger District, www.fs.fed.us/r2/arnf or (970) 295-6700

ABOUT THE HIKE
Location Roosevelt National Forest
Day hike or backpack; Moderate
3 miles or more one way
Hikable June to October
Starting elevation/High point 7800 feet/8200 feet
Accessibility None

GETTING THERE
From Estes Park, drive north on the Devils Gulch Road 6 miles to Glen Haven. Continue 2 miles past the little town to Dunraven Road, a gravel road on the left. Proceed 2.4 miles to the Forest Service parking lot on the left. The trailhead is signed "DUNRAVEN–NORTH FORK TRAIL."

LOGISTICS

Toilet facilities are provided at the trailhead. A backcountry permit is required for camping in Rocky Mountain National Park.

ON THE TRAIL

A hike to the Deserted Village, located just east of Rocky Mountain National Park, is an ideal family venture with easy access, a scenic trail, excellent fishing along the North Fork of the Big Thompson River, and a historic destination. Several designated campsites on either side of the river are available on a first-come basis.

Spruce trees tower behind a hiker on the North Fork Trail.

The trail begins in an open, grassy slope, traversing a hillside before it gently descends through a quietly shaded Douglas fir and blue spruce forest. At 0.3 mile you reach the North Fork of the Big Thompson River. The Glen Haven Trail is on the left; stay right on the North Fork Trail to reach the Deserted Village.

As the lush canyon widens, you'll cross the river twice before reaching the private land of a youth camp at 1 mile. Remind hikers to stay on the trail (right of the river) as they pass private property. The trek to either river crossing can serve as a pleasant destination for tired little legs.

Just a few yards beyond the camp, the trail crosses the river and briefly joins an old four-wheel-drive road. During late July and August, alert your crew to raspberry bushes flourishing on sun-splashed creeksides. Another food, though certainly less edible-looking, hangs in this forest year-round. Called black tree lichen, it dangles from spruce limbs in clumps of stringy moss. Kids call it old man's beard or witch's hair, and are surprised to learn Native Americans used it as food. They prepared it by soaking it in water, then baking it, sometimes with wild onions, in a fire pit. This lichen, which gets its nourishment from particles in the air, doesn't harm the tree.

At 2.5 miles, the trail enters a flower-dappled pasture called

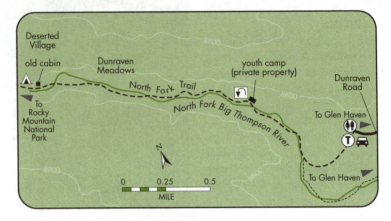

Dunraven Meadows. The area was named for the Earl of Dunraven, an Englishman who, more than 100 years ago, tried to dishonestly gain title to Estes Park and the Big Thompson River drainage. A seven-log-tall cabin, what remains of his hunting lodge, stands near the creek in the meadow's west end at 3 miles. Allow kids to look for modern stabilization techniques on the structure, while leaving the historic site undisturbed. There are no visible signs of the resort camp called Deserted Village, built in the 1890s.

Backpackers who continue their trek for 1 mile beyond the Deserted Village enter Rocky Mountain National Park, where backcountry camping permits are required.

OLD UTE TRAIL TUNDRA WALK

BEFORE YOU GO

Maps Rocky Mountain National Park brochure; USGS Fall River Pass

Information For current conditions and more information, contact the Kawuneeche Visitor Center, www.nps.gov/romo or (970) 627-3471

ABOUT THE HIKE

Location Rocky Mountain National Park
Day hike; Moderate
4 miles one way

Hikable Late June to September

Starting elevation/Low point 11,796 feet/10,758 feet

Accessibility None

GETTING THERE

From Rocky Mountain National Park's Beaver Meadows entrance station on US 36 near Estes Park, take US 34 (Trail Ridge Road) west for 22 miles to the Alpine Visitor Center and park here. From Kawuneeche Visitor Center at Rocky Mountain National Park's Grand Lake entrance, travel north on US 34 for 20.6 miles to the Alpine Visitor Center and park here. A vehicle shuttled 5 miles west on US 34 to the parking/toilet area at Milner Pass allows for one-way hikes.

LOGISTICS

Toilet facilities and drinking water are available at the Alpine Visitor Center and at Milner Pass at the end of the hike. As for all high-altitude hikes, start early in the day to avoid afternoon lightning storms. There is a national park entrance fee.

ON THE TRAIL

This "top-of-the-world" trail starts on a vast, alpine parkland speckled with miniature flowers, canopied by a mountain-rimmed skyscape. As the trail descends into the comforting confines of conifer stands, hikers discover dramatic changes in plants and weather. Families with children of mixed ages and abilities often begin their tundra trek together; while one adult descends with older kids to the Milner Pass trailhead near Poudre Lake, the other adult and younger children head back to the eastern trailhead and then drive to the Milner Pass parking area.

The trail begins in the grassland adjacent to the highway crossing opposite the Alpine Visitor Center. Wind makes itself well known as you

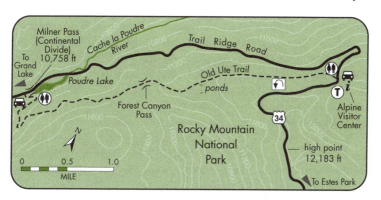

Some of the best alpine views grow at your feet.

walk the tundra stretch of the Old Ute Trail, named for the most recent tribe of American Indians to use this route to cross the mountains. Alpine flowers and grasses adapt to the relentless wind by remaining tiny. Encourage youngsters to experience this adaptation by crouching low. Ask if they feel warmer at this level or when standing tall. Have them measure the tallest flower using their finger as a ruler. Remember, the tundra ecosystem is extremely delicate; stay on the path at all times, or rock-hop to avoid trampling the vegetation.

This first 0.5 mile of trail passes through several different ecosystems. Point out small slopes littered with rocks. Explain that these areas, called fell fields, are really alpine deserts. They receive only 2 to 3 inches of precipitation a year; wind blows them free of snow and rain. Search the rocks for plants surviving these meager conditions. You're likely to find moss campion, a roundish cushion of tiny leaves. It's truly awesome to consider the ten years it took for this pioneer plant to produce its dainty, pink blossoms.

Snowbanks support another community of plants. Yellow buttercups bloom right through the snow with an alpine marsh nearby. Its wet soil supports willow, a favorite food for browsing elk. Alpine investigators can determine if *wapiti,* a Shawnee word meaning "white rump," have frequented the shrub by finding such elk evidence as nibbled leaves and stems or the animal's scat: dry, brown pellets. Very young hikers may want to turn back after exploring this first 0.5 mile of tundra.

When the road is out of sight, within the first mile, look up and southeast for a view of Longs Peak (14,259 feet), the park's tallest. Look west to see the Never Summer Range, named by Arapaho Indians for the eastern slope's year-long snowbanks.

As the trail continues its westward descent, stop periodically to measure the increasingly taller grasses and flowers. The dwarfed, wind-sculpted trees near the ponds at 1 mile are a good place to ask, "From which direction does the wind blow here?" Tree size is deceiving at high altitudes; the spruces here may be more than 100 years old.

At 1.6 miles, in Forest Canyon Pass, bright red Indian paintbrush signals the start of lush wildflower gardens. Watch for lavender-flowered chiming bells, arching 2 feet over the trail. Observant hikers will remember admiring a 3-inch version of it flowering in the tundra portion of their walk.

The trail winds through a large stand of Christmas-tree-size spruces before making its final 0.5-mile zigzag descent into what is called a climax forest. Explain that the towering firs and spruces are the tallest and biggest plants that will ever grow here. If a fire were to destroy this forest, grasses and flowers would be the first to replace the trees, followed by shrubs and aspens, with fir and spruce eventually returning. This is called plant succession, a normal process in which one plant group grows in the place where another one once grew.

At the Milner Pass parking lot, use a highway map to show your crew they have reached the Continental Divide. Using the map to demonstrate, ask, "If the rain falling on the west side of the Continental Divide eventually flows into the Pacific Ocean, where will the rain falling on the east side of the Continental Divide end up?"

 ALLUVIAL FAN TRAIL

BEFORE YOU GO
Maps Rocky Mountain National Park brochure; USGS Trail Ridge
Information For current conditions and more information, contact Beaver Meadows Visitor Center, www.nps.gov/romo or (970) 586-1206

ABOUT THE HIKE
Location Rocky Mountain National Park
Day hike; Easy
1 mile one way
Hikable Mid-May through mid-September
Starting elevation/High point 8550 feet/8670 feet
Accessibility None

GETTING THERE
From Rocky Mountain National Park's Beaver Meadows entrance station on US 36 near Estes Park, drive west on US 36 for 3 miles to

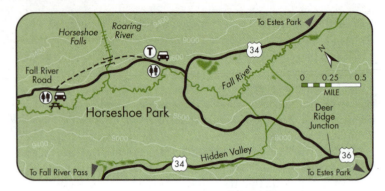

Deer Ridge Junction. Turn right onto US 34 and proceed 1.7 miles to the Fall River/Endovalley turnoff. Turn left onto Fall River Road and continue 0.5 mile to parking on the right. Parking is also available 1 mile farther at the trail's west end.

LOGISTICS

Toilet facilities are available at both parking lots; a picnic area is provided at the west parking lot. There is a national park entrance fee.

ON THE TRAIL

When Lawn Lake's dam broke in 1982, the explosion of water and rock spilled down the Roaring River valley, filling the meadow below. Today, boulders and fallen trees mark the flood's path. The Alluvial Fan Trail, named for the cone-shaped deposit formed by the river flow into lowlands, winds through a wide section of the fan. Kids like scrambling over boulders to reach the trail's huge waterfall and dipping their feet in its many cool pools. Boulders on either side of the trail shade sandy nooks that invite hikers of all sizes to stay and play.

The paved trail begins at the parking lot, winding through fallen trees and increasingly larger rocks with forested Fall River basin forming the backdrop.

Within 0.5 mile, the Roaring River, living up to its name, is heard before it's seen. The waterfall spills down a rock staircase, offering a variety of destinations. Use caution here: the river is swift and the rocks smooth. The trail branches to an interpretive sign featuring views of the lake formed by the flood. The footbridge over the Roaring River sets the stage for great family photos.

Side trails leading to mini-beaches and boulder cul-de-sacs flank the trail as it continues west to the upper parking lot and picnic area. Along the way, point out the snags, standing dead trees with numerous holes drilled into the trunk. Woodpeckers, in search of insects, spend many hours each day tapping, then listening for insect movement. Stick around long enough to watch a woodpecker drilling and listening for food.

Return via the same trail, or walk back along the road, where you'll enjoy views of Horseshoe Park and the surrounding mountains.

This hiker appreciates a quiet shore of the Roaring River.

 ## WILD BASIN TRAIL TO COPELAND FALLS AND CALYPSO CASCADES

BEFORE YOU GO
Maps Rocky Mountain National Park brochure; USGS Allen Park
Information For current conditions and more information, contact Beaver Meadows Visitor Center, www.nps.gov/romo or (970) 586-1206

ABOUT THE HIKE
Location Rocky Mountain National Park
Day hike; Easy to moderate
1.8 miles one way
Hikable Mid-May through September
Starting elevation/High point 8500 feet/9200 feet
Accessibility None

GETTING THERE

From the Beaver Meadows Visitor Center (near the Estes Park entrance to Rocky Mountain National Park), travel east on US 36 for 4 miles to the intersection of US 34, US 36, and CO-7, near the east side of downtown Estes Park. Take CO-7 south about 13 miles, turning right

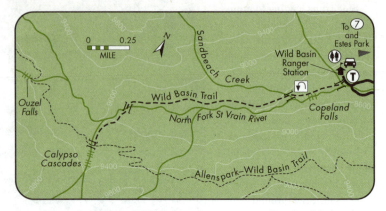

onto the road accessing Wild Basin. Continue past Copeland Lake about 2.5 miles to the parking area and Wild Basin Ranger Station.

LOGISTICS

Toilet facilities are available at the parking lot.

ON THE TRAIL

The North Fork of the St. Vrain River treats hikers to two waterfalls, each appealing in markedly different ways. The short, gentle walk to Copeland Falls invites hikers to a soothing series of pools spilling over smooth boulders. The steeper climb to Calypso Cascades greets hikers with a torrent of water crashing through jagged rocks and fallen trees. The hike is a perfect destination for families with mixed ages or ambitions.

The sound of rushing water greets hikers the second they step out of their cars in the parking lot. Ask your companions to listen and then point in the direction of a waterfall trail. The roar will direct them past several park signs to the Wild Basin trailhead. Cross several small streams on the trail before meeting a footbridge that spans a larger creek feeding into the St. Vrain.

As the trail rises to Copeland Falls, with the St. Vrain forming inviting pools below sun-baked boulders, some hikers may linger. But the splashing sounds and sights increase as the trail reaches the falls. Waterfall fanatics are appeased by following the trail's lefthand fork as it edges the cascade, then rejoins the main route. This is a good turnaround point for some hikers and a great place for photographs.

Waterfall fanatics get their fix on the trail to Calypso Cascades.

At 0.5 mile the trail's more aggressive climb to Calypso Cascades begins by winding through wildflower meadows rising above the waterway. As the trail passes through mixed forests and open areas, alternate side trails lead streamside, once again appealing to lovers of waterfalls. After crossing a rock-edged creek at 1 mile, the trail ascends the side of a hill. Passing the Pine Ridge backcountry campsite sign, continue left on the main route to a sign for Calypso Cascades, crossing the St. Vrain on a footbridge.

The trail's final ascent along a shady hillside with giant-sized steps of logs and rocks (built to minimize erosion) leads to the footbridge and trail junction just below Calypso Cascades. The dense, evergreen canopy here provides a dramatic backdrop to the scene. Note how water tumbles through deadfall and jagged rock. Encourage hikers to compare the two waterfalls and how they felt at each one.

Return via the same trail.

FERN LAKE TRAIL

BEFORE YOU GO

Maps Rocky Mountain National Park brochure; USGS McHenrys Peak

Information For current conditions and more information, contact Beaver Meadows Visitor Center, www.nps.gov/romo or (970) 586-1206

ABOUT THE HIKE

Location Rocky Mountain National Park

Day hike or backpack; Easy to challenging

1.7 miles one way to The Pool; 3.8 miles one way to Fern Lake

Hikable May through October to The Pool; June through October to Fern Lake

Starting elevation/High point 8155 feet/9530 feet

Accessibility None

GETTING THERE

From Rocky Mountain National Park's Beaver Meadows entrance station on US 36 near Estes Park, head 0.2 mile west to Bear Lake Road and continue west on Bear Lake Road 1.2 miles over a ridge to Moraine Park. A few yards past Moraine Park Visitor Center, turn right on the paved road toward the Moraine Park Campground. Pass the campground and continue on this road to its end where the Fern Lake Trail begins. The last mile and the small parking lot at the Fern Lake trailhead are not recommended for vehicles with trailers, so stop and park in the Fern Lake shuttle bus stop parking area along the way. On busy summer days be prepared to park there as well. Parking is not permitted along the roadway.

LOGISTICS

Toilet facilities are provided at the Fern Lake shuttle bus stop. A back-country permit is required for overnight stays. There is a national park entrance fee.

ON THE TRAIL

The trail to Fern Lake features the park's "best of" attractions for hikes with kids: monster-size rocks to wander among, a log bridge spanning a deep pool in the Big Thompson River, a mist-spewing waterfall, and a lake promising fishing fun. Plan to enjoy this popular trail early in the day before crowds or rain change its tone. The Pool and Fern Falls serve as turnaround points for varying energy and endurance levels. The hike to Fern Lake is an ideal overnight backpack with day-hike options to nearby alpine lakes.

Fern Lake Trail's first section meanders beside the Big Thompson River. Slow the pace on this flat section by stopping to admire small, quiet splendors flowering beside the river. At 1.1 miles, the trail winds through Arch Rocks, a collection of massive boulders tumbled from the cliffs above. Few hikers in the under-twelve set pass through here without leaping, jumping, or climbing in this natural playground.

The trail crosses the Big Thompson at 1.7 miles via a sturdy log bridge spanning The Pool. Show your companions how The Pool continues deepening and broadening as river water swirls between the steep rock walls. The bridge serves as a good destination for young hikers or those with limited time or endurance.

Just past the bridge, the trail branches, with the left fork going to Cub Lake; stay right, climbing into thick forest. Within 0.5 mile from The Pool, the trail enters a patch of Rocky Mountain maple trees intersected by a brook spilling from Mount Wuh. The trail levels some, then circles around open, south-facing slopes. The trail climbs the side of a gully and enters a thick subalpine forest.

Follow the trail across Fern Creek and climb a rather noisy ridge flanked by the roaring Spruce and Fern creeks. The steep climb warrants

Young hikers watch the Big Thompson swirl into The Pool along Fern Creek Trail.

plenty of breath-catching stops. Divert kids' attentions away from their racing hearts to the waterway's soothing array of wildflowers, to the different songs the creek provides, to the number of times they see a pink (or yellow, red, orange . . .) flower, or to a twenty-question "What in the Woods . . . ?" game about something they see frequently on the hike.

After the trail switchbacks, then curves up a hillside, Fern Falls thunders its presence at 2.5 miles. Having climbed nearly 500 feet in a mile, your group will welcome the refreshing mist from the falls. The deep shade of subalpine fir and Engelmann spruce provides a dark backdrop for portraits taken here. Fern Falls also makes a good turnaround point.

The remaining 1.4-mile stretch to Fern Lake begins with a steep climb away from the falls and into sunny warmth. Take time here to note the return to quietness and the rise in temperature. The switchbacks straighten somewhat as the trail parallels Fern Creek. However, the creek is not visible until 3.8 miles, where the trail meets the Spruce Lake Trail. Turn left, crossing Fern Creek at the outlet of Fern Lake. From the open shoreline here, ask your companions which peak seen across the lake would be named Notchtop Mountain and which one Little Matterhorn. The trail beyond Fern Lake leads to Odessa and Bear lakes.

Return the way you came.

SPRAGUE LAKE NATURE TRAIL

BEFORE YOU GO
Map Rocky Mountain National Park brochure
Information For current conditions and more information, contact Beaver Meadows Visitor Center, www.nps.gov/romo or (970) 586-1206

ABOUT THE HIKE
Location Rocky Mountain National Park
Day hike; Easy
0.5-mile loop
Hikable June to October
Starting elevation /High point 8710 feet/8710 feet
Accessibility Wheelchair-accessible

GETTING THERE

From Rocky Mountain National Park's Beaver Meadows entrance station on US 36 near Estes Park, head 0.2 mile west to Bear Lake Road and continue west on Bear Lake Road 6.4 miles to the turnoff on your left for Sprague Lake. To lessen the impact of vehicular traffic on Bear Lake Road, a shuttle bus system begins from a parking lot immediately west of the Glacier Basin Campground, on Bear Lake Road 6 miles from the Beaver Meadows entrance; parking for the Sprague Lake Nature Trail is 0.5 mile south of the Bear Lake shuttle bus parking area. There is no shuttle bus stop at Sprague Lake.

LOGISTICS

Universal-access toilet facilities and a picnic area are available at the parking lot. A backcountry permit is required for overnight stays; physically challenged individuals require a permit to use the Handicamp Backcountry Site. There is a national park entrance fee.

ON THE TRAIL

More than a century ago, homesteader Abner Sprague built a dam across a stream to form the pond we now call Sprague Lake. While trout fishing here, he undoubtedly enjoyed the views of the Continental Divide, as do countless visitors now on this fully accessible trail.

For little ones, Sprague Lake's first attraction is the resident ducklings paddling around their mothers. Father ducks are the ones

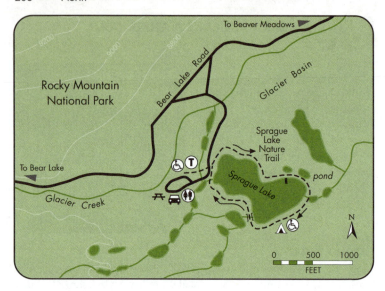

with a showy green head atop a white collar, commonly seen during the spring nesting season. When the ducks dip their heads into the water, their long, specially adapted tongues strain food (insects, tiny bits of plants, seeds, and fish eggs) from the mud.

Following the trail around the lake's north shore, point out charred tree stumps in the adjacent forest, remnants of the fire of 1900. Today's forest and undergrowth reveal the life-renewing quality that fires bring to the soil. The hearty ponderosa pine trees here survived thanks to their thick bark. Look for knots in a tree to show the bark's thickness. Aspens are newcomers in a forest, the first trees to sprout from their already established roots after a fire has cleared an area.

About 30 yards past the fishing pier, a little brown pond on your left appears lifeless but is actually home to many insects. Its prettiest resident, the brilliant blue-green dragonfly, is a favorite meal of another resident: the frog. Encourage your crew to watch the dragonfly define its hunting ground, darting after any would-be intruders with a clatter of wings. Kids of all ages are especially fond of dragonflies when they learn this iridescent insect hunts mosquitoes—eating its own weight of them in a half hour! How many mosquitoes could that be?

Before passing the pond, point out the mosses and grasses taking root around it. Explain that as plants invade this wet area, they deplete the water but build soil as they die and decay over the years. Larger

National park rangers provide a hands-on lesson on Rocky Mountain sheep.

plants eventually take root. Tell your kids that when they return here with their own children, young aspen trees may be here instead of moss.

The entrance to the wheelchair-accessible campsite is just beyond the pond, before the footbridge. On the other side of this creek draining into the lake, take a moment to enjoy great views of the Continental Divide before the trail returns you to the starting point.

GREAT GETAWAYS

There are three excellent campgrounds near Hikes 61, 62, 63, and 64. Along the eastern edge of Rocky Mountain National Park you'll find Aspenglen Campground with first-come, first-served sites (www.nps .gov/romo) and Glacier Basin and Moraine Park campgrounds, which have sites by reservation only in summer (800-365-2267).

Rocky Mountain National Park is, of course, a wonderland of adventures for your family and these are just a few highlights. Your kids will love the misty cascades of Alberta Falls, reached by an easy 0.6-mile walk from the trailhead at Glacier Gorge Junction. The Moraine Park Museum has interactive nature exhibits, bookstore, guided nature walks, and grand views of the surrounding peaks. To explore farther into the park, take Old Fall River Road (be sure to stop at Chasm Falls) or Trail Ridge Loop Drive to the top-of-the world Alpine Visitor Center.

BEAR LAKE AND GLACIER GORGE LOOP TRAILS

BEFORE YOU GO

Maps Rocky Mountain National Park brochure; USGS McHenrys Peak

Information For current conditions and more information, contact Beaver Meadows Visitor Center, www.nps.gov/romo or (970) 586-1206

ABOUT THE HIKE

Location Rocky Mountain National Park

Day hike; Easy (Bear Lake) to moderate (Glacier Gorge Loop) 0.5-mile loop, Bear Lake; 5.6-mile loop, Glacier Gorge Loop; plus 1.4 miles round-trip to Emerald Lake, 0.4 mile round-trip to Lake Haiyaha

Hikable Late June to October

Starting elevation/High point 9475 feet/10,220 feet

Accessibility None

GETTING THERE

From Rocky Mountain National Park's Beaver Meadows entrance station on US 36 near Estes Park, head 0.2 mile west to Bear Lake Road and travel west on Bear Lake Road 10 miles to the parking lot for Bear Lake. The Bear Lake trailhead is at the west end of the parking lot. See Hike 63, Sprague Lake Nature Trail, for shuttle information.

LOGISTICS

Toilet facilities are located at Bear Lake's parking area; drinking water may be available in midsummer. A backcountry permit is required for overnight stays.

ON THE TRAIL

Bear Lake and the surrounding area is a quiet showcase of Rocky Mountain National Park's ever-evolving forests and shores. The trails wander through a collage of nature's best: rainbow-making waterfalls, wildflower-bordered streams, cathedral-like forests, and mountain-mirroring lakes. A camera is almost essential for this venture. Little wonder the trails near Bear Lake are the park's most popular! Avoid crowds by starting the hike early in the morning. Any of the lakes along the trail—Bear, Nymph, Dream, Emerald, and Haiyaha—can serve as a turnaround point.

Begin on the paved 0.5-mile interpretive loop around Bear Lake. The trail's self-guiding booklet detailing the ecology of this typical high-country lake is available at the trailhead. Anglers of all ages appreciate the lake's healthy brook trout population.

Young hikers interested in exploring all or portions of the Glacier Gorge Loop continue on the 0.5-mile paved trail to Nymph Lake. Along this walk through a lodgepole forest, point out the scarred tree trunks—indicators that a porcupine dined on their bark. Pine beetles are also affecting the forest here, so be watchful of falling trees, especially on windy days. At lily pad–blanketed Nymph Lake at 0.5 mile, follow the trail around the north end of the lake to the viewpoint where Hallett Peak and Flattop Mountain add a grand background to your photographs. Have kids examine the wind-sculpted roots of the toppled spruce trees here. Ask, "What made the tree fall? Why hasn't the Park Service removed the tree? How do fallen trees help forest animals?"

Wildflowers and mini-waterfalls edge the 0.6-mile walkway to Dream Lake at 1.1 miles. On rainy afternoons, of which there are many come midsummer, this mist-shrouded destination looks much like a Japanese watercolor.

For a side trip, stay to the right of Dream Lake and just 0.7 mile beyond lies Emerald Lake, sparkling and still in its glacial cirque. Rock scramblers of all sizes have fun at this point, where the trail ends. To rejoin the Glacier Gorge Loop, head back to Dream Lake, and pick up the trail, now on your right.

From this junction, the loop trail heads south 1.1 miles toward Lake Haiyaha

Mist-shrouded limber pine edge Dream Lake in Rocky Mountain National Park.

crossing Chaos Creek. Several switchbacks through dense subalpine-fir forest (most years, snow covers the trail until July) lead to a sun-drenched viewpoint of Nymph and Bear lakes. Longs Peak looms ahead. The relatively level trail then passes through limber pines for 0.25 mile before meeting the 0.2-mile spur to Lake Haiyaha on the right at 2.1 miles. There's a lonely limber pine here, twisted and gnarled by weather's unyielding forces. A more numerous resident here, Clark's nutcracker, a bold gray bird, will literally grab your kids' attention and any food they may be carrying. Remember to honor park regulations and all wild animals' basic needs by not feeding them.

From the spur trail, the main trail leads 1.2 miles down rocky terrain, passing the trail to The Loch on the right at 3.3 miles; stay left at the Glacier Gorge Loop signs. On your right, you'll see and hear the roaring, foaming Glacier Creek. Within 0.5 mile, you pass the North Longs Peak Trail on the right at 3.8 miles, where the absence of trees is obvious, especially on a cloudless summer day; stay left on the loop trail. A forest fire in 1900 destroyed the trees, leaving behind dry turf. The cliffs to your left are called Glacier Knobs.

At 4.5 miles reach Alberta Falls, a classic aspen-clad watershow that attracts hordes of hikers who have approached it from the Glacier Gorge

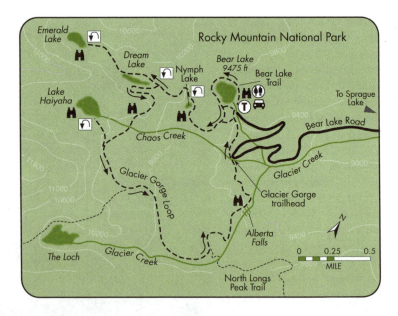

trailhead. After a photo stop here, continue walking downhill 0.8 mile to the Glacier Gorge trailhead and parking lot at 5.3 miles, then continue 0.3 mile uphill to Bear Lake's parking lot at 5.6 miles. A shuttle bus is available at Glacier Gorge trailhead that returns hikers to the Bear Lake parking lot.

 POUDRE RIVER TRAIL

BEFORE YOU GO
Map Tour de Fort bicycle map (available at local bike shops)
Information For current conditions and more information, contact Fort Collins Parks, www.fcgov.com/parks/trails or (970) 221-6660

ABOUT THE HIKE
Location Fort Collins
Day hike; Easy
Up to 10.1 miles one way
Hikable Year-round
Starting elevation/High point 4984 feet/4984 feet
Accessibility Wheelchair-accessible

GETTING THERE

In Fort Collins, follow Mulberry Street (CO-14) west to Shields Street and turn right, continuing north to Vine Drive. Parking is also available west of College Avenue (US 287) off Cherry Street; at the intersection of Mulberry Street (CO-14) and Lemay Avenue; at Seven Lakes Business Park on East Prospect Road; and at Colorado State University's Environmental Learning Center on East Drake Road. Foot access to the trail is via any of these streets.

LOGISTICS

Toilet facilities and drinking water are provided in spring, summer, and fall at the Shields Street parking area, at Lee Martinez Park (between Shields Street and College Avenue), at the Old Fort Collins Heritage Park adjacent to the Gustav Swanson Nature Center (near College and Cherry), and at the Environmental Learning Center.

ON THE TRAIL

This wide, level, paved trail near the northern city limit of Fort Collins follows the Cache la Poudre River. (The French name, meaning "where the powder is hidden," refers to the gunpowder early trappers hid prior to a snowstorm.) The Poudre River Trail is well-suited for anyone who enjoys the outdoors, from kids and grandparents to joggers and folks in wheelchairs. Environments vary along the trail, which begins at Shields Street and heads southeast, ending at Colorado State University's Environmental Learning Center (open to the public) near East Drake Road. The trail's newest 1.75-mile addition continues west from Shields Street.

From the Shields Street parking area, in the trail's first mile cottonwood and Russian olive branches frame grand views of the foothills to the west. During July and August, downy cottonwood seeds drift through the air like summer's snowflakes. Encourage youngsters to gather the airy piles of seeds collected around clumps of grass and feel the softness against their faces. Fall color walks are ideal here.

The section to College Avenue (1.4 miles) includes a working farm at Lee Martinez Park, once the site of a dairy farm. The original barn houses cows, chickens, pigs, and ponies, and the museum features old farm implements. Kids like climbing the fortlike jungle gym here. Others may relax on the benches along this most popular portion of the trail.

The next section goes under College Avenue (US 287), Fort Collins's

main street, before entering the Gustav Swanson Nature Center in Old Fort Collins Heritage Park near Linden Street. Huge, narrowleaf cottonwoods shade the nature center's 0.5-mile interpreted loop, with several bird-viewing benches shaded by the leafy canopy.

The next section to Hospital Street (0.75 mile) is less used, as it meanders through lush riverbed vegetation. To continue on to the next section, the trail goes along Hospital Street, across an overpass, and back down to the river. The 2.75-mile section of the trail from here to East Prospect Road is interpreted.

A super hiker encounters a caterpillar along the Poudre River Trail.

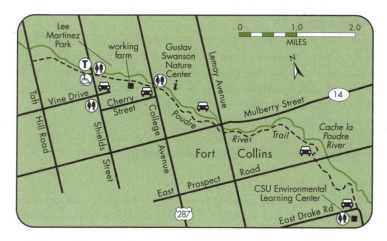

The trail here winds through open fields, under cottonwoods, and beside ponds frequented by herons, ducks, and muskrats. Before approaching the ponds, tell your companions to watch for the resident black-crowned night heron. During midday it is often seen sleeping perched on a stump in the middle of the lake. The remaining 1.2-mile portion of the trail winds south from East Prospect Road between ponds and the river, ending at the Environmental Learning Center.

 CHAPUNGU SCULPTURE PARK

BEFORE YOU GO

Map Chapungu Sculpture Park map, www.chapungusculpturepark.com/pdf/walking-map.pdf, also posted at park

Information For current conditions and more information, contact Chapungu Sculpture Park, www.chapungusculpturepark.com or (970) 461-8020

ABOUT THE HIKE

Location Loveland

Day hike; Easy

Wetlands loop 0.65 mile; Woods loop 0.35 mile; Great Lawn loop 0.3 mile

Hikable Year-round

Starting elevation/High point 4985 feet/5000 feet

Accessibility Wheelchair users have full access to the park; Braille signage throughout

GETTING THERE

From I-25 in Loveland, take exit 259 (Crossroads Boulevard/CO-68) east 0.4 mile to Centerra Parkway. Turn south (right), driving 1.4 miles to Kendall Parkway (just past the Union Pacific Railroad bridge) and turn west (right), proceeding 0.2 mile to The Promenade Shops at Centerra Shopping Mall. Ample parking is on the left.

LOGISTICS

Toilet facilities and drinking water are provided near station 6.

ON THE TRAIL

Chapungu Sculpture Park could be described as eighty-two stone sculptures informally placed in a tranquil blend of meadow, woods, and wetland. Those who've walked any of the park's paths use words like "inspiring," "relaxing," and most often, "fun, 'cuz the statues tell stories!" Imagine "Leap Frog" depicted in three stone figures or "Teen Secrets" carved into rock.

The 26-acre park exhibits the work of master stone sculptors from Zimbabwe. Each sculpture portrays a touching snapshot from African culture that reflects the universal themes of family life, nature, women, elders, and traditions. Over the past four decades, many of these sculptures

moved around the world for exhibits in gardens and parks. Their permanent home, now at Centerra, is the result of a unique partnership between Chapungu Sculpture Park of Harare, Zimbabwe; longtime art promoter McWhinney Enterprises; and the community of Loveland, considered by many "North America's sculpture capital." The park is named after the Bateleur eagle, regarded as a messenger of gods, a protective spirit in the Shona culture.

Ten "pedestrian entry" points provide access into this slice of nature and art sandwiched between the interstate and shopping mall. Station 4 is an ideal starting point between the Woods and Great Lawn

Visitors to Chapungu Sculpture Park are encouraged to "see" the art with their hands.

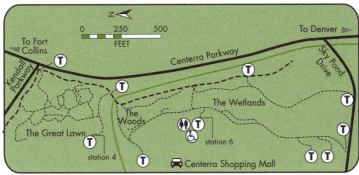

areas. A sign at each sculpture displays the artist's name and title of the piece, which is often quite literal, as in, "Me Too Mama," "Protecting the Twins," "Fetching Firewood." Imaginations and legs tend to wander freely here, so allow yourself and your companions time to explore. Unlike most "do not touch" galleries, visitors to Chapungu are encouraged to "see" with their hands. Allowing your children to feel a carving's satin-smooth finish helps them envision the artist's hand sculpting and sanding the once rough stone into the image their hands and eyes see today.

Chapungu Sculpture Park does not always remain quiet as stone. Performing artists, stone-carving workshops, school tours, an open-air African village, and a future multi-level gallery are all part of the park's mission to support African art and encourage family interaction.

67 WELL GULCH LOOP

BEFORE YOU GO
Map Lory State Park brochure, available at visitor center
Information For current conditions and more information, contact Lory State Park, lory.park@state.co.us or (970) 493-1623

ABOUT THE HIKE
Location Lory State Park
Day hike; Easy to moderate
2.2-mile loop
Hikable Year-round
Starting elevation/High point 5580 feet/5870 feet
Accessibility None

GETTING THERE
From North Fort Collins, take CO-287 north to County Road 54G (LaPorte). Go through the town of LaPorte, and turn left onto CR-52E.

Turn left again at CR-23N, drive 1.4 miles, then turn right on Lodgepole Drive. Drive another 1.6 miles to the park entrance. Park at the South Eltuck parking area, 0.6 mile south of the entrance.

From South Fort Collins, take Harmony Road/CR-38E west. Turn right onto CR-23N, driving north to a T intersection. Turn left at the stop sign onto 42C. Continue north to Lodgepole Drive and turn left. Drive 1.6 miles to the park entrance, and park as above.

LOGISTICS

The Well Gulch Self-Guided Nature Trail brochure is available at the park entrance and nature center. Bikes and horses are prohibited in Lory State Park; dogs must be on leash. Toilet facilities are provided at South Eltuck parking area. The nearest drinking water is available at the visitor center, as are interactive exhibits and guidebooks to the area.

ON THE TRAIL

Walk this interpreted loop and discover the best of what surrounds Horsetooth Reservoir; its meadows, creeks, rock formations, and view-points. Kids like stopping at the cool grotto early in the hike, later finding sparkly rocks on the trail. Many families pack a lunch for the trail's

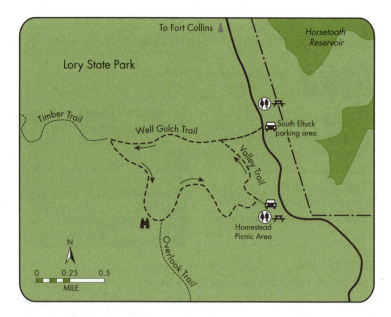

Summer hikers in Wells Gulch cool their feet in nearby Horsetooth Reservoir.

last stop, a former homestead, now a picnic area. After the trek, summer hikers often cool their feet in the reservoir, just 100 yards from the parking lot.

From the parking lot, cross the road to a short (0.2 mile) path through prairie grasses and yucca. The trailhead is at the bottom of the gulch. Two slopes converge here where a variety of trees and shrubs provide both shade and fruits including rose hips, chokecherry, gooseberry, thimbleberry, and "lemonade-berry," the dry, reddish orange fruit of a shrub with small, maple leaf–shaped leaves.

During our July visit to the gulch we spotted a yellow warbler perched in willow brush. The small, insect-eating songbird is one of 175 bird species that nest, rest, fly through, and sometimes live year-round in this diverse food and water source. The gulch is a bird-watcher's destination, but kids like counting the butterflies fluttering along the trail. Meanwhile, do keep a lookout for poison ivy. Remember, "Leaves of three, let it be."

The bubbling sounds of a small waterfall spilling into a shallow pool greet hikers at 0.2 mile. Very young hikers tend to linger here, sometimes noticing the apple tree thriving near the creek. Consider it living evidence of the 1891 homestead owned by the Howard family until 1963. The area is now part of Lory State Park, so please don't collect rocks and plants, edible and otherwise.

The trail threads among cottonwood and Rocky Mountain maple trees as it edges the streambed for 0.3 mile, then meets the Timber Trail. Turn left (south), following the Well Gulch Trail 0.4 mile as it gradually ascends through aspen and fir trees, then opens to views of Horsetooth Reservoir and Fort Collins. Some hikers will instead focus on the flickering treasures at their feet: mica bits that formed in the area's oldest rocks, gneiss and schist. (The geologist in your group may be interested in the Lory State Park field activity guide, available at the visitor center.)

From the view area, head east following the trail's 0.5-mile gradual descent along a south-facing slope. At signpost 15 encourage little hands to first feel the flat, flexible needles of the fir tree, then the sharp, round, and long needles of the adjacent ponderosa pine. The Well Gulch Trail ends in the Homestead picnic area, shaded in part by towering blue spruce trees planted by the family that first lived here starting in 1897. You'll know when you've met a spruce. When gently "shaking hands" with a branch, you'll feel its needles, sharp and spiky compared with the fir tree's flat, flexible ones.

From the picnic area, follow the roadside Valley Trail north 0.4 mile to the trailhead, turning right to return to the parking lot.

 HEWLETT GULCH TRAIL

BEFORE YOU GO
Maps Trails Illustrated #101 Cache la Poudre/Big Thompson; USGS Poudre Park
Information For current conditions and more information, contact the Canyon Lakes Ranger District, www.fs.usda.gov/hewlettgulch or (970) 295-6700

ABOUT THE HIKE
Location 22 miles northwest of Fort Collins
Day hike; Easy
2.5 miles one way
Hikable May through October
Starting elevation/High point 5672 feet/5900 feet
Accessibility None

GETTING THERE

From Fort Collins, head northwest 11 miles on US 287 to CO-14. Turn left (west) on CO-14, and travel 10.5 miles to a bridge on the right across

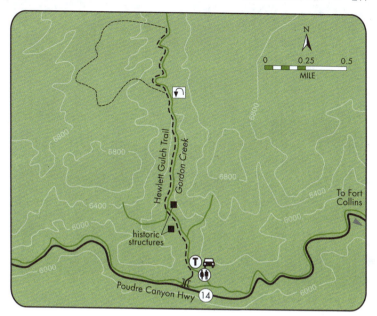

the Poudre River. Follow the paved road up a hill to the large parking lot and the trailhead.

LOGISTICS

This trail is popular with mountain bikers and deer hunters; during fall hunting season, use caution and wear an orange vest. Restroom facilities are provided at the trailhead, but no drinking water.

ON THE TRAIL

Hewlett Gulch welcomes hikers as it gently descends into a lush corridor once traveled by Native Americans, then worked as a homestead by a family of ten. Today's kids have fun playing balance games at the trail's creek crossings, most of which feature shade and an adult-sized boulder for seating. Crossings of Gordon Creek are numerous and easily navigated due to the strategically placed rocks. However, hiking the gulch after heavy rains or during the spring thaw may require wading.

The information sign at the parking lot describes the human history in the gulch, a worthy read before stepping onto the trail. The first stream crossing at 0.2 mile seems to beckon hikers to stop and play here. Instead, suggest, "Let's find out how many more times we get to cross!"

Mule deer are among the wildlife frequently seen (and hunted in fall!) in Hewlett Gulch.

Within the first 0.6 mile you'll see a lone stone-and-cement fireplace, a few rock foundations, and living proof of the gardens that once thrived here. In the spring tall stands of lilac perfume the air followed by summer's locust trees displaying fronds of lavender blossoms. And don't be surprised to see bright orange poppies amidst the wildflowers. However, kids are amazed when you point out the house foundation on the right side of the trail at 0.8 mile. Ask them, "Is your bedroom bigger than what this house once was?" Encourage your companions to imagine living, playing, and working here a hundred years ago.

At 1 mile charred tree trunks dot the slope, remnants of the 2004 wildfire here. Point out the leafy bushes at the base of the trees as signs of forest regeneration. The burned area extends to about 1.7 miles; keep a lookout here to avoid brushing against poison ivy.

At 2 miles a cairn marks a fork in the trail at the base of a hill. This can be a turnaround point, or continue to the right into a leafy area, crossing the stream several times. Where the trail veers from the stream and starts heading uphill, turn around and head back the way you came.

How many creek crossings did your group tally?

KREUTZER NATURE TRAIL AND MOUNT MCCONNEL SUMMIT

BEFORE YOU GO

Maps Roosevelt National Forest; USGS Big Narrows
Information For current conditions and more information, contact the Canyon Lakes Ranger District, www.fs.fed.us/r2/arnf or (970) 295-6700

ABOUT THE HIKE

Location Mountain Park Recreation Area
Day hike; Moderate to challenging
2.1-mile loop, Kreutzer Nature Trail; plus 1.1 miles one way to Mount McConnel summit
Hikable May to November
Starting elevation/High point 6680 feet/7200 feet on Kreutzer Nature Trail, 7960 feet at McConnel summit
Accessibility None

GETTING THERE

From I-25 near Fort Collins, take exit 269 and head west on CO-14 for 40 miles to the Mountain Park Recreation Area (at milepost 4a). Turn south into the recreation area and continue 0.2 mile to the trailhead parking lot on the right.

LOGISTICS

Drinking water and toilet, shower, and picnic facilities are available at the campground near the trailhead. Dogs must be on leashes.

ON THE TRAIL

Learn about the diverse forces that shape and lace the Poudre Canyon on the Kreutzer Nature Trail. Families with youngsters enjoy this interpreted loop trail's gentle climb through a variety of forests. Those with eager and able hikers can continue on to ascend Mount McConnel, where views of the Mummy Range and Rocky Mountain National Park are superb. Plan to also walk the interpreted nature trail at Mountain Park where fishing access is provided.

The Kreutzer Nature Trail, named after the first official forest ranger in the United States, William Kreutzer, starts at the parking area 0.2 mile past the park entrance. The hike begins in a lodgepole pine forest, leading 0.3 mile to the first of its twenty-two interpretive signs. The view here, of the Poudre River Canyon and the mountains beyond, makes this an ideal destination for beginning little hikers and their parents.

As the trail maintains an easy grade, zigzagging up the river canyon, its interpretive signs allow for frequent and interesting breath-catching stops. Topics described at each sign range from lichen to mule deer, from forest management practices to the Poudre Canyon's history. At 0.7 mile, the Kreutzer Nature Trail meets the trail to Mount McConnel's summit. This is another possible turnaround point. Those interested in completing the nature trail should follow the path to the left; mountain climbers take the path to the right.

Mount McConnel hikers follow the switchbacks up 1 mile through ponderosa-fir forest to the summit. Veer right slightly just before reaching the wooded peak at 1.1 miles. To the south is an incredible view of the Mummy Range. The distant mountains you see are in Rocky Mountain National Park. The recommended return route is to descend on the same route taken up; the trail heading east at the summit is very steep and difficult to follow before it rejoins the Kreutzer Nature Trail.

At the junction with the Kreutzer Nature Trail, continue on the same trail back to the start, or turn right to complete the loop. From the trail intersection, the Kreutzer Nature Trail heads east 0.5 mile, and then turns left, following the canyon's south-facing slope. Along this

Father and son examine an insect gall on a leaf.

sun-drenched terrain, point out examples of plants that have adapted to the climate: evening primrose, yucca, and other cacti. Children enjoy finding other examples.

At 2.5 miles, where the Mount McConnel Trail reconnects to the eastern half of the Kreutzer Nature Trail, watch for an aspen tree growing alongside the trail; stay left. The tree may appear out of place here, but encourage the kids to find its source for survival: a spring originating higher in the canyon trickles out at this point on the trail. Stop to enjoy this oasis; within a few feet the trail reenters hot, dry pinyon-juniper country.

Poison ivy and spreading dogbane pepper the trail's final 0.5 mile as it traverses a talus slope. Take time to point out poison ivy's characteristic shiny, deep-green leaves grouped in threes. Others are more interested in learning how dogbane, the compact bush with tiny pink bell-shaped flowers, got its name. It is poisonous if eaten, and its scientific name comes from the Greek words meaning "noxious to dogs."

Just after passing the talus slope, the trail meets the Mountain Park Campground road. Stop here to cool tired feet along the banks of the Cache la Poudre River, which in French means "where the powder is hidden," referring to the gunpowder early trappers once stashed prior to a snowstorm. At the road, turn left and walk 0.2 mile to the trailhead, or cross the road to walk the nature trail along the river, looping back to the trailhead in 0.2 mile.

MONTGOMERY PASS TRAIL

BEFORE YOU GO
Maps Roosevelt National Forest; USGS Clark Peak
Information For current conditions and more information, contact the Colorado State Forest State Park, www.parks.state.co.us /parks/stateforest or (970) 723-8366

ABOUT THE HIKE
Location 57 miles west of Fort Collins
Day hike; Moderate
1.9 miles one way
Hikable Mid-June to September
Starting elevation/High point 10,040 feet/11,000 feet
Accessibility None

GETTING THERE

From Fort Collins, travel west on CO-14 for 65 miles. Just past the Joe Wright Reservoir, turn left into the Zimmerman Lake parking lot.

LOGISTICS

Toilet facilities are available at the trailhead.

ON THE TRAIL

This is a short, easy walk to a grand expanse of Colorado high country. Like all high-altitude hikes, start this one on a cloudless morn. Doing so gives youngsters ample time to roam the mountaintop landscape, including stops to investigate the intimate views at their feet.

From the parking lot, cross the highway carefully and follow the edge of timber north for approximately 0.25 mile before entering the forest. To find the trailhead to Montgomery Pass, watch for blue plastic ski trail markers on the trees.

Initially the trail traverses a marshy area and parallels the highway for 0.25 mile before it joins an old logging road. The climb begins as the trail enters a forest of stately Colorado blue spruce trees. Stop to feel the sharp, pointed needles of spruce trees, which to most kids look just like Christmas trees. As the trail climbs higher, point out the spruces' cones, dangling from the tree like so many Christmas ornaments. Resident chickaree squirrels treat the cones like gift-wrapped presents, tearing them open in search of seeds. The resourceful rodents store their winter caches beneath the trees in shredded cone piles, called middens. Your

hikers may find some of the animals' entry holes into the middens.

At 0.8 mile, watch for the remains of a log cabin on the right. Bear to the right, continuing to a creek crossing. Tired hikers should turn around here.

Another 0.5 mile beyond the cabin site, the tree line gives way to an expanse of alpine tundra. The trail is not easy to discern, but head in the direction of the pass. Sedge, a family of grasslike plants, carpets much of the tundra here. Ask children to find sedges by feeling for grass that is three-sided and solid. (Remember, "Sedges have edges.") During these close searches, caution kids from accidentally injuring their eyes on these upright spiky grasses. Also, remind them to walk on rocks when possible in this fragile tundra area. Some plants here take many years of growing before they flower.

At 1.9 miles, you'll reach the pass; encourage youngsters to feel the wind's power by standing tall and stretching out their arms. When they

Child carriers give young families easy access to high mountain hikes.

inspect the tiny wildflowers, best seen from their hands and knees, they'll understand why these diminutive beauties keep a low profile. If during their exploration someone smells a skunk, they've discovered sky pilot. This alpine flower cluster with lavender-blue bell-shaped blossoms attracts bees, which favor the color.

Return via the same trail.

 LAKE AGNES TRAIL

BEFORE YOU GO
Maps Colorado State Forest; USGS Mount Richtofen, USGS Clark Peak
Information For current conditions and more information, contact Colorado State Forest State Park, www.parks.state.co.us/parks/stateforest or (970) 723-8366

ABOUT THE HIKE
Location State Forest State Park
Day hike; Moderate to challenging
1.6 miles round trip
Hikable July through September
Starting elevation/High point 10,320 feet/10,660 feet
Accessibility None

GETTING THERE
From Fort Collins, travel west on CO-14 approximately 72 miles to Cameron Pass. Continue 2.6 miles beyond the pass to a gravel road turnoff on the left. A sign for Agnes and American lakes and Crags Campground is posted just before the road. Continue 0.6 mile on this gravel road to the stop sign and entrance, proceed 0.75 mile, then turn right and proceed 1.3 miles up this very steep, two-wheel-drive road. Parking is at the road's end near a cabin.

LOGISTICS
Toilet facilities are available behind the trailhead cabin. Camping and fires are not allowed at Lake Agnes, but the Crags Campground, with drinking water and toilet facilities, is nearby.

ON THE TRAIL
The short hike to this clear, forest-fringed jewel in the high country is an alpine odyssey available to most every hiker, and so this is a popular

destination. Early in the hike the trail forks, providing options both for ambitious rock scramblers and for those drawn to forest serenity. Agnes Lake's two-fish limit (flies and lures only) and stunning sur-roundings satisfy anglers of all ages.

The Lake Agnes Trail begins behind the cabin on the left side of the Middle Fork of Michigan Creek. The jagged profile of the crags that rim the lake's alpine basin is visible from here.

Alpine wildflowers like lupine and paintbrush greet hikers on the Lake Agnes Trail.

Point out these rock pinnacle formations, explaining that the hike's lake destination sits below and to the right of the Nokhu Crags.

Beginning in the spruce-fir forest, the trail crosses the creek and within 0.2 mile forks. Follow the trail to the right for 0.5 mile, climbing 400 feet through the hushed corridor of towering trees. The trail to the left, though a bit shorter (0.4 mile), follows a rocky ravine to the lake. Snowbanks remain in the protected areas of this drainage late in the summer, which may limit your return route to the same trail you hiked up.

The few furred and feathered residents of this high timber area have left their mark. During the walk, encourage youngsters to look

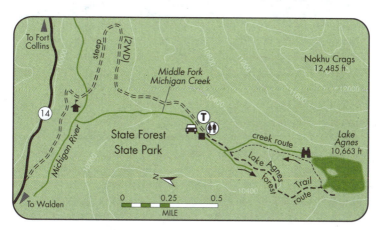

and listen for signs of wildlife. Spiderwebs, woodpecker-dimpled tree trunks, deer scat, and birdcalls are among the signs they may find. The creek splashes down the ravine on the left. But do look up and to the left where the Nokhu Crags (12,485 feet) pierce the sky like so many stone fingers. The other high summit here is Mount Richtofen (12,940 feet), the highest in the Never Summer Range.

Patches of snow linger through some summers, giving little human hands a chance to throw snowballs. Ask kids if all the patches of snow will melt away during the summer. Why not? How can today's snow here help them find north? Here and in other high-altitude walks, watch for pink-tinged "watermelon snow," colored by the cold-tolerant algae. It's not recommended for human consumption, but you might see snow worms or snow fleas consuming the snow algae.

As the Lake Agnes Trail nears a flattened talus rock area at 0.7 mile, watch for the headgate that steers a portion of the creek into a pipe. This water will eventually flow through water faucets in Fort Collins, nearly 100 miles away. Where the trail meets the lake, talus slopes lead to the water's edge, which invites fishing or simply rock skipping. Note the island in the lake forested with *krummholz*, trees shaped and stunted by winds.

The trail heading left (east, with the lake on your right) leads in 0.1 mile to the lake's outlet and the creek, and the beginning of the optional return route via the rocky, avalanche-swept creek bottom—a fun 0.4-mile path for those with strong knees. For the forest alternative, turn around and follow the same trail back.

GREAT GETAWAYS

To camp close to Hikes 70, 71, and 72, pitch your tent at Ranger Lakes Campground, my favorite of the four campgrounds located in State Forest State Park (970-723-8366), 75 miles west of Fort Collins. To reserve sites go to www.reserveAmerica.com or call (303) 470-1144 or (800) 678-2267.

Within the park you can follow the Beaver Lodge Nature Trail, a 0.7-mile interpretive loop or watch for signs of moose along the 2-mile, wheelchair-accessible Gould Trail loop. At Moose Visitor Center, Colorado's moose viewing capital, try on moose ears, listen to moose calls, and check out the forest's furred creatures, or head to the stocked Ranger Lakes for some fishing. Near the park you'll also find the Colorado Duck Refuge.

7 2 STATE FOREST STATE PARK, NATURE TRAILS

BEFORE YOU GO
Map State Forest State Park brochure
Information For current conditions and more information, contact Colorado State Forest State Park, www.parks.state.co.us/parks/stateforest or (970) 723-8366

ABOUT THE HIKE
Location Gould
Day hike; Easy
1.5 miles round-trip, Ranger Lakes Nature Trail; 0.5 mile, Mountain View Nature Trail; 0.7 mile, Beaver Lodge Trail
Hikable June to October, park open year-round
Starting elevation/High point 9280 feet/9380 feet
Accessibility None

GETTING THERE
From Fort Collins on CO-14, drive west 75 miles, passing through Rustic and continuing 8 miles west of Cameron Pass. Watch on the left for Colorado State Forest State Park's Moose Visitor Center, a large green-roofed building with wire-sculptured moose out front. The park entrance is on the left. The Ranger Lakes trailhead and parking area is 2.5 miles east of the visitor center.

LOGISTICS
Restrooms, drinking water, and parking are provided at the Moose Visitor Center, with ample parking available at each trailhead. Bring raingear, fishing gear, binoculars, and bug repellent. Several campgrounds as well as a yurt and cabins are available for rent here; call (800) 678-2267.

ON THE TRAIL
Consider the following three trails the "best of" introduction to Colorado's largest state park (71,000 acres). The interpretive trails feature family-friendly routes through forests and around lakes perfect for young anglers and the occasional moose grazing on willow. The trails are located in the park's southwest portion, easily accessed from Moose Visitor Center.

Before stepping onto a trail, step into the park's Moose Visitor Center. Here, while kids stand nose-to-nose with a stuffed moose, they'll see the sign posting the latest sighting of a real moose, elk, mink, otter, coyote,

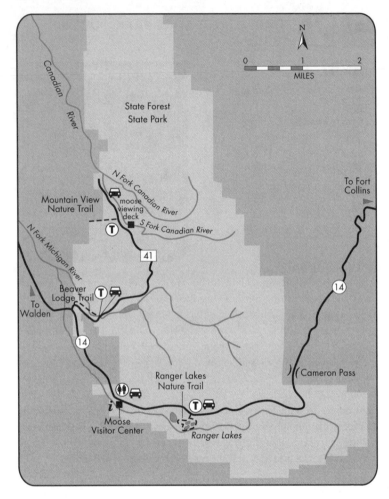

or fox in the park. You'll learn about the day's activities, like "Intro to GeoCaching," "Outdoor Cooking," and "Let's Get Humming." While wandering the center's extensive collection of guidebooks, nature gifts, and interactive exhibits, you'll discover the park's winter attractions, like glow stick–lit ski trails and the network of yurts, huts, and cabins to rent. Fishing licenses and geocache units are also available here.

Families with time for just one hike head to the Ranger Lakes trailhead, 2.5 miles east of the visitor center on CO-14. The trail's interpretive brochure alerts hikers to the subtleties of an ever-changing forest. They'll learn to spot a "nursery log" and how to feel a tree's needles to know if it's spruce, fir, or pine. (Spruce needles are square and spiky. Fir needles are flat and flexible. Lodgepole pine needles come in packages of two.) They'll see signs of dramatic changes in the managed forest, such as logging and thinning to allow sunlight on healthy trees. However, your crew will have witnessed a grand-scale shift in forest health during the drive to the park along CO-14, where massive swaths of dead trees are left standing as a result of the mountain pine beetle epidemic. Reassure your kids that the beetles are a

Columbines flower between large-leafed false hellebore.

natural force, affecting mostly crowded and aged trees. As the trees die, conditions change to allow a new forest to begin.

As the trail edges the trout-stocked lakes, the anglers in your group may see fish feeding, and fortunately, several fishing docks from which to cast their lines.

When nearing an area of lakeside willows, let the kids know they're in Colorado's "Moose Viewing Capital." They're likely to find moose scat (one-inch-long dry pellets) and tracks (two-toed hooves the length of a child's hand or longer). But their best chance at spotting a moose grazing in willows is during the twilight time around sunrise and sunset. Watch for subtle movements and sounds, like the flick of a moose's ear or the rustling of antlers moving through willow branches. Your family will want to try their luck at the park's moose viewing deck, located adjacent to the parking area for the Mountain View Nature Trail. To access the viewing deck and nature trail from Moose Visitor Center, drive 3 miles west on CO-14 to the junction of County Road 41, turn right and proceed about 7 miles. The viewing deck and parking are on the right and the trailhead is on the left. The platform overlooks willow-lined streams along the South Fork Canadian River, prime moose habitat. On the 1-mile Mountain View Nature Trail, your crew will discover geocaching, a fun hide-and-seek-in-nature game using GPS units, available to rent at the Moose Visitor Center.

On your return to CO-14, stop at the Beaver Lodge Trail (0.7 mile), located near the CO-14 and CR-41 intersection. The views of alpine wildflowers along the North Fork Michigan River, and perhaps a moose grazing by the river, will be your best memories of Colorado's State Forest State Park.

PAWNEE NATIONAL GRASSLANDS

BEFORE YOU GO
Map Pawnee National Grasslands brochure
Information For current conditions and more information, contact Pawnee National Grasslands, www.fs.fed.us/r2/arnf or (970) 346-5000

ABOUT THE HIKE
Location Pawnee National Grasslands
Day hike or backpack; Easy to moderate
1.5 miles one way to western butte; 2 miles one way to eastern butte
Hikable Year-round
Starting elevation/High point 5420 feet/5420 feet
Accessibility None

GETTING THERE

From Fort Collins, head east on CO-14 to Briggsdale, then continue east 13 miles to County Road 103; turn left. Drive 4 miles, and then turn right on CR-98; drive 0.75 mile to CR-105 in Keota. Follow CR-105 for 2.5 miles out of Keota; turn right on CR-104. Drive 3 miles to CR-111; turn left. Continue driving north 4.5 miles until the road takes a sharp bend to the west. Park in the lower lot or follow short, steep Forest Road 685 up and around to the top of the hill, where a windmill and signs mark the upper parking area and trailhead just north of it.

LOGISTICS

A portable toilet is available at the trailhead. Bring plenty of water, sunscreen, and a hat. Binoculars are recommended. This area is surrounded by private land; please respect landowners' rights. Camping

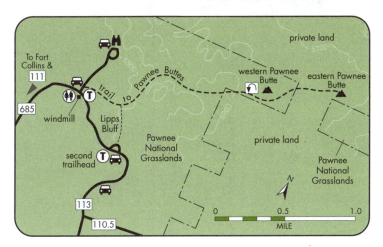

within the Pawnee Buttes area is not encouraged; developed camping facilities are provided at Crow Valley Campground in Briggsdale, off CO-14.

ON THE TRAIL

Pawnee National Grasslands is the prairie gem of northeastern Colorado. The trail leading to the two wind-scoured buttes crosses fields and gullies with limitless views in all directions. For kids, this nationally known study area for birds of prey is a wildlife wonderland to explore. A night visit under the grasslands' star canopy is long remembered.

Before starting your hike, drive or walk 0.3 mile to the overlook located just northeast of the trailhead parking area for a sweeping view of the Pawnee Buttes and the grasslands. Exploring kids should be warned that prairie rattlers tend to hang out in gullies and rock outcrops. Remind your climbers to place their hands only in places they can see clearly. The overlook and Lipps Bluff are closed from March 1 to June 30 for raptor nesting season. Do not climb through the fence if it is closed. Raptors such as golden eagles, prairie falcons, and ferringous hawks nest in the cliffs along the overlook. If people get close, raptors will abandon their nests, leaving their eggs and fledglings unprotected.

From the parking area near the windmill, follow the trail 0.2 mile down the small draw and across the prairie. You may encounter cows grazing here. Cross a gully and pass through a gate at 0.5 mile before reaching a saddle separating two bluffs.

Birds of prey nest on the bluffs of Pawnee Buttes.

The yucca plants here indicate the presence of the yucca moth, without which the yucca could not exist. During July nights, the female moth lays her eggs in the yucca flower. In doing so, she fertilizes the flower, which forms the yucca seeds. As the seeds ripen, the moth larvae feed on them, leaving enough for the plant to reseed year after year. North American Indians relied on yucca flowers and fruit as foods, crushed its roots to make soap, and used its leaves to make brooms, sandals, and rope. Ask kids to feel the sharp-bladed leaves and describe how they would use the plant.

At 0.7 mile, the trail descends into a badlands area, which is simply hills that have eroded over a long period of time. Explain that these landforms are composed of sediments (rock and sand) from a vast sea that covered this area 70 million to 90 million years ago when dinosaurs still roamed the region.

From here the trail dips into a gully twice before it enters a grassland near Lipps Bluff (on your right) with views of the westernmost of the two Pawnee Buttes. Continue on the recently reconstructed gravel trail toward the buttes. Great horned owls nest on the bluffs; their screeching may signal you are too near their territory. Watch for golden eagles that nest on the eastern buttes.

As the trail skirts the western butte at 1.5 miles, spring and summer visitors see swallows sweeping the sky near their mud-pellet nests in the cliffs. Bison roamed this area only 125 years ago; today you may see antelope grazing or the occasional deer in the draws. The western butte is a good turnaround point for a shorter hike.

One or both buttes may be the destination for some hikers; however, climbing them is not recommended due to their crumbly siltstone and sandstone composition. (Silt-laden streams left their sediment here between 5 million and 38 million years ago.) As this part of the trail crosses private property between the two buttes, please respect property rights.

In another 0.5 mile you reach the eastern butte, where prairie falcons that nest in the eastern bluff are particularly sensitive to intruders. (To protect raptor nesting habitat, some bluffs are closed to public access from March 1 to June 30. During the closure, please stay on the trail.) Stop to have the kids use binoculars to watch a bird circle over its prey, then swoop down to feed.

Return via the same trail.

BEST RIVERSIDE WALKS

Greeley

Local Greeley families know where to take the kids on the 20-mile Poudre River Trail. They park at the Poudre River Ranch Natural Area, then walk west exploring a narrow, river-edging path with sandstone bluffs on the left nearly touching their shoulders. This 1.5-mile section crosses the southern edge of the natural area with dirt trails leading to a small willow-framed lake perfect for young anglers. The cottonwood-shaded corridor leads to the Poudre Learning Center, another restroom, parking, play, and information source. Access the trail from the parking lot at North 71st Avenue and Cache la Poudre River Road.

www.poudretrail.org   (970) 336-4044

Fort Collins

See Hike 65, Poudre River Trail.

Steamboat Springs

The Yampa River Core Trail edges the town's waterway for 6 miles, from Walton Creek Road at CO-40 to the James Brown Bridge on Shield Drive. Many families begin their walk at the free Yampa River Botanic Garden, located just south of downtown off Trafalgar Drive. Sculptures, ponds, and earthen berms enhance the 6-acre park where dragonflies and butterflies enchant the kids while thirty different high-altitude gardens amaze the grown-ups. Continuing north on the river trail leads to downtown Steamboat Springs and parking at the 9th Street kiosk. Restrooms are seasonally available at the Trillium House in the botanic park.

www.steamboatsprings.net   (970) 879-4300

Estes Park

The River Walk along the Big Thompson River starts many families' visits to Rocky Mountain National Park. Beginning from the Estes Park Visitor Center, located just off CO-34, the 2-mile trail heads west through a shopping district adjacent to the lively river. Those walking east from the visitor center circle Lake Estes, where fishing and play boats can be rented. Restrooms, drinking water, and parking are provided at the Estes Park Visitor Center.

www.EstesParkCVB.com   (970) 577-9900

Opposite: Wildflowers tower over a toddler exploring Pass Creek Trail in the San Juan Mountains.

WEST/SOUTHWEST

GRAND JUNCTION, BLACK CANYON OF THE GUNNISON NATIONAL PARK, DURANGO AND THE SAN JUAN MOUNTAINS, AND MESA VERDE NATIONAL PARK

74 TRAIL THROUGH TIME

BEFORE YOU GO
Maps Colorado State Highway; Trail Through Time brochure (available at trailhead)
Information For current conditions and more information, contact the Bureau of Land Management, www.co.blm.gov/gjre or (970) 244-3000

ABOUT THE HIKE
Location Rabbit Valley Day hike; Moderate 1.5-mile loop
Hikable March to November
Starting elevation/High point 4700 feet/4820 feet
Accessibility None

GETTING THERE

From Grand Junction, take I-70 west 30 miles to the Rabbit Valley exit (exit 2). Turn right and park near the gate, but do not block it.

LOGISTICS

Toilet facilities are located near the trailhead, but bring your own drinking water. A perfect accompaniment to this hike is a visit to the Dinosaur Journey of the Museum of Western Colorado, a 17-mile drive east on I-70 to exit 19 at Fruita. Huge roboticized dinosaurs and paleontologists examining their finds are among the attractions at the hands-on science museum. Call (888) 488-3466 for information.

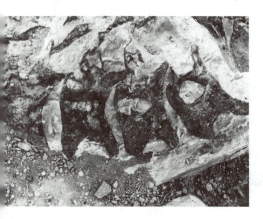

ON THE TRAIL

Imagine walking across a dry, windswept, rocky mesa, the drone of an interstate just out of earshot, and discovering dinosaur bones! Located only 30 miles west of Grand Junction in Rabbit

Fossilized Camarasaurus vertebrae are found along the Trail Through Time.

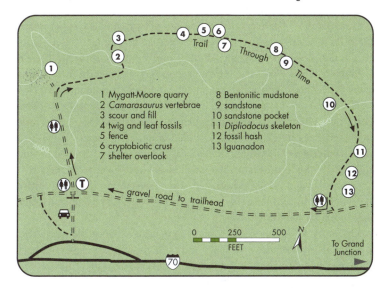

1 Mygatt-Moore quarry
2 *Camarasaurus* vertebrae
3 scour and fill
4 twig and leaf fossils
5 fence
6 cryptobiotic crust
7 shelter overlook
8 Bentonitic mudstone
9 sandstone
10 sandstone pocket
11 *Diplodocus* skeleton
12 fossil hash
13 Iguanodon

gravel road to trailhead

0   250   500   FEET

N

To Grand Junction

70

Valley, this interpreted stroll along a trail through a dinosaur quarry is a rewarding diversion for both dinosaur fans and rock hounds. Considered the southeastern tip of the Dinosaur Diamond—which extends southwest to Moab, Utah, north to Vernal, Utah, and west to Price, Utah—the Trail Through Time is riddled with fossilized dinosaur bones and plant material.

Before beginning the Trail Through Time, tell children that 140 million years ago this high desert was a lush floodplain dotted with lakes, forests, rivers, and ponds where dinosaurs roamed and flying reptiles soared. Amid giant ferns and heavy clouds, all that could be heard was the rumble of thunder, the buzz of insects, and the roar of prehistoric creatures. Perhaps the dinosaur devotee of your group can add to the picture.

At the parking area, an informative sign highlights the geologic history of the Rabbit Valley region. The trail brochure, available in a stand behind the sign, points out the geological and paleontological sites that might otherwise be overlooked. Go around the gate and walk the road 250 feet north of the parking area to where the trail begins. After seeing the 18-foot stretch of *Camarasaurus* vertebrae imbedded in rock at signpost 2, most hikers stay tuned for more signs of ancient remnants. Encourage youngsters to examine rocks along the trail, many of which are imprinted with plant fossils, the remnants of a dinosaur's diet.

Near signpost 4 are several impressions of twigs and leaves deposited 135 million years ago. Fossils were formed long, long ago when plants or animals were trapped, then buried under layers of dirt and sand (sediment). Over time, the layers turned to rock and the impression made by the plant or animal remained. Are fossils being made now?

Near signpost 6, take time to examine the dry, sandy soil. It's alive! The black, crusty stuff covering much of the untrampled terrain here is biological soil crust (sometimes called cryptobiotic crust). It is like a plant, composed of lichen, fungi, mosses, and algae that combine to bind and anchor the loose grains of sand. The spongy crust holds moisture, prevents erosion, and sometimes traps seeds. Plant communities develop from this vital soil layer. Advise children not to tread on it—this very valuable soil takes years to restore.

On rainy days, use caution near signpost 8. Bentonitic mudstone, a decomposed volcanic ash deposited millions of years ago, gets very slippery when wet. Stop to feel this fine-textured deposit.

At the trail's end, turn right and follow the gravel road 0.3 mile back to the parking area, looking skyward for eagles, hawks, and ravens soaring much higher than flying reptiles once did.

GREAT GETAWAYS

To round out Hike 74, add an overnight at Highline Lake State Park. Head 16 miles west of Grand Junction on I-70; take Loma exit 15; then go 6 miles north on CO-139. Reserve a site at www.coloradostateparks .reserveAmerica.com.

The two lakes in the park make it an ideal destination for boating, birding (200 bird species have been observed at the park), and swimming. There's also biking and hiking (kids love the 1-mile Blue Heron Pond Loop).

If you've got budding paleontologists in your family, there are several fantastic dinosaur destinations nearby. Four miles southwest of Fruita, you'll find a 0.5-mile interpretive loop trail at the Fruita Paleontological Site and 1.5 miles south of Fruita on CO-340 is the 1-mile Dinosaur Hill Interpretive Trail. At the interactive-oriented Museum of Western Colorado (www.museumofwesternco.com), located off I-70 in Fruita, you can check out the real bones of dinosaurs such as apatosaurus, stegosaurus, and allosaurus or walk the 0.75-mile Riggs Hill Loop Trail.

ALCOVE NATURE, CANYON RIM, AND WINDOW ROCK LOOP TRAILS

BEFORE YOU GO

Maps Colorado National Monument brochure; USGS Colorado National Monument
Information For current conditions and more information, contact Colorado National Monument Visitor Center, www.nps.gov/com or (970) 858-3617

ABOUT THE HIKE

Location Colorado National Monument
Day hike; Easy
0.3 mile one way, Alcove Nature Trail; 1.5-mile loop, Canyon Rim and Window Rock Trails
Hikable Year-round
Starting elevation/High point 5787 feet/5787 feet
Accessibility Wheelchair-accessible at visitor center

GETTING THERE

From Grand Junction, drive 12 miles west on I-70 and take exit 19 to Fruita, then continue for 2 miles on CO-340 to Colorado National Monument's west entrance. Proceed 4 very winding miles to the visitor center parking lot and park headquarters.

LOGISTICS

Toilet facilities and drinking water are available at the visitor center and at the campground west of the Window Rock Trail. There is a national monument entrance fee.

ON THE TRAIL

This collection of rambles through Colorado's high desert leads to overlook points that most kids say are "really cool." One of the few trails in Colorado National Monument far from a precipitous canyon rim, the Alcove Nature Trail serves as a delightful introduction to desert wildlife and geology. A loop on Canyon Rim and Window Rock trails rewards with views of the distant Book Cliffs and closer formations.

The Alcove Nature Trail begins just across from the visitor center. Two brochures accompany this thirty-one-site interpreted trail, the "Junior Ranger" version aimed at young hikers. Kids make their own discoveries along the trail, and the sagebrush lizard darting straight up a cliff is likely to delight them. Your companions can "feel" where the insect predator

Prickly pear cacti flower in the high desert of Colorado National Monument.

prefers to live by placing their hands on sand exposed to sun and in the shade. Encourage kids to imagine that the sand remaining on their hands is composed of granules from the bottom of lakes that covered this dry landscape millions of years ago. Return via the same trail.

The Canyon Rim Trail begins behind the visitor center at the bottom of the stairs. From a safe distance, the trail parallels Wedding Canyon with a view of Independence Monument, once part of the massive rock wall between Wedding and Independence canyons. Weathering forces eroded most of the wall, leaving behind the remaining freestanding monolith.

Utah juniper, the most common tree here, is best known by humans and animals for its frosty blue berries. Explain to your companions that Native Americans ground the seeds of the fruit into a meal. The berries, when crushed, produce a distinctive odor. Point out the tree's fibrous bark. Imagine pounding it, as the Ute Indians did, into a soft diaper for babies!

Within 0.5 mile, the trail heads northeast to a car-accessible overlook where panoramic views of the Book Cliffs line the horizon. Why do you think this towering palisade that extends into Utah was so named? From here the sandstone artistry of spires within Colorado National Monument can be viewed. Shaped by wind, water, ice, and heat, only

stone fingers remain where a plateau of less weather-resistant rock once stood. Look for the slender monoliths named Kissing Couple, Praying Hands, and Pipe Organ. Kids often have different names for the images they see in the formations.

Continue on the brief paved portion of the trail, which overlooks the Book Cliffs. Below, the Colorado River serpentines the Grand Valley's rich farmland. After leaving the Book Cliffs viewpoint, the short route to Window Rock becomes a dirt pathway, not well defined but usually marked by footprints. However, do stay on the trail. Biological soil crust (also called cryptobiotic crust), the dark, lumpy crust that "holds the place in place," takes years to reestablish itself after it's been damaged. Allow kids a close investigation of this plant community composed of fungi, moss, algae, and lichen.

When you intersect the Window Rock Trail, turn right, and at 0.7 mile the "window" of Window Rock appears in the stone wall, seen from behind a fence at the trail's end. The window began as a crack and has been carved out over thousands of years by the relentless forces of wind and water erosion.

To return, follow the Window Rock Trail back to the sheltered Book Cliff overlook at about 1 mile, and turn right to walk west on the roadside back to the visitor center parking lot.

 MICA MINE

GETTING THERE

In Grand Junction at First Street and Grand Avenue, head west 1 mile on Grand Avenue (CO-340) and turn left on Monument Road. Turn left

Bits of sunlit mica glisten near the mouth of Mica Mine.

at D Road, which becomes Rosevale Road. Turn right onto Little Park Road, driving 5.5 miles to the Bangs Canyon trailhead and the parking lot on the left.

LOGISTICS

The trail is open to pedestrians and horseback riders; bicycles are prohibited, however. Water facilities are not provided, so bring plenty of drinking water.

ON THE TRAIL

A ten-year-old told me, "It's a trail covered in sparkly fairy dust that goes to a cool, shiny cave." Her mom added, "The trail to Mica Mine gives me a good dose of sandstone serenity." Considered Grand Junction's classic, and no doubt prettiest hike, the trail follows Ladder Canyon's shaded streambed to the Mica Mine. It's best experienced in spring or fall, when the stream flows or the cottonwoods glow in shades of gold. However, a cloudy, breezy summer day can be comfortable in the canyon, as it was during our midday hike in July.

From the parking lot, follow the wide, rocky path as it descends 0.1 mile to the junction of the Rough Canyon and Mica Mine trails. Head right on the Mica Mine Trail, entering the leafy canyon bottom. Throughout the hike the trail threads stands of cottonwood, sage, pinyon, and juniper, edging the stream and then following a less rocky route. The first stream crossing is at 0.5 mile. Depending on the season and the age of your crew, expect to stop for balance games on rocks

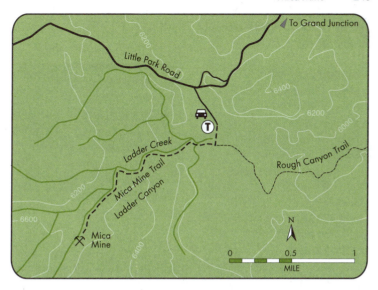

spanning a pool or to scramble up to a kid-sized overhang in the canyon wall. Numerous spur trails lead to and from the stream, but there's little concern of losing someone in this narrow canyon.

Looking up at about 0.9 mile, watch for large thumbs of sandstone along the horizon. At your feet you'll start to see flecks of mica sparkling amidst milky white quartz fragments scattered on the trail. Kids will want to pocket these treasures, but encourage them to keep walking; there's much more in store. As the trail nears the mine, mica and quartz particles become so thick, it appears to be a snow-covered path.

With a bit of mica, show your companions how it splits, paper thin, into distinct layers. Explain that mica is also called isinglass and was used as small windows in wood- or coal-burning stoves. To appreciate its glass-like characteristic, hold a thin layer of mica up to the sun. Note how mica glimmers in sunlight, then becomes a plain gray rock when clouds diminish the light. Save this mica close-up until after the kids have had a chance to explore the mine.

Where the canyon walls seem to converge into a cluster of oak and cottonwood, look up and to the left. The cliff of pink, rose, bright white, and gray rock is the source of all the mica and quartz. The two alcoves you see are the areas once mined, inviting the climber in your group, eager to explore the seemingly endless supply of shiny booty.

Return via the same trail.

WEST BENCH TRAIL

BEFORE YOU GO
Maps Grand Mesa National Forest; USGS Mesa Lakes, USGS Lands End
Information For current conditions and more information, contact Grand Valley Ranger District, www.fs.fed.us/r2/gmug or (970) 242-8211

ABOUT THE HIKE
Location Grand Mesa
Day hike; Easy to moderate
3.4 miles one way
Hikable Year-round
Starting elevation/High point 9800 feet/9900 feet
Accessibility None

GETTING THERE
From Grand Junction, travel east on I-70 24 miles to exit 49, turning right onto CO-65. Drive south 25 miles to Jumbo Reservoir near Mesa Lakes Resort. Turn right and follow the road to the Mesa Lakes Ranger Station, where parking is provided. Or, from the Grand Mesa Visitor Center, travel north on CO-65 for 8 miles to Jumbo Reservoir and follow the directions above.

LOGISTICS
Drinking water and toilet facilities are provided at Jumbo Reservoir and Glacier Springs campgrounds.

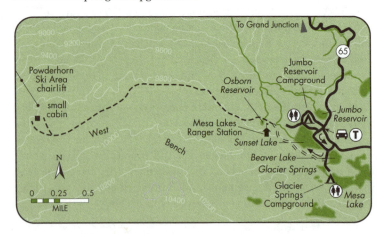

ON THE TRAIL

A popular path for hikers, bikers, and skiers, the West Bench Trail leads through aspen forest and groves of spruce and fir before ending in the meadows at the top of Powderhorn Ski Area. Summer's wildflowers and autumn's aspen glow add memorable color to every hike on this trail.

Starting at Sunset Lake, cross its dam into a residential cabin area, arriving at a gravel road in 0.4 mile; follow this to the right about 0.6 mile to the trailhead. The trail begins in a wooded area just beyond the group of vacation cabins.

During my late-summer visit here, I watched a short-tailed weasel, also called an ermine, dart through the downed trees and brush of this area. Colorado's smallest carnivore, less than 10 inches long and weighing only 6 ounces, swiftly attacks animals several times its size. Quiet hikers on talus slopes or around rocky outcroppings are rewarded with sightings of weasels hunting mice, pikas, and chipmunks. Colorado has two species of weasel. The long-tailed weasel, two times larger, lives at elevations lower than 8000 feet. In winter both weasel species turn white, with just the tip of their tail remaining black.

The trail's first 0.2 mile edges Osborn Reservoir, a small, often dry pond, as it rises gently to the West Bench, a long, elevated portion of Grand Mesa. The black boulders and rocks here are remnants of the volcanic rock layer that capped this region 10 million years ago. Encourage your companions to watch for rocks that look like black sponges. Help them understand how hot lava in contact with water caused steam to form holes in the rocks.

Skiers, however, watch the blue markers tagging trees and tall poles as the trail continues placidly through aspen forest and open fields. Does the pole height give clues to the winter snow depth here? Note the difference in air temperature as the trail begins a gentle climb from a sunny field into the shaded forest. At about 2 miles the trail reaches its high point (9900 feet).

In aspen forests like these, hikers

Views from the West Bench Trail include the Book Cliffs, Roan Cliffs, and chairlifts of Powderhorn Ski Area.

often claim "eyes" (limb scars) on aspen trees are following them. Instead, ask your hikers to keep their eyes open for clawlike scarring on the aspen trunks. In August, male elk rub the blood-gorged velvet off their antlers, leaving scarred trees. Female deer gnawing on aspen bark also leave their mark, as does a bear swiping its claws across the trunk. Can your sleuths tell the difference?

At about 2.5 miles, the trail crosses a shallow creek and winds through aspens for 0.2 mile, then forks into a meadow. Follow the route to the right to a small ski patrol cabin and the top of a chairlift, your destination. (Some hikers bypass the right turn and continue hiking 2 miles to Powderhorn Ski Area's second chairlift to the bench.) While you enjoy lunch here, views of Book Cliffs to the left, separated by the Colorado River (which cannot be seen) from the Roan Cliffs on the right, are worth noting.

Return via the same trail.

 MESA LAKE SHORELINE TRAIL

BEFORE YOU GO
Map Grand Mesa brochure
Information For current conditions and more information, contact the Grand Mesa Visitor Center, www.fs.usda.gov/gmug or (970) 856-4153

ABOUT THE HIKE
Location Grand Mesa
Day hike; Easy
1.5-mile loop
Hikable Mid-June through September
Starting elevation/High point 9900 feet/9900 feet
Accessibility Paved picnic area adjacent to trailhead

GETTING THERE
From Grand Junction, take I-70 east to exit 49 (CO-65) and Mesa. Drive southeast on CO-65 for about 25 miles. Turn right at the Forest Service sign for Mesa Lake, passing a cabin and resort area and turning left at the bottom of a hill. In 0.5 mile, you will arrive at Glacier Springs Picnic Grounds and parking area located between Mesa and Beaver lakes.

From Delta, head east on CO-92 approximately 4 miles to CO-65. Turn left (north) and travel 25 miles to Mesa Lake.

LOGISTICS
Restrooms are provided at trailhead. No drinking water is available here.

ON THE TRAIL

Of Grand Mesa's many family-friendly destinations, the Mesa Lake Shoreline Trail tops the list for hikers, anglers, solitude seekers, and the kid in anyone. It's a high-country sampler that threads forests of aspen and spruce, crosses streams, traverses a talus slope, and passes a beaver pond while edging a trout-stocked lake.

To circle the lake in a clockwise direction, head east (left) from the trailhead, located behind the restroom. Within 0.2 mile you'll meet pavement; veer left about 50 yards to return to the Mesa Lake Shoreline Trail (#503).

Anglers of all ages fish the many lakes of Grand Mesa.

While edging the lake's eastern shore at 0.6 mile, you'll cross the bottom of a talus slope smothered in large, sharp-edged rocks. The path made through the talus allows for easy walking.

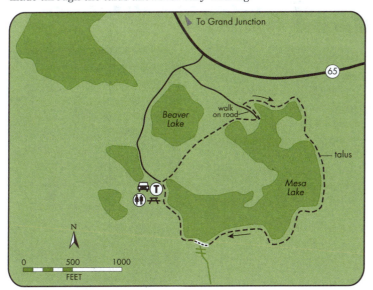

Listen for the high-pitched whistle of a yellow-bellied marmot, and you're likely to spot the chunky ground squirrel lounging on a sunny rock. Commonly called "whistle pigs," marmots spend their summers preparing for winter by eating, storing up to 60 percent of their body weight in fat. Your kids may see this rodent's smaller rock-dwelling neighbor, the pika, scampering across the slope. They have a better chance of seeing this "haymaker's" trademark, a bundle of grasses drying on rocks before it's cached deep in the talus.

Just beyond the rock slope, point out the spruce trees growing within a mature aspen stand, soon to crowd them out. In this way, forests are continually regenerating.

Several drainages spill into Mesa Lake, often spanned by a boardwalk. At 1.3 miles children tend to stop where a small waterfall, originating from Lost Lake, spills alongside and under the boardwalk. From here the trail returns to the start, with Beaver Lake on your left.

For more fun on Grand Mesa, head to the Grand Mesa Visitor Center, located at the junction of CO-65 and Forest Road 121 near Island and Ward lakes (see Hike 79). Numerous kid-friendly trails originate here with staff on hand to answer questions and lead interpretive programs.

CRAG CREST NATIONAL RECREATION TRAIL

BEFORE YOU GO
Maps Grand Mesa National Forest; USGS Grand Mesa
Information For current conditions and more information, contact the Grand Mesa Visitor Center, www.fs.fed.us/r2/gmug or (970) 856-4153

ABOUT THE HIKE
Location Grand Mesa
Day hike; Moderate to challenging
1.4 miles one way to Forrest Lake; 2 miles one way to Crag Crest; 6.5 miles one way to west trailhead; 9.4-mile loop
Hikable Late June to mid-September
Starting elevation/High point 10,150 feet/11,189 feet
Accessibility None

Ward Lake Recreation Area

GETTING THERE

From I-70 east of Grand Junction, take CO-65 east 35 miles to the Grand Mesa Visitor Center. Turn east on FR 121, traveling 3.5 miles, passing Eggleston Lake. Continue on to the Crag Crest Campground. Parking for hikers is in the lot opposite the campground. For a 6.5-mile one-way hike, leave a shuttle vehicle parked at the west trailhead, located on CO-65, 0.5 mile west of the Grand Mesa Visitor Center.

LOGISTICS

Toilet facilities and drinking water are available at the campground. Mosquito repellent is advised for most hikes on the Grand Mesa.

ON THE TRAIL

Whether you hike a gentle trail to secluded Forrest Lake or make the vigorous climb to Crag Crest on the world's largest flattop mountain, hikers of all abilities can enjoy Grand Mesa. Colorado's evergreen island in the sky is home to more than 300 lakes.

From the eastern trailhead adjacent to Crag Crest Campground, the trail forks within 0.1 mile. To the right is the route to Crag Crest, described below.

To the left, a mellow 1.4-mile trail heads west to Forrest Lake, a fine destination for those with shorter legs and less endurance. (On some USGS maps, this lake is labeled Upper Hotel Lake.) The first 0.3 mile of the Forrest Lake Trail requires a bit of exertion before it levels off in an old-growth spruce forest. Clumps of stringy moss hanging from these

Marmots typically perch on the rocky terrain above the treeline at Crag Crest.

trees intrigue young hikers. This growth, which some call old man's beard, is actually named black lichen, at one time an important food for Native Americans. Tell children the lichen was traditionally prepared by stewing it with onions over low heat. Ask, "Does that sound like something you would like to eat?" Time spent splashing in the creek that drains from this forest-fringed lake, followed by a picnic lunch on its shore, is a delightful way to enjoy this destination.

From the eastern trailhead, those taking the right fork to hike to Crag Crest or the entire loop first meet Upper Eggleston Lake within 0.7 mile, its still waters rippled by jumping trout; Bullfinch Reservoir is 0.5 mile farther. Dog-toothed violets (or glacier lily, a yellow lily with two long, shiny leaves) flower as the snow melts in the forest undergrowth here. This edible plant has a potato-like bulb and a seed pod that when cooked tastes similar to green beans.

After passing the sign for Butts Lake at 1.2 miles, the trail continues heading north, zigzagging 1000 feet to the crest. Soon the aspen-fir forest gives way to open, treeless vistas. Stay tuned to the trail here and watch for steep drop-offs on both sides. As the trail passes an area covered with lava rock, tell kids that the rocks are indicators of the 400-foot-thick lava layer that blanketed this mountain 10 million years ago. Have them feel the surprisingly lightweight red-black lava.

At 2 miles, the 360-degree view from Crag Crest, a rocky pinnacle surrounded by outstanding mountain vistas, includes the Book and Roan cliffs to the northwest. The rugged, lava-topped mountain directly north is Battlement Mesa. The highest point to the east is 11,234-foot Leon Peak. Also in this direction are the Elk Mountains and the Anthracite Range. To the south are Gunnison Peak, Uncompahgre Peak, the San Juan Mountains, and Lone Cone. Far to the west are the Uncompahgre Plateau and the La Sal Mountains of eastern Utah. Some hikers head back from here on the same trail.

Those continuing the hike to Crag Crest's western trailhead follow its narrow spine for 3 miles. At the sign for the Cottonwood Lakes Trail at 5 miles, turn left. Continue heading south for 1 mile as the trail gradually descends to the quiet confines of spruce and fir forest. At the next trail intersection, at 6 miles, turn right to reach the west trailhead in 0.5 mile; to return to the eastern trailhead via the loop route, turn left. This 3.4-mile trail heads east with several short climbs and descents as it passes through meadows and forest.

At about 8 miles, near the north–south trail to Forrest Lake, continue heading east (straight ahead) 1.4 miles before meeting the eastern trailhead.

GREAT GETAWAYS

No reservations are required at Jumbo Reservoir Campground, 45 miles east of Grand Junction in Grand Mesa National Forest (www.fs.fed.us /r2.gmug, 970-242-8211), which is your best bet near Hikes 77, 78, and 79.

There are a couple of excellent short hikes in this national forest: the 0.5-mile guided Discovery Trail that begins at Grand Mesa Visitor Center, and the 0.5-mile paved Land o' Lakes Trail, which has three awesome overlooks of the San Juan Mountains, Roan Cliffs, and Grand Mesa's lakes.

Grand Mesa's lakes offer opportunities for non-motorized boating and are a fishing paradise, especially Ward and Alexander lakes. And don't miss the Grand Mesa Visitor Center for its broad selection of nature books and interactive exhibits.

 WARNER POINT NATURE TRAIL

BEFORE YOU GO
Map Black Canyon of the Gunnison National Park brochure
Information For current conditions and more information, contact Black Canyon of the Gunnison National Park, www.nps.gov /blca or (970) 641-2337

ABOUT THE HIKE
Location Black Canyon of the Gunnison National Park
Day hike; Easy to moderate
0.7 mile one way
Hikable May to October
Starting elevation/High point 8289 feet/8302 feet
Accessibility None

GETTING THERE

From Montrose, drive east on US 50 for 6 miles to CO-347. Turn left and continue 7.5 miles to the Black Canyon of the Gunnison National Park visitor center. Then proceed another 6.2 miles to the trailhead parking area.

LOGISTICS

Toilet facilities are available near the parking area. Drinking water is available at the visitor center. There is a national park entrance fee.

ON THE TRAIL

The walk to Warner Point follows a roller-coaster path along a ridge offering awesome views of the Black Canyon. Kids love exploring the varied terrain, scrambling up and down each little summit on the trail. Benches along the way serve as destinations for small hikers or as delightful spots from which to enjoy this high-desert garden.

At the trailhead, you can pick up a copy of the Warner Point Nature Trail guidebook. Stop here to have children experience the spicy fragrance of sagebrush by rubbing a few of its gray-green leaves between their fingers.

The trail begins in a stand of pinyons and junipers, many of which are gnarled and twisted by the area's weather extremes. Size can be deceiving under such conditions. These trees, though short in stature,

Views from Warner Point Nature Trail include the Gunnison River snaking through the Black Canyon.

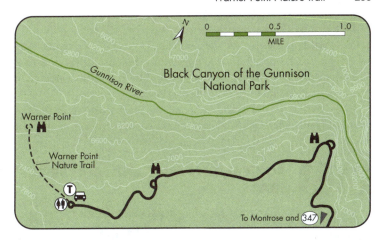

are hundreds of years old. What makes them look so old? Pinyons along the trail bear scars made by porcupines dining on their bark. Watch for trees that are girdled by porcupine gnawings. In such cases, the tree's water and nutrient system has been cut off and the ancient tree will die. Decaying trees host many species of insects and animals, which explains why park officials do not remove them.

Another common inhabitant here is the mountain mahogany bush. During summer months, the bush's long (2 to 3 inches), feathery seed tails coil and straighten in response to changes in moisture. Have kids look for seed plumes that have started working their way into the ground. As you look skyward at signpost 4, the San Juan Mountains etch the horizon. Below them are green, irrigated meadows that contrast with the surrounding dry land.

After signpost 5, the trail follows a narrow hogback with dizzying views into Black Canyon. Guardrails do not edge these cliffs and overlooks, so keep an eye on little ones. From this perspective, kids see why the canyon was named "Black." In 1881 the railroad construction crew laying rails for the "Scenic Line of the World," which ran at the eastern end of the canyon, called their workplace the Black Canyon because, they complained, they never saw the sun during their winter's work. (A number of early workers and explorers claim this story true; however, the railroad did not run in this part of the canyon.) The mountain range in the distance is called the West Elks. Look to the right for views of the Gunnison River while walking toward signpost 7. It took 2 million years for the river to carve this gorge called the Black Canyon.

Just beyond the rest bench between signposts 13 and 14, the trail becomes flat as it approaches Warner Point. This wide-open vista allows an unparalleled look at the Gunnison River and the varying rock formations of this canyon. Be extra watchful here of those who tend to roam; there are no guardrails at the overlook.

Return via the same trail, and leave the trail brochure in the box near the trailhead. If you wish to keep it, leave the requested amount in the box.

81 BOX CANYON FALLS AND HIGH BRIDGE TRAILS

BEFORE YOU GO
Map City of Ouray Box Canyon Park
Information For current conditions and more information, contact the City of Ouray, www.ci.ouray.co.us or (970) 325-7211

ABOUT THE HIKE
Location Box Canyon Park
Day hike; Easy
1.1 miles round-trip
Hikable May to October
Starting elevation/High point 7900 feet/8100 feet
Accessibility first 0.1 mile

GETTING THERE

On US 550, 0.5 mile south of Ouray, turn right onto the Camp Bird Road/County Road 361, then turn right again onto the one-way loop road leading to Box Canyon Park's visitor center and ample parking.

LOGISTICS

Toilet facilities, interpretive information, and a trail guide are available at the visitor center. There is a park entrance fee.

ON THE TRAIL

Nestled in the heart of the San Juan Skyway, one of America's most scenic drives, the two trails to Box Canyon Falls offer equal impact. The cool, misty (and easy) walk to the falls leads deep into a cleft in the canyon where Canyon Creek thunders 285 feet from the creek bed above. The sunny but steep portion of the hike offers grand views of the region as it leads to the top of the falls.

From the visitor center, turn right onto the Native Plant Loop that connects to the Box Canyon Falls Trail. Interpretive panels guide hikers

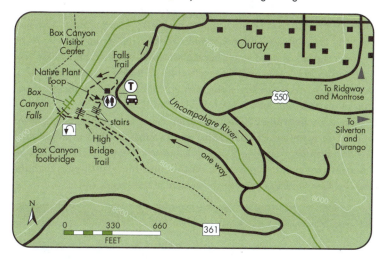

along the 0.1-mile walk to the falls. The rock wall to the west of the falls, as seen from the suspension bridge, shows a famous "discontinuity" of 1.6 billion years, evidenced in the lower vertical strata and the upper horizontal one. Perhaps the young geologists in your group will find the differences.

Despite being short and easy, the Falls Trail requires adult supervision. Steep cliffs and swift running water are the attractions here but also the danger to kids who step away from the fenced walkway. Also, many youngsters need an adult's hand to hold as they approach the roaring falls on a walkway suspended over rushing Canyon Creek. After they've reached the falls, many scamper down the stairs to a rocky, unfenced area near the creek. Supervision is necessary here as well.

Let your companions know the rock that forms this canyon is Colorado's

A hiker in Box Canyon watches Canyon Creek thunder down 285 feet of Precambrian rock.

oldest, formed in the Precambrian era nearly 2 billion years ago. Explain that the force of water from Canyon Creek eroded a fault in the rock, shaping the box-shaped slot. This high-altitude riparian area hosts two rare fern species that may be spotted in a shaded rock nook. Return via the same trail veering right, turning right up the metal staircase marked with a sign for the High Bridge Trail.

The 0.5-mile trail's 200-foot elevation gain offers unparalleled views of the Ouray valley, Cascade Falls, and two major volcanic formations, the Amphitheater and the Blowout. Enjoy the breath-catching views at the trail's top point, then return via the same route, turning right onto the Box Canyon Falls Trail at the bottom of the stairs.

GREAT GETAWAYS

Close to Hikes 81 and 82 you'll find Ridgway State Park (970-626-5822), which is 16 miles north of Ouray. Go to www.reserveAmerica.com or call (303) 470-1144 or (800) 678-2267 to reserve campsites.

At Ridgway Reservoir you can swim or rent paddleboats, aqua-cycles, kayaks, or canoes at Ridgway Marina. Or head to Ouray for a splash at Ouray Natural Hot Springs pool or for a 0.2-mile hike to Lower Cascade Falls and Trail (the trailhead is at the east end of Eighth Avenue in Ouray).

 BABY BATHTUBS TRAIL

BEFORE YOU GO
Map USGS Ouray
Information For current conditions and more information, contact Ouray Trails, www.ouraytrails.org or (970) 626-3399

ABOUT THE HIKE
Location Ouray
Day hike; Easy
0.3 mile one way
Hikable Mid-May through September
Starting elevation/High point 8100 feet/8280 feet
Accessibility None

GETTING THERE
From Ouray, take US 550 south 1.1 miles, turning east (left) on to the Amphitheater Campground Road. Continue approximately 0.2 mile to just before the bridge; park on the left.

LOGISTICS

Drinking water and toilet facilities are available at the Amphitheater Campground, another 0.6 mile east on the right.

ON THE TRAIL

Youngsters are eager to hike this irresistibly named trail along Portland Creek. They also love to dip their feet in the water-scoured pockets

A beginning hiker with big companions explores the edges of Portland Creek.

in the colorful rock of the streambed. On sunny summer days, this short hike often becomes an afternoon's delight.

The trailhead is on the right just past the bridge. In 500 feet, the trail crosses the North Fork Portland Creek, allowing many options for feet bathing as well as mountain viewing. The trail then follows the main fork of Portland Creek to a footbridge over the creek at 0.3 mile. The Baby Bathtubs Trail is a small part of the Ouray Perimeter Trail, a 4.2-mile loop that when completed will feature the town's waterfalls, a walk through a tunnel, and magnificent views of the area. Information on the trail is available at the Ouray Chamber Resort Visitor Center (1230 Main Street) and at the website above.

From the footbridge, return via the same trail.

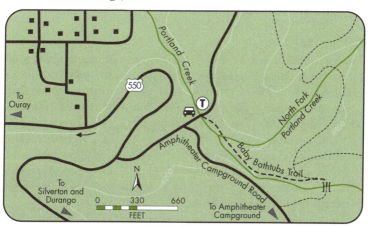

83 ICE LAKE TRAIL

BEFORE YOU GO

Maps San Juan National Forest; USGS Ophir

Information For current conditions and more information, contact the Columbine Ranger District, www.fs.fed.us/r2/sanjuan or (970) 247-4874

ABOUT THE HIKE

Location San Juan National Forest

Day hike or backpack; Challenging

0.6 mile one way to waterfall;
2.5 miles one way to lower lake;
3.5 miles one way to upper lake

Hikable Mid-June to mid-September

Starting elevation/High point 9850 feet/12,257 feet

Accessibility None

GETTING THERE

From Silverton, take US 550 northeast for 2 miles and turn left on Forest Road 585 leading to the South Mineral Campground. Drive 4.1 miles to a parking area alongside the road across from the campground.

LOGISTICS

Toilet facilities are available at the campground. As with all high-altitude hikes, begin this one early in the day before afternoon thunderstorms. Camp at least 200 feet away from lakeshores to protect the fragile environment.

ON THE TRAIL

The Ice Lake Trail is a deceptively challenging walk to a decidedly magnificent destination. Engineered with shallow switchbacks to minimize steepness, the trail leads to two Ice Lake basins, lower and upper. Both are rewarding destinations for eager day hikers or overnight campers. This is a popular trail throughout the summer.

From the parking area, gentle switchbacks through a softly padded forest floor begin the trail as it heads west. At 0.6 mile, a spur trail to the right leads about 0.1 mile to a destination for little hikers: a waterfall splashing 400 feet down a granite wall. Hold on to little hands for this view. Return to the Ice Lake Trail.

The trail continues switchbacking for another 0.8 mile to where

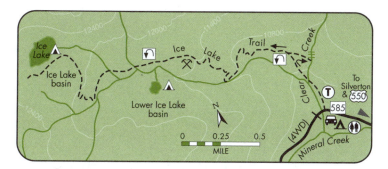

a stout railroad tie serves as a footbridge across a clear creek at 1.1 miles. About 0.5 mile from here, the remnants of a mining structure stand nestled in aspens on the left side of the trail at 1.6 miles. Remind your companions that this and other patented mining claims should be treated with the same respect as private property.

The trail continues westerly through a spruce-fir forest until it opens to the panorama of the lower basin at 2 miles. Though too shallow for fishing, Lower Ice Lake sits in a verdant basin offering splendid views of the mountains that rim this valley. The area surrounding the lake is flat, affording a multitude of campsites, rest spots, or day-hike destinations.

The trail to Ice Lake remains relatively level until it reaches the rocky hillside at the end of the lower basin at 3 miles. Bright blue columbine and red Indian paintbrush canopy the trail as it climbs for the last 0.5 mile.

During breath-catching stops, it's fun to watch and listen for noisy rock-dwelling rodents, the pika and the yellow-bellied marmot. More often heard than seen, the pika keeps busy all summer gathering its winter stash, which amounts to as much as five bushels! Look for its miniature bundles of grass drying on the rocks. In contrast is the marmot, lazily sunning itself while accumulating his winter food— nothing more than extra layers of fat! When snow blankets these mountains, the marmot's heart slows down to one beat every twelve to fifteen seconds. Have kids compare that number to their own heart rates. The pika, however, scampers about year-round, its furry claws helping it grip ice. Ask which of the two mountain dwellers they'd like to be, and why.

When you reach the (upper) Ice Lake basin, help your crew identify each of the surrounding peaks. They are, from the south around west

Columbines line the trail to Ice Lake.

to the north: Fuller Peak (13,767 feet), Vermilion Peak (13,894 feet), Golden Horn (13,600 feet), Pilot Knob (13,738 feet), and Ulysses S. Grant Peak (13,767 feet). Watch for an equally grand show at your feet. During mid- to late summer, herds of "little red elephants" show their rows of pink spikes to admirers who kneel close. King's crown, with its fleshy leaves and maroon top hat, reigns over the wet soils.

Return via the same path.

GREAT GETAWAYS

The stunning mountain setting of South Mineral Campground, 7 miles west of Silverton on FR 585, is the place to grab a first-come, first-served campsite near Hikes 83 and 84.

From the campground you can enjoy hiking along the popular, unmaintained 0.5-mile trail alongside Mineral Creek to South Mineral Waterfalls or fishing for brook and rainbow trout in South Mineral Creek.

If the gold mining history of the region sparks your kids' curiosity, head to Animas Forks, a well-preserved historic town 12 miles northeast of Silverton off CR-2 or take the Old Hundred Gold Mine tour (970-387-5444), 5 miles northeast of Silverton on CR-2, where you can ride the mine's original battery-powered train 1600 feet into Galena Mountain and see gold flakes shimmer in your pan at the mine's sluice boxes.

 HIGHLAND MARY LAKES TRAIL

BEFORE YOU GO
Map USGS Howardsville
Information For current conditions and more information, contact the Columbine Ranger District, www.fs.fed.us/r2 /sanjuan or (970) 247-4874

ABOUT THE HIKE
Location Weminuche Wilderness
Day hike or backpack; Moderate to challenging 3.5 miles one way
Hikabie Late June through September
Starting elevation/High point 10,478 feet/12,090 feet
Accessibility None

GETTING THERE
From Silverton, take Greene Street north, turning right on County Road 2 (formerly CO-110). Follow this road 4.2 miles east, turning right (south) at Cunningham Gulch. Continue another 4 miles on Forest Road 589, Cunningham Gulch Road, bypassing the four-wheel-drive roads turning up the mountainside. All but the last 0.7 mile of the drive is passable for two-wheel-drives; parking is available here. Those in four-wheel-drive vehicles continue driving on the road, crossing Cunningham Creek, and park by the registration box.

An elk grazes on highland grasses and willows.

LOGISTICS

Raingear is recommended for all high-altitude explorations; start this one early and don't proceed if the sky looks threatening. The Highland Mary Trail is in the Weminuche Wilderness; please respect regulations that protect this fragile area. Campsites at the Highland Mary Lakes must be at least 200 feet from the lakeshore. Firewood is not available above timberline.

ON THE TRAIL

This alpine hike leads to several lakes that jewel a large and open tundra basin above timberline. The trail climbs steadily uphill, crossing and recrossing Cunningham Creek and several side streams; pack extra socks and a walking stick for the wet conditions. Include a camera and flower guide in your pack as well. Fishing is rated fair at the lakes for rainbow, brook, and cutthroat trout. Nights here are remembered as stellar events.

The trail begins its climb on the west side of Cunningham Creek. At about 0.5 mile it passes a trail heading east to the Continental Divide. The Highland Mary Trail levels briefly before reaching another eastbound route at 1 mile (both of these connect a short distance east). Continue heading south, ascending 800 feet up Cunningham Gulch over the next 2 miles through highlands, marshes, and meadows. Ask your companions to count the number of times they cross the creek, promising an award (an extra energy bar?) to the hiker with the driest feet for the day. Scan the mountainsides for old mines, remnants of the mining frenzy that took place here and in most parts of the San Juan Mountains.

Wildflowers appear to compete for "best in show" along much of the trail, providing another breath-catching diversion for your group as they judge for "brightest pinks," "tallest blues," "most columbines," or categories they choose. During these and other pauses in wet alpine terrain, remind hikers to stay on the trail or a rock when possible; the plants here face enough challenges already.

At 3.5 miles the first and smallest of the Highland Mary Lakes is on your left, followed by the second largest on your right. Continue on the

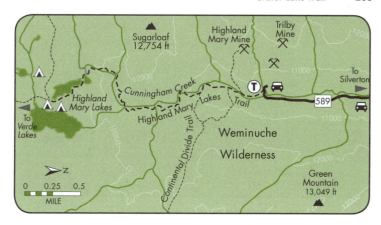

main trail as it passes between the two lakes, then heads south to reach the third and largest of the lakes. The lush green alpine landscape surrounding the lakes promises excellent fishing, regardless of the catch. Hikers eager to explore this relatively level alpine basin can walk 0.5 mile south to the Verde Lakes. Views of the prominent peaks here include Sugarloaf (12,754 feet) to the northwest and Whitehead Peak (13,225 feet) to the west.

85 CRATER LAKE TRAIL

BEFORE YOU GO
Map USGS Snowden Peak
Information For current conditions and more information, contact the Columbine Ranger District, www.fs.fed.us/r2/sanjuan or (970) 247-4874

ABOUT THE HIKE
Location Weminuche Wilderness
Day hike or overnight backpack; Moderate to challenging
5.5 miles one way
Hikable Late May to mid-October
Starting elevation/High point 10,744 feet/11,634 feet
Accessibility Wheelchair-accessible fishing pier at Andrews Lake

GETTING THERE
From Durango, drive US 550 north about 45 miles to the Andrews Lake turnoff on the east (right) side. From Silverton, drive US 550 south 8

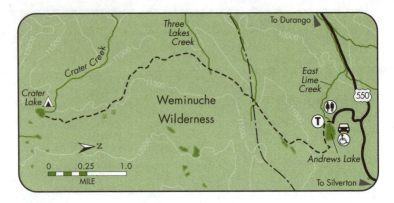

miles to the turnoff to the left. Follow this road 1 mile to the upper parking lot, designed for overnight or day hiking.

LOGISTICS

Toilet facilities are provided near the parking lot. Two access points to the trail begin at the parking lot: a paved trail begins near the toilets, and a gravel trail starts near the horse hitching post; both trails skirt the south end of Andrews Lake. Crater Lake is in the Weminuche Wilderness; regulations protecting this area are posted at the registration box about 100 yards from the lake—please sign in here. Practice leave-no-trace outdoor skills.

ON THE TRAIL

This popular trail climbs steadily to alpine Crater Lake, nestled in the base of North Twilight Peak. Hikers enjoy top-of-the-world views along the trail, interspersed with passages through wildflower meadows and dense spruce-fir forest. Fishing at the forest-edged lake or climbing above timberline to a saddle between peaks highlights this one- or two-day trip.

From the parking lot, both trails contour the south end of Andrews Lake, where the paved wheelchair-accessible trail ends. The gravel trail then edges the ridge of a marshy area. Some 10,000 years ago, the Animas Glacier began retreating, carving the pinnacles, crests, and lakes of this region. The geologist in your group may point out evidence of the glacier's rocky path, or moraine, on this landscape. At 0.25 mile, the trail begins its steepest ascent by switchbacking up a 500-foot ridge.

During breath-catching stops, your companions will first spot tiny cars following US 550 over Molas Pass. Looking north toward Silverton, they'll see Sultan and Kendall mountains; to the west is the Lime Creek valley, topped by Engineer Mountain, Twin Sisters, and Jura Knob. Views east feature Snowden Peak. After establishing the four directions, ask your pathfinders to point to them at various stops along the way. Foot-high

An interpretive sign near the start of Crater Lake Trail captures the interest of a young hiker.

wildflower panoramas begin after 1 mile, when the trail tops a ridge and then begins crossing streams and threading meadows. At about 1.75 miles, you cross into the Weminuche Wilderness.

The trail also traverses forests dominated by Englemann spruce and subalpine fir, the only trees in the Rocky Mountains thriving in elevations at 9000 feet and above. Help your companions identify the trees by their cones. Spruce cones hang downward from branches and are purple when immature, papery as they age. Fir cones stand upright on the tree's upper branches, appearing as fat, dark purple fingers that by early fall have aged to brown. A black, spiky cone core often remains on the tree after the cone has fallen apart, scale-by-scale, releasing its winged seeds. Chipmunks and their larger look-alikes, golden-mantled ground squirrels, gather cones of all ages, caching them in the loose, thick duff under trees. When your group hears the familiar chipmunk chatter, look to see if the call is from a ground squirrel, identified by a lack of stripes on its head and dorsal stripes from hip to shoulder, or the smaller chipmunk, with stripes on its head.

The trail maintains a steady grade as it heads south for 1.5 miles, winding through dense forest and open meadows equally thick with wildflowers. At 3.25 miles the trail veers east for 0.5 mile where views of the near-vertical north face of the Twilight Peaks inspires tired hikers. The three Twilight Peaks that form this massif called the West Needle Mountains are all over 13,000 feet. As the trail veers south again, it crosses several small streams and forested areas in the last 1.5 miles to the lake. Marshy areas here blur the trail somewhat, so look around for the route, maintaining a southerly direction.

Crater Lake sits just below timberline, offering a variety of tree-shaded campsites. The lake's still waters mirror the rugged north face of Twilight Peak, offering stunning views, especially at dawn or dusk. Fishing from the shoreline is reportedly good in this stocked lake. The climb to the small saddle just above the lake rewards hikers with views of the Needle Mountains to the east.

Return via the same trail.

PASS CREEK TRAIL TO ENGINEER MEADOWS

BEFORE YOU GO
Map USGS Engineer Mountain
Information For current conditions and more information, contact the Columbine Ranger District, www.fs.fed.us/r2/sanjuan or (970) 247-4874

ABOUT THE HIKE
Location Coal Bank Pass, north of Durango
Day hike, Moderate
2.5 miles one way
Hikable Mid-June to October
Starting elevation/High point 10,660 feet/11,680 feet
Accessibility none

GETTING THERE
In Durango, at Main Avenue and 32nd Street, drive north 33 miles on US 550 to Coal Bank Pass, turning right into the rest stop and parking area. Just ahead on the left is the 200-yard road and parking area adjacent to the trailhead.

LOGISTICS
Toilet facilities are provided at the rest area, but water is not. As in all high-altitude hikes, start early in the day, bring raingear, and be prepared to turn around if clouds begin building rapidly. Bring a camera to capture the spectacular wildflowers and mountain views.

ON THE TRAIL
Quick, easy access and the promise of high-country bliss pull countless hikers of all ages to the Pass Creek Trail, better known as "We're hiking

Engineer." The under-an-hour drive from Durango to the trailhead via the San Juan Skyway (US 550) whets the visual appetite with mountain views, including on your left, at about mile 30, the pyramid-shaped Engineer Mountain rising up out of a flower-studded meadow.

Though numerous kids have climbed the nearly 13,000-foot peak along a continuation of the Pass Creek Trail, the final ascent is precarious, requiring hand and foot holds on loose rock, a "best hike" for seasoned rock climbers only. "Make it to the meadows" defines the trail's delight for most hikers.

Look for the Pass Creek trailhead sign on the left (west) side of parking area and road. Follow the trail east and north as it traverses the bottom of a slope. Towering purple larkspur, white umbrellas of cow parsnip, and flames of bright orange paintbrush canopy even the adults in your group here. False hellebore (aka skunk cabbage)

Hikers walk through head-high wildflowers at the start of Pass Creek Trail.

adds a tropical look to the mix with its huge, slightly pleated leaves.

The trail soon enters the shade of a spruce-and-fir forest, ascending while it contours the base of the mountain. Numerous forest nooks dotted with mushrooms in late summer provide quiet rest stops for those not accustomed to the altitude.

At about 0.8 mile, the climb begins easing via switchbacks, leading to what we now would call "a small lake" on the left at 1.3 miles. Over the thirty-some years I've walked this trail, the lake size has decreased

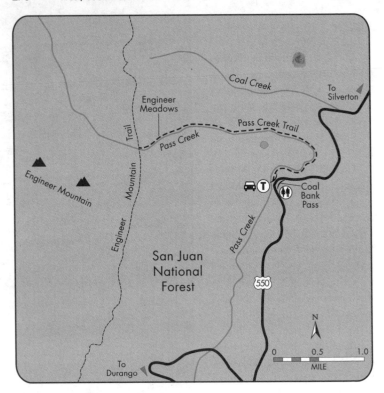

as the marsh has expanded, a natural course of forest health. Perhaps, when your kids hike Engineer in a decade or two, a grassy meadow will have claimed much of the pond.

Along the popular path numerous timbers, long enough to host a team of backpackers, lay cut and cleared by trail maintenance crews. For hikers, the logs serve as places to stop, breathe, and take in the views. However, at 2 miles the first glimpse of Engineer Mountain, artfully framed by a few spruce trees, motivates everyone out of the trees and into the field of alpine flowers, commonly called Engineer Meadows. Continue another 0.5 mile on the Pass Creek Trail to its junction with the Engineer Mountain Trail, an ideal destination for most hikers. (Climbers ascending Engineer Mountain follow the rough route up the mountain's northeast ridge.)

Return via the same trail.

87 POTATO LAKE TRAIL

BEFORE YOU GO
Maps San Juan National Forest; USGS Engineer Mountain
Information For current conditions and more information, contact the Columbine Ranger District, www.fs.fed.us/r2/sanjuan or (970) 247-4874

ABOUT THE HIKE
Location San Juan National Forest
Day hike or backpack; Easy
1 mile one way
Hikable May to October
Starting elevation/High point 9360 feet/9800 feet
Accessibility None

GETTING THERE

From Durango, drive north on US 550 for 28 miles and turn east (right) onto signed Lime Creek Road. Continue 3.5 miles on this gravel road to a large lily pond on the right. The trailhead and parking area are just past this pond, on the left. From Silverton, drive south on US 550 for 20 miles to Lime Creek Road and turn east (left), following the directions above.

LOGISTICS

The lake has several nearby level campsites, and camping permits are not required.

ON THE TRAIL

The trail leading to Potato Lake (commonly called Spud Lake) is as friendly and fringed with interesting diversions as the sparkling destination itself, which can serve as a lunch site, a fishing spot, or an overnight campsite. Recently regraded

Rock skipping at Potato Lake entertains big and little hikers.

and rerouted, this popular trail is now easy enough for beginning hikers.

Before setting foot on the trail, most kids like to inspect the lily pond across from the trailhead. While they throw pebbles into the water (as most everyone seems compelled to do at the sight of a pond), explain that the blanket of lily pads actually protects the fish and plants living under them from the heating effects of the high-altitude sun. The seeds of the lily's yellow flower were once gathered by Native Americans and ground into flour or roasted—with a flavor, some say, like popcorn.

A medley of aspen and spruce flanks both sides of the rocky path that climbs gently for 0.25 mile to the smooth, wide trail on the right. Potato Mountain, also called Spud Mountain, peeks through the trees straight ahead. Engineer Mountain (see Hike 86), a popularly photographed peak prominently visible from US 550, appears to the west of the trail, followed by Graysill and Grizzly peaks.

Within 0.5 mile, the trail turns to the northwest, where the amazing architecture of beavers awaits your inspection. In the recent past, only a few abandoned lodges remained in the pools on both sides of the trail. Now, prominent stick-and-mud structures bulge from the ponds' still waters. Beavers store their food—aspen twigs and stems—in the lodge, which they enter via an underwater door. Gnawing aspen trees keeps the beavers' teeth trimmed. Otherwise their choppers would grow so long they'd be useless and the animal would die of starvation! To feel the jaw power these dam builders employ in their construction, have kids touch the toothmarks gouged into aspen stumps littering the pond region.

Just beyond the beaver ponds, the lake opens to its full panorama. Potato Mountain (11,871 feet), a small spud compared to its 13,000-foot neighbors to the east, the West Needle Mountains, is reflected in this spring-fed lake. The lake offers a beachlike entry for wading on either side of the creek draining it. In early July, the lake's water temperature is warm enough for a refreshing dip. Young anglers like to settle into the chair-size rocks along the lake's shore for a relaxing afternoon fishing its trout-stocked waters. The trail around the lake can be followed in either direction, following the shore-side path and crossing a marshy area near the lake's northeast shore. Raspberries and strawberries growing along the shore are free to keen-eyed, nimble-fingered pickers.

Return via the same trail.

 ANIMAS OVERLOOK TRAIL

BEFORE YOU GO
Map San Juan National Forest
Information For current conditions and more information, contact the Columbine Ranger District, www.fs.fed.us/r2/sanjuan or (970) 247-4874

ABOUT THE HIKE
Location San Juan National Forest
Day hike; Easy
0.8-mile loop
Hikable May to October
Starting elevation/High point 8000 feet/8080 feet
Accessibility Wheelchair-accessible

GETTING THERE
From the Durango town center, head north on Main Street to 25th Street (Junction Creek Road); turn left (west). Follow this street for 3.5 miles, to where it enters the San Juan National Forest. Continue on this gravel road, now called Forest Road 171, to milepost 8, where wheelchair-accessible parking for the Animas Overlook Trail is on the right.

LOGISTICS
Universal-access toilet facilities are available at the trailhead.

ON THE TRAIL
The Animas Overlook Trail is a short, very pleasurable trail that shows the diverse forces that shaped this corner of the state. Nine interpretive signposts along this wheelchair-accessible path provide the kind of geological, ecological, and historical information that normally requires

San Juan Mountain
Overlook

Robertas
Point

171

Junction
Creek
Road

one way

Animas Overlook Trail

one way

To Durango

N

0   250   500
FEET

paging through several guidebooks. This recently completed trail is a cooperative project initiated by the area's Business and Professional Women. It was designed and developed by members of the San Juan Forest Service and completed by a crew of developmentally disabled adults from Durango. Ultimately, Braille guides will be available for the trail. This forest trail is rich with signs of wildlife.

From the trailhead, the trail veers left. Mullein, the tall, woolly "weed" growing beside the trailhead post, is best appreciated when kids touch its soft leaves against their cheeks. After experiencing the plant in this way, they understand why the plant is collected for use in making skin-softening lotions.

 In a few yards the trail reaches the San Juan Mountain Overlook, providing views of the Animas valley, crowned by the San Juan Mountains to the north, with the Animas River flashing like a huge silver snake through its middle. Point out the river's lazy, winding path through the flat valley below. Ask, "Why doesn't the river follow a straight line?"

As the trail winds through the mixed conifer forest, look for charred bark on tree trunks—evidence of the controlled burn here in 1977. You may find tree stumps decorated with conspicuous little piles of descaled pinecones, remnants of the chickaree squirrel feeding on the cones' seeds. More often heard than seen, this common reddish-brown squirrel frequently calls from a tree in scolding *tsk, tsk, chrrr* notes.

At the trail junction at a little past 0.1 mile, turn left to follow the

Interpretive signs introduce nature's secrets to all hikers.

one-way loop. A common sound is the *rat-a-tat* drills of a downy woodpecker in search of an insect meal or declaring its territory. Imagine being a woodpecker beating its beak against wood twenty times a second, in uninterrupted bursts, for almost an hour! Woodpeckers have special feet to give them a good grip on the tree, and their long, stiff tails help hold them in place.

At about 0.3 mile you reach Robertas Point, with an interpretive sign that directs eyes to the valley to the south, where the area's earliest inhabitants, the Ancestral Pueblo, once thrived. Animal signs to look for are the dry pellets of the mule deer left near oak brush. Examine the leaves of this deer forage to see if it has been nibbled on recently. Look skyward, where a large black bird might be soaring overhead; it may be a turkey vulture riding a thermal. At dusk, quiet hikers often hear the resonant *hoo hoo-oo* of a great horned owl.

Picnic tables are scattered alongside the trail, inviting a snack break. At 0.7 mile, the trail loops back to the trail fork near the beginning; turn left to return to the trailhead.

 FIRST FORK TRAIL

BEFORE YOU GO
Maps San Juan National Forest; USGS Rules Hill, USGS Durango East, USGS Hermosa
Information For current conditions and more information, contact the Columbine Ranger District, www.fs.fed.us/r2/sanjuan or (970) 247-4874

ABOUT THE HIKE
Location San Juan National Forest
Day hike or backpack; Moderate to challenging
3 miles one way
Hikable May to October
Starting elevation/High point 8080 feet/9856 feet
Accessibility None

Forest floor views of aspen splendor

GETTING THERE

From Durango, take East Third Avenue north to its end, bearing right (northeast) on Florida Road (County Road 240). Follow this road 9.6 miles, just past a steep uphill curve where a sign on the left reads "COLVIG SILVER CAMPS." Turn left on this wide gravel road and travel almost 2 miles. The road appears to end at the camp's barn building, but continues about 0.75 mile farther on this narrow road suitable for two-wheel-drive vehicles in dry weather. Stop at the cattle fence that crosses the road, where parking is allowed on either side.

LOGISTICS

Please close all gates and fences. Water and toilet facilities are not available here.

ON THE TRAIL

The splashing, gurgling sounds of First Fork Creek, the stream that joins Red Creek at the trail's beginning, accompany hikers most of the way to Missionary Ridge. The trail climbs gradually, with numerous creekside destinations along the way. The last 0.5-mile hike to the ridge can be challenging.

Watch for the "FIRST FORK" trailhead sign on the left side of the road across from Red Creek, about 0.25 mile past the parking area. Pass through a barbed-wire gate to start the trail. The easy-to-follow trail winds through a narrow, red-walled canyon shaded by towering aspen and spruce.

Keep an eye open for green tree saplings emerging from blackened stumps, an example of forest regeneration after the 70,000-acre Missionary Ridge Fire of 2002 scorched portions of this trail. On very windy days, be aware that burned tree snags can be hazardous. After climbing several short hills, at 0.7 mile the trail wanders through a lovely aspen stand. Ask your crew to look for signs of the Missionary Ridge fire on the surrounding hillsides.

Among the many wildflowers lacing this wooded canyon is the wild rose, so common it's hardly noticed by many hikers. But a careful look at a rose in flower or fruit may reveal an insect gall, an elongated swelling about the size of a cherry. Explain that a gall is formed when an insect lays its eggs on the plant.

The aspen-shaded trail continues its gentle climb west for another 1.3 miles. Along the way few hikers resist stopping to admire the First Fork as the creek spills into fern-laced pools or edges mossy red rock walls. Many leaf boats and elfin fantasies are launched along this lovely section of the trail. At 2 miles the trail enters an aspen meadow and veers north (right) as it ascends toward Missionary Ridge. Those preferring streamside explorations should turn around at the meadow. The last mile climbs several heavily wooded knolls before reaching the Missionary Ridge Trail, a former stock trail. Turnaround points are many along this section, promising surprisingly new and stunning views as you descend the canyon.

Return the way you came.

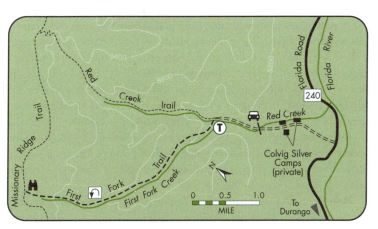

90 JUNCTION CREEK TRAIL

BEFORE YOU GO
Map USGS Durango West,
Trails Illustrated Durango, Cortez
Information For current
conditions and more
information, contact the
Columbine Ranger District or
(970) 247-4874

ABOUT THE HIKE
Location Durango
Day hike; Easy to moderate
3 miles one way
Hikable April to November
**Starting elevation/High
point** 6950 feet/7150 feet,
8000 feet at Gudy's Rest
Accessibility None

GETTING THERE

From Durango, head north on US 550 (Main Avenue). Turn left (west) on 25th Street. Drive 3 miles (the road becomes County Road 204), passing through residential areas, to the parking lot on the left.

LOGISTICS

Toilets are provided in the parking lot. Drinking water is not available here. Mountain bikers frequent the trail, commonly yielding to hikers, resulting in multi-use compatibility.

ON THE TRAIL

Experience the Junction Creek Trail as a streamside stroll or as a day hike on the Colorado Trail, and your whole family will be hooked. Along the way you'll meet smiling hikers, bikers, joggers, babies-in-packs, and kids-in-tow, as well as the occasional backpacker hiking the final portion of the 487-mile Denver-to-Durango trek. Yet, just off the trail, clear-water pools and forest nooks serve as destinations and sanctuaries for all ages. Indeed, at the 3-mile bridge crossing Junction Creek, a three-generation French family told me their hike was *"le meilleur!"*

From the parking lot, the trail crosses a sunny meadow before entering the leafy canyon at 0.3 mile. Summer hikers will see plenty of "lemonberry" bushes (three-leaf sumac) bearing tiny orange-red berries with a lemon tart taste.

Branches of oak, cottonwood, Rocky Mountain maple, and red-twigged dogwood shade the trail, providing a fall-color hike after high-country aspens drop their gold leaves. As with many popular trails, poison ivy thrives here. In autumn, it too shifts to shades of glossy bronze and orange, becoming a colorful but toxic candidate for a child's "pretty leaf" collection.

At 0.5 mile, on the right, kids like to check out the boulder topped with stacks of balanced rocks. This ever-changing attraction is also a distraction and a good place to talk to kids about leave-no-trace ethics. Is it okay to stack rocks here just because a lot of people use the trail? Would the flat-topped boulder look more natural without the people-made topping? Where is it okay to stack rocks?

As the trail continues through patches of sun and shade, numerous spur trails lure hikers to inviting pools rimmed with boulders, some family-sized, others perfect for little bare feet to balance on.

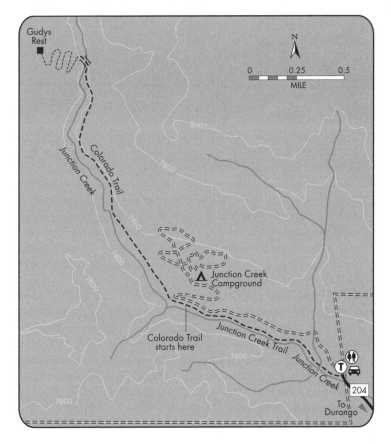

Hikers play balance games on a Junction Creek spur trail.

Ponderosa pines yield to fir trees as the trail ascends, meeting the official start of the Colorado Trail (CT) portion at 1.4 miles. The CT starts southwest of Denver in Waterton Canyon (at the time of publication, this trailhead was not accessible), passing through seven national forests, six wilderness areas, and five major river systems. Though some hikers complete the trail in as little as a month, many walk portions of the CT each summer. Today's hike could be the first of many for someone in your group.

Beyond the CT sign the trail ascends in earnest, then levels, passing intriguing cliff formations on the right. Today's destination, the bridge crossing at 3 miles, is a welcome pause for cooling feet in Junction Creek's pools. Return via the same trail.

Those wanting to continue their day hike on the CT, follow the trail over the bridge as it switchbacks 1 mile to Gudy's Rest, named for Gudy Gaskill who devoted thirty years to making the Colorado Trail a reality for countless hikers, bikers, and equestrians.

91 HIGHLINE TRAIL TO TAYLOR LAKE

BEFORE YOU GO
Map USGS LaPlata
Information For current conditions and more information, contact the Dolores Public Lands Center, www.fs.fed.us/r2/sanjuan or (970) 882-7296

ABOUT THE HIKE
Location Plata Mountains
Day hike; Easy
1 mile one way with 4WD; 3 miles one way with 2WD
Hikable Mid-June through September
Starting elevation/ High point 10,479 feet with 2WD; 11,615 feet with 4WD/11,650 feet
Accessibility None

GETTING THERE

From Durango, travel west on US 160 for 11 miles to County Road 124, turning north toward the La Plata Mountains. After 4 miles this paved road turns to gravel; continue another 5 miles to the sign for Cumberland Basin. Four-wheel-drive vehicles are required beyond this point. For those in two-wheel-drive vehicles, park here and walk these last 2 miles to Kennebec Pass on the popular, though very rough four-wheel-drive Forest Road 571. Those in four-wheel-drive vehicles will find ample parking at the pass.

LOGISTICS

Nearest toilet facilities and drinking water are seasonally available in forest service camp-grounds in La Plata Canyon. As with all high-altitude hikes, start this one early in the day, before afternoon storms develop.

The most colorful of alpine wild-flowers, Indian paintbrush, blooms in shades of yellow, red, and coral.

ON THE TRAIL

A 2-mile walk or a rollicking four-wheel-drive ride leads to Kennebec Pass, where grand views of the La Plata and San Juan mountains reward hikers and drivers. The trail starts at Kennebec Pass. Wildflowers stand tall and colorful along the gentle 1-mile trail to Taylor Lake, which serves as a perfect lunch, photo, and feet-cooling spot.

Those who must hike the last 2 miles of FR 571, a steep, rocky route to Kennebec Pass, enjoy views of the La Plata Mountains framed by dense stands of spruce trees. On the northwest edge of the parking area at Kennebec Pass, to your left, find the Highline trailhead to Taylor Lake. Before joining the trail, orient yourself and your companions to the mountain profile featured on the large interpretive sign just 50 yards north of the parking area. Those who have hiked the Potato Lake Trail (Hike 87) may recognize Potato or "Spud" Mountain in the foreground.

As your crew walks through shoulder-high and taller stands of false hellebore, erroneously called skunk cabbage, watch for places where deer or elk have bedded down. These and other animals do not eat this plant because its roots and new shoots are poisonous. Native Americans used small amounts of the plant's large, pleated leaves as a medicine for the heart. Dried and powdered, this plant becomes the garden insecticide called hellebore. I've seen more than a few kids wear the large leaf as a sun-shielding hat.

Some kids and their parents can't resist picking a cluster of the trail's lavender beauty, columbine. Removing Colorado's state flower in any form is unlawful—and "awful," according to my twelve-year-old companion, after a young couple with two fistfuls of columbines passed us on the trail. A better memory is the flower's sweet, delicate fragrance.

Taylor Lake is not visible from the trail, so ask your hikers to look ahead for a straight line of brush, behind which is the lake. Alpine willows flourish in the wet soils of the dam that formed the lake in the 1950s for irrigation storage. The lake, with a maximum depth of 6 feet, is not stocked, nor does it currently serve farming purposes.

After the trail crosses a small shallow stream made muddy by foot traffic, it heads into the willows where it's easily lost. Continue walking through the brush to the lake's shore. The sandy shallow shore to your left (south) is ideal for photos, pebble skipping, and wading. Return via the same trail.

 SHARKSTOOTH TRAIL TO CENTENNIAL PEAK

BEFORE YOU GO
Maps San Juan National Forest; USGS La Plata
Information For current conditions and more information, contact the Dolores Public Lands Center, www.fs.fed.us/r2/sanjuan or (970) 882-7296

ABOUT THE HIKE
Location San Juan National Forest
Day hike or backpack; Moderate to challenging 2.5 miles one way
Hikable Mid-June to October
Starting elevation/High point 10,900 feet/13,062 feet
Accessibility None

GETTING THERE
From Durango, travel west on US 160 for 29 miles to Mancos. Turn right (north) on CO-184, driving 0.4 mile to County Road 42 on the right, marked by the sign for Jackson Reservoir and Transfer Campground. Follow this road (it becomes Forest Road 561 after it enters the national forest) for 12.5 miles, passing Transfer Campground (at 10 miles) and continuing to 0.5 mile beyond the Aspen Guard Station on the right. Bear right at the road intersection with FR 350 (Spruce Mill Road), following the sign to the Sharkstooth Trail and Windy Gap. Drive 6.5

Sharkstooth Trail hikers sample top-of-the-world views at the saddle of Centennial Peak.

miles, staying on FR 250, veering right onto FR 346 at a sign for Twin Lakes. The trailhead is 2 miles from here. Deep ruts and mud puddles may require low-clearance vehicles to park alongside this road. Limited parking is available at the trailhead.

LOGISTICS

As with all high-altitude hikes, start this one early in the day. Allow four to five hours to complete the peak climb and return to the trailhead. The nearest toilet facilities and drinking water are available at Transfer Campground.

ON THE TRAIL

Besides having a name kids like, the Sharkstooth Trail leads them to destinations all hikers enjoy: a flower-filled forest jeweled by streams, a signed loop trail around a historic mining claim, a spectacular saddle for resting and lunching, and, finally, a relatively easy 13,000-foot peak to climb.

The first half of the hike begins in the shade of spruce trees. Purple flowering monkshood and larkspur touch the shoulders of some hikers, come late July and August. Within the first 0.5 mile you pass a talus slope on your left. Let your group know they are walking the edge of a rock glacier that blankets the mountain above the trail. Ice holds the talus rock together; however, summer hikers would have to search 3 to 5 feet beneath the surface of this sun-baked slope to find it. High-altitude hikers see rock glaciers on relatively shallow slopes (less than 45 degrees).

As the trail continues switchbacking through the forest and over streams, watch for the first glimpse of Centennial Peak and Hesperus Peak at about 0.7 mile. Triangular-shaped and banded with different layers of sedimentary rock, Hesperus Peak stands to the right of Centennial, which has a long, gradual slope. Though Hesperus appears to be the big brother of Centennial, your companions will be surprised to learn Centennial is only 200 feet shorter than Hesperus. Ask why the two appear so different in height.

Beyond this view, at 1.1 miles, is the beginning of the interpreted historic loop trail around the Windy Williams Mine site. Hikers should conserve their energy for the uphill climb by taking this signed loop trail on the return hike. Some hikers may want to head back here.

As the trail rises above timberline, stop to point out how it climbs to the lowest point between two peaks, called a saddle—at 1.8 miles, this is a good place to sit, snack, and rest. The peaks on either side of the saddle are Sharkstooth to the left and Centennial to the right. The saddle can be a turnaround point for hikers not interested in bagging a peak, or those uncomfortable with heights or unstable footing. This

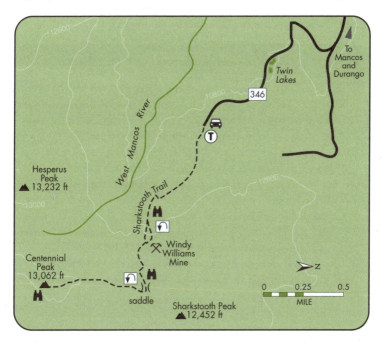

point and higher are good places to see the extent of the rock glacier with its "feet" edging the trail's beginning.

From the saddle, the 0.7-mile trail leading to the summit of Centennial is often faint or nonexistent as it climbs over steep talus slopes. However, when we climbed this with our then-seven-year-old son, Niko, we found subtle paths through the rock just below the right side of the crest. During ascents and descents, the rocks' unstable conditions require that hikers not line up behind one another; rather, they should stagger themselves while hiking to prevent potential injuries from falling rock. The most challenging portion of the climb leads to a false summit. From here, the trail's last 200 yards follow the top of the ridge and make the initial struggle worthwhile.

Views from the summit of Centennial include the La Plata Mountains encircled by the entire San Juan Mountain range to the north, with The Needles to the northeast and the San Miguels northwest. Looking south, the mesa above Durango where Fort Lewis College is located can be seen. Sleeping Ute Mountain lies to the west. On clear days, the far western views include those of southeastern Utah's Abajo and Henry mountains.

Return via the same trail, allowing time for a casual stroll along the signed historic 0.3-mile trail around the mining site.

GREAT GETAWAYS

To camp within striking distance of Hikes 92, 94, and 96, head to Transfer Park Recreation Area (www.fs.fed.us/r2/sanjuan, 970-882-7296) for a first-come, first-served campsite. This campground is 39 miles northwest of Durango or 11 miles northeast of Mancos via CO-184 then County Road 42.

Hiking opportunities at the campground include the 0.5-mile barrier-free Big Al Trail, featuring dramatic views of La Plata Mountains, or the 3-mile loop Transfer Trail, which winds down to the West Mancos River and heads uphill on Box Canyon Trail.

Nearby you'll find stocked trout in Jackson Lake at Mancos State Park (http://parks.state.co.us), located off mile 4 on CR-42, or, of course, you can take advantage of your proximity to Mesa Verde National Park (www.nps.gov/meve) and the Anasazi Heritage Center (www.co.blm.gov/ahc/hmepge.htm).

93 BEAR CREEK PRESERVE

BEFORE YOU GO
Map USGS Telluride
Information For current conditions and more information, contact the Norwood Ranger District, www.fs.fed.us/us/r2/gmug or (970) 327-4261

ABOUT THE HIKE
Location Bear Creek Preserve
Day hike; Easy to moderate
Up to 2.6 miles one way
Hikable Late April through October
Starting elevation/High point 8750 feet/9500 feet
Accessibility None

GETTING THERE

From Colorado Avenue (CO-145) in downtown Telluride, turn south on Pine Street and drive three blocks, crossing the San Miguel River to the small clearing where the street ends and the trail begins. Use the public parking spaces along the nearby streets.

LOGISTICS

Toilet facilities, drinking water, sport fields, and the innovative playground called Imagination Station are located in Town Park. The Scenic Gondola (7:00 AM–11:00 PM; free to foot passengers) is located in downtown Telluride on San Juan Street. (For more details, see the Telluride riverside walk at the end of this section.)

ON THE TRAIL

An abandoned jeep trail brings pedestrians of all sizes and stamina to magnificent views of

Tots in tow, families enjoy the mist from Bear Creek Falls.

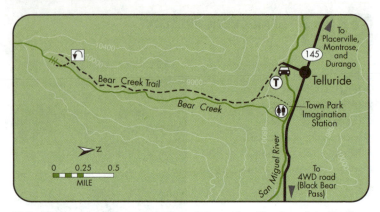

Telluride's waterfalls and surrounding peaks. The broad trail allows groups to talk, walk, and investigate nature together as they enter a finger of the hanging valley in which Telluride so beautifully sits. The Bear Creek Trail lies within the 325-acre mountain canyon called Bear Creek Preserve, protected by the Telluride Land Trust. In Town Park, which edges Bear Creek Preserve, kids crawl, leap, swing, and climb with abandon at the Imagination Station. Another reward can be planned for after the hike: a free gondola ride that connects the towns of Telluride and Mountain Village, promising a memorable 1750-foot climb above town and back.

As the trail begins its gradual staircase climb, views of town and the beaver ponds on the west edge of Town Park appear. Wildflowers seem to nod their approval with your passing; stop to admire any or all of the many varieties that lace this walk. Purple monkshood and larkspur greet summer visitors; cow parsnip appears as stands of parasols composed of tiny white flowers. Wild, light-pink geraniums interest the budding pilot in your group when you point out the tiny lines on its petals. These markings act as runway lines, attracting insects to land and feed on the flower's nectar. What else happens as a result of the insect's visitation?

Thanks to the number and variety of flowers along this trail, beginning hikers will enjoy matching the colors found in nature with those on their clothing. Others like watching for their favorite color; is it found on a flower, sparkly rock, or butterfly?

As the trail continues along Bear Creek, the sound of waterfalls increases, as does the number of side trails, most of which lead to Bear Creek tumbling below. These "social" trails are not maintained and can be quite steep. Remind lagging hikers that their payoff for finishing the hike is to stand in the mist of a waterfall described as awesome by the preteens visiting the site during our hike.

Nearing the last 0.25 mile, watch on the left for distant views of a three-tiered waterfall—they are a suggestion of what's to come. Upon reaching the trail's waterfall climax, many groups picnic on the area's large flat rocks. Adventurous hikers may seek a closer, misty sampling of the waterfall by hiking an additional 0.2-mile trail, climbing up the knoll to the left of the main trail.

Return as you came. Returning hikers can access the Imagination Station playground by veering off the Bear Creek Trail onto a side trail leading downhill into the Bear Creek Preserve.

GREAT GETAWAYS

There are two campgrounds close to Hike 93. Southwest of Telluride off CO-145 you'll find Sunshine Campground at 8 miles and Matterhorn Campground at 12 miles. Sites at both are first-come, first-served.

For some extra fun, head to Telluride and explore the 2.7-mile Jud Weibe Trail, which loops above town with awesome views of two waterfalls and the Telluride Ski Area. (The trailhead is at the north end of Aspen Street) or jump on the San Miguel River Trail, an easy 6-mile round-trip trail that winds through town. At Telluride's east end you can stand in the way-cool mist of 300-foot Bridal Veil Falls or go downtown and take the only free gondola ride in North America or visit the Imagination Station at Town Park, which awakens the inner child in every visitor.

 DOMINGUEZ-ESCALANTE TRAIL

BEFORE YOU GO
Map None
Information For current conditions and more information, contact the Anasazi Heritage Center, www.co.blm.gov/ahc or (970) 882-5600

ABOUT THE HIKE
Location Dolores
Day hike; Easy
0.5 mile one way
Hikable Year-round
Starting elevation/High point 7100 feet/7200 feet
Accessibility Wheelchair-accessible

A family hikes along the trail through sage and sagebrush.

GETTING THERE
From Cortez, head north on CO-145 for 8 miles. Turn left onto CO-184 and continue 1.5 miles to the turnoff for the Anasazi Heritage Center on the right.

LOGISTICS
Toilet facilities and drinking water are available at the Anasazi Heritage Center (9:00 AM–5:00 PM in summer, 10:00 AM–4:00 PM in winter).

ON THE TRAIL
This paved, wheelchair-accessible trail to an ancient dwelling site overlooking several mountain ranges will delight children of all ages. Interpretive signs along the way identify the local plants and explain how the Ancestral Puebloan people (formerly called Anasazi) used them about 1000 years ago. See the following hike (Hike 95) for an overview of the Ancestral Puebloan culture.

Before visiting the Dominguez and Escalante pueblos, be sure to visit the museum at the Anasazi Heritage Center. Operated by the Bureau of Land Management, the center houses more than 3 million artifacts, including one of the largest archaeological projects in the United States. Kids like to enter the center's rebuilt Pueblo I Pithouse or try their hands at grinding corn using a mano and metate—just as the Ancestral Puebloans used their stone tools more than a thousand years ago. Don't miss the interactive sections of the new timeline exhibit, and the ten-minute film *Visit with Respect* featuring a modern Hopi archaeologist and his six-year-old son.

For a preview of what lies ahead on the trail, stop at the Dominguez Pueblo, located in front of the Anasazi Heritage Center. Ask your crew to point out the site's four rectangular rooms and the circular kiva, a ceremonial room. Examine the stonework here. Encourage them to compare it to the masonry at the Escalante Pueblo.

The trail to the Escalante Pueblo begins at the picnic site just west of the Anasazi Heritage Center. This gently graded 0.5-mile trail ascends through stands of scrub oak, pinyon, and juniper. Yucca and cactus are also part of the undergrowth here.

All the plants you see on this trail were important to the people who once lived here. Imaginative young hikers might hear stone tools grinding corn or children chasing a wild turkey through the brush. If they are especially quiet and watchful, they may see a horned lizard sunning itself.

Escalante Pueblo, named for the Franciscan priest who may have discovered this site in 1776, is at the top of a hill. The area around the site and a nearby overlook offer a panoramic view of the area's peaks. Sleeping Ute Mountain, identified by its silhouette of a reclining Native American, is directly west. Help children find north by locating Lone Cone, once an active volcano millions of years ago and now a triangular peak located between two mountain ranges, the San Juans (northeast) and the Abajos (northwest). Mesa Verde National Park and the Ute Mountain Ute Tribal Park are directly south. The lake below is McPhee Reservoir. Completed in 1985, it flooded many Ancestral Puebloan sites. Artifacts collected and studied during the McPhee Project are housed at the Anasazi Heritage Center.

Escalante Pueblo contains the remains of an Ancestral Puebloan "Great House"—a block of rectangular rooms, the larger ones used for living, the smaller for storage. Kids questioning the petite size of the rooms should be told that most early Puebloan activities took place outdoors, sleeping being reserved for indoors on cold nights. Some walls form circular underground rooms called kivas. Ask children to point out the two kivas (one excavated and one unexcavated depression to the south). Observant youngsters may notice the masonry here is fancy, made up of rows of blocky rocks alternated with bands of smaller stones called chinking stones. This masonry style is one of the many signs indicating that the early Puebloans who lived here traded with Puebloans of the Chaco area (100 miles south) and tried to maintain a similar lifestyle. Ask your crew to compare the masonry of this ruin to that of the Dominguez site seen at the trail's start.

Return as you came.

SAND CANYON AND EAST ROCK CREEK LOOP

BEFORE YOU GO
Map Sand Canyon and Rock Creek trails brochure
Information For current conditions and more information, contact Canyons of the Ancients National Monument, www.co.blm.gov /canm or (970) 882-5600

ABOUT THE HIKE
Location Bureau of Land Management's Canyons of the Ancients National Monument, Cortez
Day hike; Moderate
4.75-mile loop
Hikable Year-round, though summer can be very hot
Starting elevation/High point 5472 feet/6300 feet
Accessibility None

GETTING THERE

From Cortez, head south on CO-491. Turn right (west) on County Road G at the signs for the airport and/or Hovenweep National Monument. Drive 12.5 miles on this paved, curving road. Sand Canyon trailhead parking is on the right (north) on an unimproved slickrock surface, not suitable for low-clearance vehicles. Use caution when parking. Do not park on the road or on adjacent private property. As of press time, a new parking area is in the planning stages.

LOGISTICS

Prior to hiking Sand Canyon, plan a visit to the Bureau of Land Management's Anasazi Heritage Center, 10 miles north of Cortez. The center, headquarters for Canyons of the Ancients National Monument, features interactive displays and information about early life in the

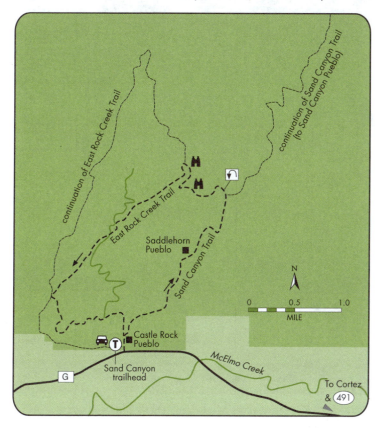

Southwest (see Hike 94, Dominguez-Escalante Trail). Bring plenty of water, sunscreen, hats, and binoculars. No water or toilet facilities are provided. All hikers, bicylists, and horse riders must stay on the formal, marked trails. Before you begin the hike, remember to sign in at the trail register.

ON THE TRAIL

From about 900 to 1300 AD, the Four Corners area, where Colorado, Utah, Arizona, and New Mexico abut, was home to a vast group of people now called the Ancestral Pueblo. Many of their cliff houses, towers, rock art, and pottery are currently preserved in places like Mesa Verde National Park and the Anasazi Heritage Center. Yet much of the area remains as an unsigned outdoor museum and laboratory featuring

Saddlehorn Pueblo remains protected, yet very fragile, in an alcove above Sand Canyon.

the cliff dwellings that represent the culmination of an ancient culture. Sand Canyon is one such unlabeled monument of Pueblo history.

Few signs identify the hundreds of archaeological sites in this one-time home for the Ancestral Puebloans. Yet, every Sand Canyon hiker discovers ancient towers, rock walls, and cliff dwellings while walking the trail's path over slickrock and through stands of pinyon and juniper trees. Observation skills are needed at each of the spur trails where few signs tell you what to look for. Discovery is what this hike is about.

Prior to 1200 AD the Ancestral Puebloans lived in scattered settlements in canyon bottoms and on mesa tops. They moved to the cliffs late in the twelfth century, sustaining themselves by raising and gathering food. Soon years of drought, combined with other factors, forced the cliff dwellers to leave their homes in favor of river corridors to the south.

Today, many American Indians regard the region as their ancestral homeland. Blessings and seasonal ceremonies continue here, maintaining oral traditions while respecting those who came before.

Begin the hike with a "Don't bust the crust!" shout-out, reminding your companions to stay on the trail and off the dark, lumpy surface of the soil, called biological soil crust (also called cryptobiotic crust). Also remind them not to disturb the stone ruins or remove any material from the area.

As you ascend the Sand Canyon Trail, behind you, to the south, looms the head of Sleeping Ute Mountain. When viewed from a distance, the small range appears to be a person lying down. Legend has it that when clouds gather on the highest peak, the "Sleeping Ute," a war god, is letting rain clouds slip from his pockets. Do your kids see rain in the forecast?

From the trailhead, follow the cairns stacked on slickrock to the large sandstone butte known as Castle Rock Pueblo. Hikers get their first chance at finding ancient clues at this village dated 1250–1280 AD. A spur trail on the north side of the butte provides access to the site. In 1993–94 archaeologists from nearby Crow Canyon Archaeological Center conducted limited excavations here, finding remnants of over forty above-ground rooms, nine towers, and sixteen or more kivas, special underground rooms. Your companions may spot a wall of rectangular rocks set in the ground, but archaeologists have carefully documented and removed most of the site's other artifacts, now curated at the Anasazi Heritage Center.

Return to the trail where cairns mark the gently sloping slickrock, leading to a trail signpost for East Rock and Sand Canyon. Follow the Sand Canyon Trail to the right through clusters of pinyon and juniper trees. Within a mile a spur trail veers left accessing Saddlehorn Pueblo, one of Sand Canyon's many dwellings tucked into a protective alcove high in the sandstone embankment. Many cliff dwellings appear well preserved, but they remain quite fragile. Use your binoculars to get a better view of each ancient home, and please stay out of the sites.

At 1.5 miles, you'll reach a signpost pointing west to East Rock Creek Canyon. For a shorter hike, this signpost can be a turnaround point. If you were to continue on the main trail about 5 miles north beyond the signpost, a steep trail would lead you to the expansive Sand Canyon Pueblo. (Contact the Anasazi Heritage Center for driving and hiking directions to the pueblo.) In 1275 AD nearly 600 people lived in this compact, walled village tending their cornfields and flocks of turkeys.

Continuing west along the 0.75-mile section of trail as it climbs to East Rock Creek, you'll encounter two spur trails leading to views of Sand Canyon. Remind your companions that every plant they see today was a source of food, medicine, shelter materials, and building supplies for the Ancestral Puebloans. Nuts from the cones of a nearby pinyon tree were their food, just as they are today. Fibers from yucca spikes became sandals, and its roots made soap.

Turn left at the sign for East Rock Creek Trail. The trail's last 2.5 miles offer numerous "scoping stops" into East Rock Creek Canyon, but please stay on the main trail. Spotting a rock home tucked in a distant alcove or "discovering" a tower perched on a high point thrills many hikers in this canyon. However, plan a lunch stop along this final portion to refuel the interest and energy levels of young discoverers.

As the trail returns to slickrock, watch for sky-mirroring pools dimpling its surface. Called potholes, these occasional oases are more than water holes for animals. Close-up investigation often reveals such tiny creatures as worms, snails, and tadpoles. But keep both little and big hands and feet out of potholes, because oils from human skin can damage any form of life in the water.

The final 0.25 mile contours the opposite side of Castle Rock Pueblo, returning to the trailhead on the slickrock surface that began the hike.

 ## PETROGLYPH POINT LOOP TRAIL

BEFORE YOU GO
Map Mesa Verde National Park brochure
Information For current conditions and more information, contact Mesa Verde National Park, www.nps.gov/meve or (970) 529-4465

ABOUT THE HIKE
Location Mesa Verde National Park
Day hike; Moderate
2.8-mile loop
Hikable Mid-April to October
Starting elevation/High point 6850 feet/6970 feet
Accessibility Wheelchair-accessible, with assistance, to Spruce Tree House

Petroglyphs—images pecked in the rock— depict Ancestral Puebloan life.

GETTING THERE

From Durango, drive US 160 west 36 miles; from Cortez, drive US 160 east 10 miles. At the entrance to Mesa Verde National Park, drive 20 miles to the parking area at Chapin Mesa Museum.

LOGISTICS

Toilet facilities and drinking water are available at the museum. The park is open year-round, but the trail is closed after snow falls. Hikers register at the sign-up stand at the ranger station adjacent to the museum. During hot summer months, plan to explore this trail in the cool of morning.

ON THE TRAIL

On this loop trail, hikers discover how prehistoric American Indians fulfilled their needs for food, shelter, and clothing while living in the high desert canyons of the Southwest. The trail circles a canyon and mesa top occupied by Ancestral Puebloans from around 600 AD until early in the thirteenth century (for an overview of this ancient culture of cliff-dwelling people, formerly called the Anasazi, see Hike 95). The Petroglyph Point guidebook, available at the museum and ranger station, highlights the interesting plants and geology seen from the trail.

The loop begins on the wheelchair-accessible Spruce Tree House Trail. Descend 0.25 mile to the impressive Ancestral Puebloan dwelling surrounded by tan sandstone cliffs and lush vegetation. A spring trickling through the rock wall supplied water to a community of some 100 people living here 1400 years ago

As the trail leaves this oasis, it meanders past stands of scrub oak, mountain mahogany, bitterbrush, serviceberry, yucca, and cactus. Explain that the Puebloan people incorporated each of these seemingly fruitless plants into their daily lives. Ask your kids "How could you use any of these plants?"At 1.1 miles, watch for the four-room dwelling perched on a ledge above sign 18. Point out the structure's height, asking questions such as, "How tall were the original walls? What do you think the rooms were used for?" Hikers are asked not to walk close to the fragile walls of this ancient dwelling. Please respect the fragile nature of this unprotected prehistoric structure by staying on the trail.

Grooves carved in a sandstone boulder at sign 19 fuel imaginations when hikers learn the rock was a prehistoric stone tool–sharpening site.

At 1.5 miles, sign 24, is Petroglyph Point, the park's largest and best-known group of petroglyphs, images carved in rock. The Ancestral Puebloans stood on a ledge or rope ladder here to chip a collage of designs or messages through the darker layer of desert varnish and into the lighter sandstone beneath.

Park Service personnel made this trail, not the early Puebloans, who were adept at scrambling up slopes and leaping over boulders. When faced with a steep cliff wall, the "ancient ones" chipped notches into the sandstone, just deep enough to hold the front part of a hand or foot. Watch for this type of stone ladder in a small section of the trail just beyond the petroglyphs.

From this point, the trail traverses the pinyon-juniper mesa top, circling back around to the parking lot. Encourage kids to feel the spirit of "those who came before" as they quietly stalk this dry forest like the inhabitants once did.

GREAT KIVA AND CHIMNEY ROCK TRAILS

BEFORE YOU GO
Map Chimney Rock brochure
Information For current conditions and more information, contact the Chimney Rock Interpretive Program, www.chimneyrockco.org or (970) 883-5359

ABOUT THE HIKE
Location Chimney Rock Archaeological Area
Day hike; Easy (lower ruins) to moderate (upper ruins)
0.25-mile loop, Great Kiva Loop Trail; 1 mile (round trip), Pueblo Trail, by guided tour only
Hikable May 15 through September
Starting elevation/High point 7400 feet/7600 feet
Accessibility Great Kiva Loop Trail

GETTING THERE

From Durango, drive US 160 east 45 miles; from Pagosa Springs, drive US 160 west 17 miles. Turn south on CO-151, driving 3 miles to the Chimney Rock entrance gate with a parking area on the right. The visitor "welcome cabin" is located in about 0.5 mile on the left. Stop here to arrange for a tour.

LOGISTICS

The visitor welcome cabin provides toilet facilities, bottled water, books, and souvenirs but no running water. Access to the ancient sites is only through daily 2.5-hour tours (starting at 9:30 AM) sponsored by the Chimney Rock Interpretive Association, May 15 through September 30. After your tour has gathered, you will drive another 3 miles to the upper parking lot. Call (970) 883-5359 for information on guided tours.

ON THE TRAIL

During this guided walk, it's easy to imagine the era when the Ancestral Puebloans (formerly called Anasazi, see Hike 95) occupied this high point, grinding corn in the shade of a juniper tree, performing rituals in a smoke-filled kiva, keeping watch over their land from the twin spires known as Chimney Rock. Hikers are intrigued by unexplained

Chimney Rock's highest known Ancestral Pueblo site overlooks the Piedra River valley.

remnants found at the area's two separate early Pueblo II structures (circa 925–1125 AD).

The high mesa of Chimney Rock holds sixteen individual sites, fourteen of which are residential. On the tour you will visit four of these sites that have been excavated and stabilized: the Great Kiva and the Pit House on the Great Kiva Trail, and the Ridge House and the Great House on the Pueblo Trail. Other sites have been excavated and studied, then reburied to protect them and the valuable information they hold.

The tour starts west of the upper parking lot, following the paved, wheelchair-accessible Great Kiva Loop Trail around a cluster of Pueblo II sites including a "Chimney Rock Style" pit house. The Great Kiva was an important part of the community here. Encourage your companions to imagine the site as it appeared 1000 years ago.

One puzzling prehistoric feature is the circular basin ground into a rock slab near the end of the paved trail. It is considered to have astronomical significance. This loop portion of the trail ends back at the parking lot.

From the Great Kiva loop, the tour to the Great House continues 1 mile and 200 feet up the Pueblo Trail. Along the way, point out to your kids the Piedra River valley to the west, farmed by an estimated 1000 Native Americans. Share with them the special feeling of knowing they are walking the same path the Ancestral Puebloans used daily in carrying jugs of water from the river to their homes. At your feet, look for fossils in the rock that hint of the inland sea that covered this region millions of years ago. Count the number of unexcavated prehistoric structures you walk through.

The Great House, situated near the two Chimney Rock pinnacles, is "Chacoan" in construction style. Notice the walls made of small rock layers alternated with large ones. How might this structure have been used? Encourage your kids to find the similarities and differences of the upper and lower sites. Marvel at the astronomical knowledge of people living here 1000 years ago; they observed the lunar standstill, equinoxes, and summer solstice, building their settlement in locations best situated to watch them year after year. Explore why marking the seasons and recognizing lunar events would be important to Ancestral Puebloans as they farmed? Ask, "Do you think you know the sky as well as those living here a thousand years ago? Why?"

Those who focus their sights (binoculars needed) on Companion Rock, the wider pinnacle next to Chimney Rock, may see the peregrine falcons that summer there. Their nest is merely a depression in the rock. Because this bird of prey migrates to Mexico, where use of the pesticide DDT is extensive, its eggs break easily. Listed as an endangered species, the peregrine falcon population is increasing due to federal and state laws protecting it.

Your guide will lead you back via the same trail.

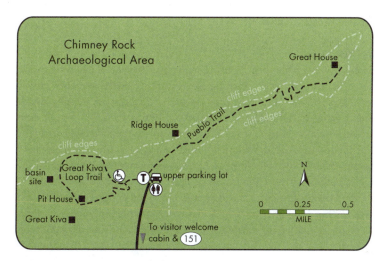

PIEDRA RIVER TRAIL

BEFORE YOU GO
Map USGS Oakbrush Ridge
Information For current conditions and more information, contact the Pagosa Ranger District, www.fs.fed.us/r2/sanjuan or (970) 264-2268

ABOUT THE HIKE
Location San Juan National Forest
Day hike or backpack; Easy
2.8 miles one way
Hikable Mid-May to mid-October
Starting elevation/Low Point 7636 feet/7460 feet
Accessibility None

GETTING THERE

From Pagosa Springs, take CO-160 west 2 miles to Piedra Road (County Road 600/Forest Road 631) and turn right (north). Follow this paved then gravel road northwest 17 miles to where it crosses the Piedra River. Parking is on the left, 200 yards from the bridge.

LOGISTICS

Toilet facilities are at the Piedra Picnic Area, located just before the bridge crossing the Piedra River. Water and toilet facilities are seasonally available at Bridge Campground, located across the parking area on the east side of FR 631.

ON THE TRAIL

From its canyon-rim beginnings, the Piedra River Trail follows a gentle descent through towering cliffs, along inviting pools, and into grassy meadows. Boulder outcrops and footpaths to the river happily divert kids hoping to find signs of river otters. The destination for the first 1.5-mile section of the Piedra River Trail is a large meadow framed by the Piedra River and Williams Creek, an ideal setting for beginning backpackers—with a fishing pole! Similar sites are available east of the trail junction with the Piedra Stock Trail at 2.8 miles.

Find the trailhead in a meadow adjacent to the parking lot's southwest side. Within 100 yards, knee-high sandstone outcrops on your right serve as stops for tightening shoelaces. However, the river's first of many pools attracts attention to the left, where dramatic desert varnish stripes the cliffs above a small waterfall. The trail then winds through a collection of boulders. In about 200 yards, a sign points left for the "main trail," the Piedra River Trail, which you follow (the smaller trail to the right is the Piedra Ice Fissures Trail, Hike 99).

At about 0.5 mile, watch on the right for a seep in the cliff wall, marked by a buttress of rocks. The water dripping here could be traced to leaks from the ice fissures on the ridge above the trail.

Inviting meadows frequented by deer and elk flank either side of the river as the trail continues its gradual descent. At just before 1 mile the river curves west, making way, it appears, for O'Neal Creek coming in from the left. Continue to a large footbridge spanning Williams Creek at 1.5 miles. The bridge can serve as a turnaround point for tired hikers.

The Piedra River slices through steep cliffs before entering open meadows.

Your chances of seeing a river otter are slim, but the budding biologists in your group may find its scat or tracks on "landings," favorite pullout spots on the river's banks. In addition, at creek crossings along the trail, look for a small area of matted grass in the shade of a tree. River otters rest in areas such as these where water flow on either side allows for a quick escape. Be aware of poison ivy in this area!

The trail maintains its easy route along the river, at 2.3 miles meeting the Trail Creek Trail on the right; stay left. About 0.5 mile beyond that is the junction with the Piedra Stock Trail on the left where a footbridge crosses the Piedra River; the Piedra River Trail continues to the right. It begins climbing just beyond here via a vague, unmaintained trail, so this is another good turnaround point.

Return via the same trail.

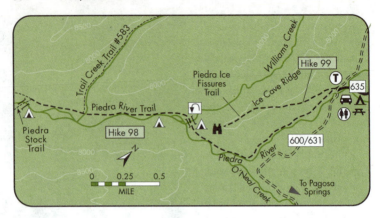

PIEDRA ICE FISSURES TRAIL

BEFORE YOU GO
Map USGS Oak Brush
Information For current conditions and more information, contact the Pagosa Ranger District, www.fs.fed.us/r2/sanjuan or (970) 264-2268

ABOUT THE HIKE
Location San Juan National Forest
Day hike; Easy
Up to 1 mile one way
Hikable Late May to mid-October
Starting elevation/High point 7636 feet/8050 feet
Accessibility None

GETTING THERE

From Pagosa Springs, take CO-160 west 2 miles to Piedra Road (County Road 600/Forest Road 631) and turn right (north). Follow this paved then gravel road northwest 17 miles to where it crosses the Piedra River. Parking is on the left, 200 yards from the bridge.

LOGISTICS

Bring a house thermometer on a string 3 or more yards long so your kids can have fun finding the "iciest" or coldest caves. A headlamp is also useful for looking into these deep slices in the earth. Nearest toilet facilities and drinking water are available seasonally at Bridge

Campground, located across the parking area, on the east side of FR 631. Toilets are also available at the Piedra Picnic Area.

ON THE TRAIL

For a "really cool" close-up look and feel of the Pagosa region's unique geology, your kids will want to check out this historic offshoot of the Piedra River Trail. This is not a Forest Service–maintained trail, and little ones who tend to wander are not advised here due to the unprotected nature of the ice fissures. It's a short walk to the fissures, followed by an easy ascent that levels to an aspen-shaded overlook of the Piedra River valley.

The trail starts near the parking lot in an open meadow and continues about 200 yards to a sign pointing to the left for the

Deep fissures in sandstone were ice sources for early homesteaders to the Piedra River area.

"main trail," the Piedra River Trail. Follow the smaller trail to the right and uphill on the remains of an 1880s wagon road turned logging road in the 1960s.

Within 0.5 mile, the trail enters a mixed forest. You may find cleanly cut tree stumps, evidence of the logging that occurred here. But your crew will almost certainly find a large hole in the center of the road with logs laid across it. Look to the left, where more long cracks or fissures fracture the forest floor. Explain that the breaks were caused by the overlayment of sandstone, which is more brittle than the pliable or bendable shale layer beneath it, shifting downslope and cracking. It's like trying to plaster-coat a balloon filled with air. Walk carefully around this network of fissures, which are not fenced and contain loose rock.

Historically, homesteaders used this area as their ice source in early summer. In the 1880s families would picnic here, then lower their brave gatherer in a bucket down nearly 30 feet, where he or she would hack at the ice. Today, while it is unsafe to enter any of the fissures, your kids can take the temperature of the forest's freezer, using their thermometer dangled into one or more of the fissures.

The gentle slope beyond the fissures lures hikers about another 0.5 mile to the tip of Ice Cave Ridge, which offers a variety of views of the Piedra River valley and surrounding peaks.

Return via the same route.

GREAT GETAWAYS

To make Hikes 98 and 99 into a fun weekend trip, camp at the first-come, first-served sites at Bridge Campground, 19 miles north of Pagosa Springs on County Road 361/Piedra Road.

The best part about this location is that there are a lot of ways to cool off. The 0.5-mile trail to thundering Piedra Falls (970-264-2268) is a great option. At mile 17 on CR-631, north of Pagosa Springs, turn right on CR-636 and right on CR-637. At mile 20 on CR-361, you'll find the turnoff for Williams Creek Reservoir—a perfect spot for a dip surrounded by stunning views of the San Juan Mountains. You can also relax at the Pagosa Hot Springs (970-264-4168) in Pagosa Springs for the ideal finish to a long day of hiking.

LOBO OVERLOOK AND CONTINENTAL DIVIDE TRAIL

BEFORE YOU GO
Maps Rio Grande National Forest; USGS Wolf Creek Pass
Information For current conditions and more information, contact the Divide Ranger District, www.fs.fed.us/r2/riogrande or (719) 657-3321

ABOUT THE HIKE
Location Rio Grande National Forest
Day hike or backpack; Moderate
0.5-mile loop, Lobo Overlook; 2 miles one way, Continental Divide Trail
Hikable Mid- to late June to mid-September
Starting elevation/High point 11,700 feet/12,000 feet
Accessibility None

GETTING THERE

Drive to Wolf Creek Pass on US 160, 36 miles west of Del Norte and 28 miles east of Pagosa Springs. The road to Lobo Overlook is just east of the pass, on the north side of the highway. The road is accessible to passenger cars after the snow is cleared in early to midsummer. Drive 2.5 miles up this steep, two-wheel-drive road to the radio tower, where the parking area is located.

LOGISTICS

Picnic tables and a vault toilet are provided at the Lobo Overlook. Bring plenty of drinking water.

ON THE TRAIL

This easily accessible trail along the spine of the Rocky Mountains is open to most anyone destined for the southwest corner of the state. Little ones may walk as far as the Lobo Overlook where lines of peaks and ridges fill the skyscape like an ocean of rough waters. Meadows bursting with showy wildflowers lure their bigger brothers and sisters following the trail to the west.

From the radio tower parking lot, the 0.3-mile walk south to the Lobo Overlook whets the visual appetite. Guardrails edge this cliff-top viewpoint, but eager little hikers may need special watching. The sea of mountains here means more to very young lookers when Wolf Creek Ski Area and the thin stripe of US 160 are pointed out. Explain to young

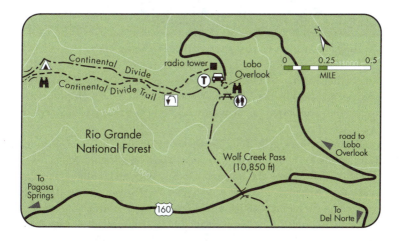

Relaxing in a meadow of wildflowers rewards an alpine hiker.

hikers that Wolf Creek Pass (10,850 feet) is actually a low place between the east and west sides of the Rocky Mountains, and the highway allows people to travel across the mountains. Loop back to the parking area in 0.2 mile.

Begin your hike on the Continental Divide Trail in the stand of spruce trees on the west side of the radio tower. The trail's first 0.5 mile is easy to follow as it crosses the ridgetop winding through an alpine meadow and enters a cluster of spruce and fir trees. In this coniferous gathering, your companions may notice a tarlike substance coating the ends of the lowest spruce branches; it's called black snow mold. Spruce trees can reproduce when the snowpack holds a branch against the ground through the spring months. But if the snow lingers too long, snow mold takes hold, which can eventually kill the tree. Look for spruce seedlings started from mature branches.

At 0.5 mile is the start of a large meadow just past the spruce-fir forest. This makes a good destination for some hikers.

Within the next 0.5 mile, the trail dips down to the south, avoiding a steep ridge climb. It then enters a flower-painted alpine bowl. Point to Treasure Mountain across this valley. Its tresses of timber have been cut in a more natural fashion, rather than the square blocks usually used in clear-cutting. Ask, "What is the purpose of clear-cutting?" (Almost always: logging. Occasionally: fire prevention and habitat improvement.) "Does this clear-cut look natural?"

While peering across these mountainscapes, chances are good you'll spy a small group of elk grazing. The high-altitude food (grasses and shrubs) they're stocking up on contains as much as 40 percent more nutritional value than that found at lower elevations. This is because plants of this terrain are generally small, so their food value is concentrated. What other reasons might cause animals to live at high altitudes during the summer? (Besides cooler temperatures and fewer people, fewer insects are the driving force. In addition to biting elks' face and eyes, the flying pests lay eggs on the animals' skin.)

After climbing back to the ridge top at 1.6 miles and then descending 0.4 mile into a long valley, the trail meets a saddle, or low point, along the Continental Divide. Numerous campsites and top-of-the-world views make this 2-mile walk an ideal destination for day hikers and backpackers alike, though unlimited opportunities for longer treks exist on this trail.

Return via the same trail.

BEST RIVERSIDE WALKS

Grand Junction

The 1.5-mile Audubon Trail, a section of Grand Junction's extensive Colorado River Trail, gives walkers a leafy passage that edges cattail marshes singing with red-winged blackbirds. The trail parallels the tailrace (canal) from the hydroelectric plant where the chance of spotting a great blue heron, red-tailed hawk, magpie, mallard duck, or woodpecker sparks interest in beginning birders of any age. Parking is available near the trailhead at the Albertsons shopping center at the northwest corner of Broadway (CO-340) and Dike Road on the Redlands in Grand Junction. In addition, restrooms, picnic tables, and fishing access are available in Connected Lakes State Park (with a valid State Parks pass or paid entry fee).

www.riverfrontproject.org   (970) 683-4333

Durango

The 7-mile Animas River Trail (ART), over thirty-six years in the making, brings families through twelve city parks and over five pedestrian bridges. Along the way they pass the town's library, high school, a waterfall, several grocery and retail stores, a children's museum, a shopping center, a dog park, and Whitewater Park where kayakers paddle Smelter Rapid well into the river's icy winter chapter. The historic Durango & Silverton Narrow Gauge Railroad parallels portions of ART, while rafters and tubers paddle the Animas spring through fall. Anglers fish the Animas's "Gold Medal" waters almost year-round. Public toilets and drinking water are seasonally available at Santa Rita Park (0.5 mile south of the US 160/550 junction) and year-round at the Durango Public Library (1900 East Third Avenue). Downtown trail access and parking are available at Rotary Park, 15th Street and East Second Avenue and at the Durango Discovery Museum, 1333 Camino Del Rio.

www.durangogov.org/parks/trails   (970) 373-7300

Montrose

The Uncompahgre RiverWay Trail gives families 3 miles of year-round riverside views of the San Juan Mountains with access to two parks and the Ute Indian Museum. Restrooms and parking are provided at the Cerise Park on West Main and CO-90, and at the museum (US 550 and Chipeta Road), located on the 8.65-acre homestead owned by Chief Ouray and his wife, Chipeta. The Uncompahgre RiverWay will eventually form a 37-mile "Rails-to-Trails" connection between the cities of Montrose and Ouray.

www.cityofmontrose.org   (970) 240-1400

Telluride

The San Miguel River Trail, 4.25 miles one way, can begin in Town Park, a summer fun center featuring the Trout Pond for kids' fishing, the Imagination Station playground, a swimming pool, and several ball fields. Walking east just a few blocks leads to the shopping district and scenic gondola. Kids of all ages remain thrilled long past the free, thirteen-minute ride capturing 360-degree views of surrounding 14,000-foot peaks as the gondola climbs 1750 feet to Mountain Village. Dog-friendly with handicap access, the gondola ride is a "must-do" in Telluride. See Hike 93, the Bear Creek Trail, for another, nearby family-friendly hike in Telluride.

www.visittelluride.com   (888) 605-2578

TRAIL TALES

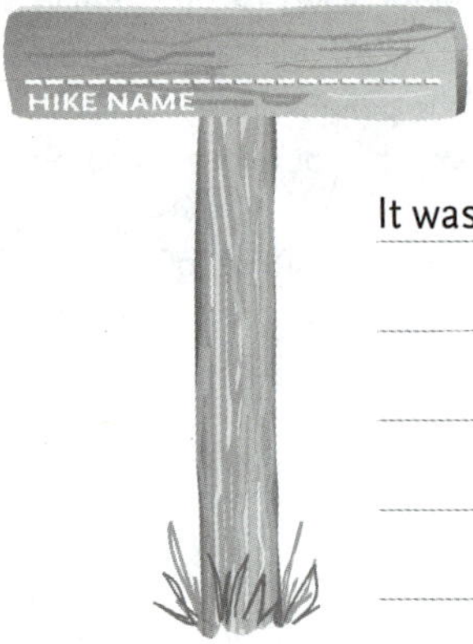

HIKE NAME

Date hiked: _____

It was really cool when…

_____
_____
_____
_____
_____
_____
_____
_____

HIKE NAME

Date hiked: _____

It was really cool when…

_____
_____
_____
_____
_____
_____
_____

HIKE NAME

Date hiked: _____

It was really cool when... _____

_____

_____

_____

_____

_____

_____

HIKE NAME

Date hiked: _____

It was really cool when... _____

_____

_____

_____

_____

_____

INDEX

ABOUT THE AUTHOR

Maureen Keilty is a writer based in Durango, Colorado. Her interests in the diverse landscapes and cultural heritages of the Southwest have long fueled her work as a writer, an outdoor educator, and a wilderness guide. Maureen has also written *Best Hikes with Children in Utah* (1993, 2000), *Durango* (Desert Dolphin 1993, 1998), and *National Geographic's Guide to the Outdoors, Southern Rockies* (2000). Her husband, Dan Peha, is equally inspired by the mountains and deserts near Durango. His photographs have appeared in numerous books (including this one), magazines, and calendars. Their son, Niko, who child-tested many of the "best hikes" in Colorado and Utah, now explores rivers and routes on his own.

THE MOUNTAINEERS, founded in 1906, is a nonprofit outdoor activity and conservation organization whose mission is "to explore, study, preserve, and enjoy the natural beauty of the outdoors . . . . " Based in Seattle, Washington, it is now one of the largest such organizations in the United States, with seven branches throughout Washington State.

The Mountaineers sponsors both classes and year-round outdoor activities in the Pacific Northwest, which include hiking, mountain climbing, ski-touring, snowshoeing, bicycling, camping, canoeing and kayaking, nature study, sailing, and adventure travel. The Mountaineers' conservation division supports environmental causes through educational activities, sponsoring legislation, and presenting informational programs.

All activities are led by skilled, experienced volunteers, who are dedicated to promoting safe and responsible enjoyment and preservation of the outdoors.

If you would like to participate in these organized outdoor activities or programs, consider a membership in The Mountaineers. For information and an application, write or call The Mountaineers Program Center, 7700 Sand Point Way NE, Seattle, WA 98115-3996; phone 206-521-6001; visit www.mountaineers.org; or email info@mountaineers.org.

The Mountaineers Books, an active, nonprofit publisher, produces guidebooks, instructional texts, historical works, natural history guides, and works on environmental conservation. All books produced by The Mountaineers Books fulfill the mission of The Mountaineers. Visit www.mountaineersbooks.org to find details about all our titles and the latest author events.

 The Mountaineers Books
1001 SW Klickitat Way, Suite 201
Seattle, WA 98134
800-553-4453
mbooks@mountaineersbooks.org

The Mountaineers Books is proud to be a corporate sponsor of The Leave No Trace Center for Outdoor Ethics, whose mission is to promote and inspire responsible outdoor recreation through education, research, and partnerships. The Leave No Trace program is focused specifically on human-powered (nonmotorized) recreation.

Leave No Trace strives to educate visitors about the nature of their recreational impacts and offers techniques to prevent and minimize such impacts. Leave No Trace is best understood as an educational and ethical program, not as a set of rules and regulations.

For more information, visit www.lnt.org, or call 800-332-4100.

OTHER TITLES YOU MIGHT ENJOY FROM THE MOUNTAINEERS BOOKS

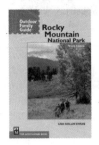

Outdoor Family Guide to Rocky Mountain National Park, 3rd Edition
Lisa Gollin Evans
A family-focused guidebook to one of the country's most popular national parks

100 Classic Hikes Colorado, 3rd Edition
Scott S. Warren
Full-color guide to the best of the best and featuring ten new hikes

Best Loop Hikes Colorado
Steve Johnson & David Weinstein
Loop hikes for all ability levels, plus great snowshoe loops for winter outings

Babes in the Woods Hiking, Camping, and Boating with Babies and Young Children
Jennifer Aist
A detailed guide on introducing very young children to outdoor experiences